THOSE
WHO
STAYED

THOSE WHO STAYED

THE SIKHS OF KASHMIR

BUPINDER SINGH BALI

AMARYLLIS

AMARYLLIS

An imprint of Manjul Publishing House Pvt. Ltd.
• C-16, Sector 3, Noida, Uttar Pradesh 201 301, India
Website: www.manjulindia.com
Registered Office:
• 10, Nishat Colony, Bhopal 462 003 – India
Distribution Centres
Ahmedabad, Bengaluru, Bhopal, Chennai, Hyderabad,
Kolkata, Mumbai, Noida, Pune

Those Who Stayed – The Sikhs of Kashmir by Bupinder Singh Bali

Copyright © Bupinder Singh Bali, 2024

Bupinder Singh Bali asserts the moral right to be
identified as the author of this work

This paperback edition first published in India in 2024

ISBN 978-93-5543-629-0

This is a work of creative non-fiction and is based on personal interactions and experiences of the Author and materials collected by the Author through verifiable research. The views and opinions expressed in this book are those of the Author and do not reflect or represent the views of the Publisher or any other person. The intention is not to hurt the sentiments of anyone but to provide information. Some names and identifying features have been changed to protect the identity of certain individuals.

No warranties or guarantees are expressed or implied by the Publisher's choice to include any of the content that is in this volume. Neither the Publisher nor the Author shall be liable for any physical, psychological, emotional, financial, or commercial damages, including but not limited to, special, incidental, consequential or other damages.

All rights reserved. No part of this book may be used or reproduced, stored in or introduced into a retrieval system, or transmitted, in any form, or by any means (electronic, mechanical, photocopying, recording or otherwise) without the prior written permission of the Author and or the Publisher. Any person who does any unauthorized act in relation to this publication may be liable to criminal prosecution and civil claims for damages.

This book is dedicated to the minorities of the world.

Contents

Timeline of Events ix
Introduction xii

1	A Phone Call	1
2	Kerala to Kashmir	10
3	Sacrificial Lambs	21
4	From Landlords to Tenants	33
5	Home and Homeland	39
6	Invisible	49
7	A Red Winter	60
8	Aspirations and Options	68
9	Nada	75
10	Azaadi	82
11	Daydreams	96
12	Lives and Livelihood	105
13	Those Who Cannot Foresee	114
14	Unearthing Chithisinghpora	122
15	Paranoia, Alms and Pistols	135
16	Men Are From Mars, Women Are From Venus, Sikhs Are From Punjab	147
17	The Sikhs of Kashmir, Circa 1490 to Present	156
18	The ISI Blueprint	168
19	Survivor Stories	175
20	Battle of Ichahama and Attina	187
21	Closures Matter	198

22	Aftermath of 1947	204
23	To Leave or Not to Leave	214
24	The Good Old Days	220
25	Better Left Unsaid	227
26	A Silent Migration	241
27	Articles 370 and 35(a)	249
28	Opinions and Options	260
29	Deluge and Delusions	266
30	Goodbyes	271

Epilogue		276
Acknowledgements		280
References		282

Timeline of Events

Srinagar, Kashmir, 7 October 2021: A phone call, some shocking news, panic

Srinagar, Kashmir, 7 October 2021: The news reaches my wife Indu and parents

Srinagar, Kashmir, 7 October 2021: TV and print media dissect the news

Srinagar, Kashmir, 1989–1991: Migration to Jammu for four years

Srinagar, Kashmir, 8 October 2021: Lives in Kashmir affected, especially from the socio-economic point of view

Srinagar, Kashmir, 9 October 2021: Discussing school life, childhood as a Sikh in Kashmir

Srinagar, Kashmir, December 2000–March 2001: Mehjoor Nagar Sikh massacre incident, eyewitness accounts

Srinagar, Kashmir, 9 October 2021: Indu and I discuss future opportunities, dreams and aspirations of the Kashmiri Sikhs

Srinagar, Kashmir, 10 October 2021: Peace and turmoil go hand in hand

Jammu, 2001–2010: My newfound freedom in Jammu, how different it was from living in Kashmir

Srinagar, Kashmir, 11–16 October 2021: New army-militant encounters, further panic

Srinagar, Kashmir, 16 October 2021: Problems related to livelihood, employment, education, other socio-economic challenges faced by our community, arguments

Srinagar, Kashmir, 16 October 2021: A new incident, our future, options in and out of Kashmir

Srinagar, March 2015: The massacre of Chithisinghpora, survivor stories

Srinagar, Kashmir, 17 October 2021: Paranoia, Indu and father discuss second migration out of Kashmir in 2001

Srinagar, Kashmir, 18 October 2021: I visit my school after two weeks

Kashmir, 1490–present: History of the Sikhs in Kashmir

Srinagar, Kashmir, 19 October 2021: ISI's blueprint about civilian killings in Kashmir appears in media outlets, our future in Kashmir comes into question

Baramulla, Kashmir, October–November 1947: The Kabali Raid in Kashmir

Budgam, Kashmir, November 1947: Battle of Ichahama and Attina between the Kabalis and the Sikhs of Kashmir

Srinagar, Kashmir, 19 October 2021: The uncertainty of living in Kashmir, further anxiety

Kashmir, 1947 and its aftermath

Srinagar, Kashmir, 20 October 2021: Indecisiveness about the future and life

Srinagar, Kashmir, 21 October 2021: Some normalcy

Srinagar, Kashmir, 24 October 2021: Dinner at an uncle's home

Srinagar, Kashmir, 29 October 2021: Discussing Article 370, its effect on the community

Srinagar, Kashmir, August 2019: The Revocation of Article 370 and Article 35(a), its effect on our lives

Srinagar, Kashmir, 30–31 October 2021: Life in Kashmir, the silent migration of the Sikh community

Kashmir, September 2014: The Kashmir Floods, response of the micro-community

Srinagar, Kashmir, 1 November 2021: Thinking about the future

Kashmir, October 2022: New cycle of civilian killings, renewed paranoia

Introduction

When Nehru made his famous speech, '*At the stroke of the midnight hour when the world sleeps, India will awake to life and freedom*,' most of Kashmir was still in a deep sleep. A sleep that was broken months later when thousands of armed tribal men from Pakistan and Afghanistan poured into Kashmir. They turned the beautiful Valley which was red with apples and orange with the retreating autumn into one red with blood and orange with arsons.

In the year 1947, during October and November, when every other state decided to either side with India or Pakistan, the King of Jammu and Kashmir, Maharaja Hari Singh, kept everything in limbo until armed mercenaries came roaring into the Valley, killing thousands of people, and destroying everything in their way. The Maharaja had no other option but to accede to India to protect his territory and his citizens. But the then Governor-General, Lord Mountbatten, wrote to the Maharaja, 'It is my government's wish that as soon as law and order have been restored in Jammu and Kashmir and her soil cleared of the invaders, the question of the State's accession should be settled by a reference to the people.'

Pakistan, going by this letter which said accession should be settled by a reference to the people, claimed that the accession to India was fraudulent. Ever since Kashmir has become the bone of contention between the two countries, and a living hell for its citizens. Time and again, Pakistan had tried to wage wars to occupy the territory of Kashmir, the primary posit being that Kashmir was a Muslim-majority state and should have acceded to Pakistan, a Muslim country.

The war of 1965, also called the Second Kashmir War, began after Pakistan tried to infiltrate into Kashmir to precipitate an insurgency against Indian rule. The war ended when a ceasefire was attained under United Nations Security Council resolutions and then the Tashkent Declaration.

Another war took place between India and Pakistan in the year 1971, during the Bangladesh Liberation War, which resulted in the Simla Pact and defining of the Line of Control (LOC), which remains the most disputed line on earth. No pact or declaration was strong enough to contain the Kashmir issue.

The occasional pacts and declarations and treaties and ceasefires that followed only metamorphosed into an eternal insurgency and militancy which is still ongoing in Kashmir.

In 1989, Pakistan shifted and channelled its efforts through the Inter-Services Intelligence (ISI), aiding Pakistan-based militant groups who are waging a proxy war against Indian security forces in the state. The proxy war claimed more than 48,000 lives between 1988 and 2023 in an estimated 65,600 incidents of terrorist violence. The thirty-plus years of turmoil had left the citizens of Kashmir miserable. The Kashmiri Pandits who had been in Kashmir for generations were ousted from their homes and had to face an exodus in their own country. The Kashmiri Muslims suffer on a day-to-day basis, losing their lives, livelihood and peace of mind, and much more.

We, the Kashmiri Sikhs, are stepping on two boats, undergoing a slow migration, suffering mentally, physically, economically and socially. We are neither happy in Kashmir, nor can we leave Kashmir and migrate elsewhere. We are rooted in Kashmir though our present and our future does not seem bright if we stay. Once in a while, something happens that makes us wonder again and again—Should we stay in Kashmir or leave? Is it safe for us? Can we flourish here or not?

What pushed me to write this book was an incident that happened on 8 October 2021—the killing of a Sikh school teacher for being a Sikh. Yes. Just for being a Sikh. But while writing this book, I understood that I was writing it as a response to the accumulated angst and the everyday suffocation we all were enduring for having lived in Kashmir since the last thirty years. It should have been written much sooner, not just as a reaction to some killing, but to bring to the world the plight and suffering, the challenges and problems, the courage and stubbornness, the daily life and its trivialities, the sorrow and dismay of the Sikh community living in the Valley.

During the last two years, targeted killings of non-locals and non-Muslims have gained momentum in Kashmir. Over twenty people from the section of minorities have been killed. Sikhs, who comprise less than 1 per cent of the total population of Kashmir, are the main minorities living in Kashmir. Sikhs continue to live here despite decades of conflict in the area, and a mass execution of around 20,000 Sikhs in 1947.

Through this book, I want to provide a holistic look at the lives of the Sikhs in Kashmir, a micro-minority in a conflict zone where the majority are fighting for freedom from India and hoping for a future with Pakistan. The fear of death, another Partition-like bloodshed looms over us if we are ever faced with such a future.

According to the official portal of the Government of Jammu and Kashmir, the population of Sikhs in Kashmir is only 0.88 per cent. Even in the age of the internet, when information is abundantly available, not much of it comes up when we type 'Sikhs in Kashmir'. The only search results that return are the sporadic incidents that came in the news. Kashmiri Sikhs as they are called, are a community living or rather surviving in the conflict-torn area, and their narrative is either lost or ignored. When the whole world is keenly looking at Kashmir, they look only at the majority community, its issues and problems. The lens they use does not focus on the Sikhs. With a unique identity, this micro-minority, wherever they live, does not camouflage well with the general population, for which they sometimes must pay a hefty price.

Our narrative has been lost, and through this book, I wanted to reclaim a portion of it.

1

A Phone Call

Srinagar, Kashmir
7 October 2021, Thursday
Morning

I was teaching carbon and its compounds to my class. Third period, Class X, chemistry. 'This chair, these mats, your clothes, your books, this marker in my hand, everything has carbon in it.'

My phone rang incessantly, so I kept pressing the power button to silence it. But the vibration sounded louder than the ringer in the pin-drop silence of the classroom.

'All living beings, all dead, non-living things, almost every single thing has carbon.' There were only seven students in the class, three girls and four boys, sitting cross-legged on the floor. Two of the seven classrooms had proper furniture, like chairs and benches. The remaining had mats on the floor on which the students sat.

Like most government schools in Kashmir, the school I was teaching in had a very low enrolment statistic. There were only eighty-three students in the whole school. Government schools catered to the local population belonging to the area, which meant low enrolment. Though there were no guidelines and provisions, the general policy of the government was to open primary and middle schools in every locality. A group of ten to fifteen middle schools form a cluster. Every cluster had one or two high schools, in which successful students from middle schools were admitted. Similarly, for every three to four clusters, there was one higher secondary school where students from high schools could advance their education. This kept the overall enrolment at the government school very low. People with means and money preferred private education for their children because the facilities and infrastructure in private schools were much better than those in government schools.

This was our first Class X batch after the school had been upgraded to high school recently. To accommodate the batch, the staff strength had been increased and new facilities like a science lab, a computer lab and a bigger collection of library books were introduced. The building, however, was not expanded, which led to temporary partitions of bigger classrooms to accommodate two separate classes. A large classroom was designated as an all-in-one lab, library, and smart classroom.

It was around 11.30 a.m. when my phone vibrated again and I excused myself to look at the screen and saw that it was Veerji who was calling. I declined the call with a custom message—In class, will call back later— and turned on the Do Not Disturb mode on the phone. Whatever it was, it could wait, I thought to myself.

Veerji used to call me sometimes, unexpectedly, whenever some new idea struck him. Over the years, he had become a close friend, a mentor, and a teacher. As a kid, I used to go to the community library, where he taught us Punjabi. His real name was Jagjit Singh, but all of us called him Veerji—elder brother—as a mark of respect.

'So, who will tell me why carbon is so common? Why is it found in everything around us?' I asked.

Silence.

'No one?' Silence again.

'Make a little effort at least. Why am I wasting my energy if you won't even try to answer? I have even told you so many times that I don't dislike wrong answers yet you people keep mum.'

'Sir, carbon is in everything because it is too much in quantity,' Mujeeb replied. In my twelve years of teaching, I had developed one thing for sure. Patience. Many students in most of the government schools were below average, but this was a batch that had several disadvantages.

This batch had joined school after two years due to subsequent lockdowns. These students were out of school twice. First, on account of the revocation of Article 370, from August 2019 through February 2020, and then due to Covid, for the next one and a half years.

'Okay. At least, write ten examples of things containing carbon. Do that much,' I said. The classroom was devoid of any furniture. The walls had a timetable, a student performance chart, and an old skeleton chart torn in a way that the right knee was missing. The windows were just frames, the glass had been long broken. As winter was approaching, the staff proposed to fix polythene sheets on them to keep the cold out. The students had no reference in the class to write.

'And five examples of things you think will not have it,' I added.

Among these seven students, only two girls, Nashma and Shabu, were interested in education. The rest just wanted to pass the exams and move on with their lives. During the lockdown, when we taught the students online using Zoom, only one or two students joined the classes.

I had a sudden urge to check the phone again, and when I did, there were seven missed calls from Veerji, two from Gurmeet ma'am, a colleague who was teaching in another class, and several WhatsApp messages. Waheguru, everything should be fine, I prayed.

'Danish, you come here and mind the class. I have to go to the principal's office now.'

I have learned to make the unruliest student in-charge of maintaining discipline in the class. There was an old saying in our place, '*Chor ko hi rakhwali dedo to chori kaun kaun karega* (If you make the robber in-charge of security, who will do the robbing then?') Danish was wearing his shirt out, with the cuffs rolled-up. Two of the top buttons were undone. With no tie and belt, he looked like a hooligan. But that was how most students came dressed to school.

We, as teachers, were happy that they were coming at all, uniform or not, studies or not. Everything else was secondary. The primary aim was to make them attend the school. If we started scolding them, they would stop coming to school.

I immediately called Veerji. 'Are you in school?' he asked without ceremony.

'Yes.'

'Go home quickly.'

'What, why? Is everything alright?'

All imaginary scenarios swam in my mind. My mother was electrocuted while using the immersion rod. The gas cylinder had exploded. Father had collapsed. He was in an accident. My stomach twitched and my heart raced.

'I'll call you back in some time. But you leave now,' he replied.

'But what, tell me if...'

He hung up on me. I opened my WhatsApp, anticipating something, some clue of what was happening. I hoped everything was alright. There was a message from my masi, '*Suna kuchh*, did you hear anything?' A few more messages on different groups, but nothing unusual. I called him again, but he was on another call.

I walked to the office to find Gurmeet ma'am, who was busy on a call. She signalled me to sit on the chair next to hers.

'*Kaand hogaya*. There has been an attack in some school in the city,' she told me, holding the call she was on. She gestured for me to wait till she finished it. I felt a sigh of relief. My parents were fine. Everything was OK. All the horrible thoughts about my family and friends disappeared. I tried Veerji's number again.

'What happened? I heard there was an attack somewhere,' I told him.

'Two people have been killed, shot dead at point-blank range—school teachers,' he replied.

'You kept calling. I thought something bad had happened. Don't scare me like that,' I said. Killings were common in Kashmir.

'No, my dear, you don't understand. The killings have started again. Targeted killings. Go home now,' he ordered.

'Started again? What do you mean by that? It can be an isolated incident. Why are you jumping to conclusions?'

'Seven civilian killings in the last week alone. What do you think? And today, one is a Sikh teacher, and the other is a Hindu. Rumours are they checked their IDs and then killed them. I'll call you back, but leave now.'

A Sikh teacher? I didn't have any relatives who was a teacher. Masi was. But she had messaged me, so she was fine. No one I knew could be hurt. The relief I felt evaporated suddenly. Why would they kill a Sikh teacher? Why should I go home? Was there any intelligence input that more attacks would happen? And should I return home now or wait till the class was over? I was still on the phone with Veerji as these thoughts went through my mind. I wiped my sweaty palm on my shirt. I could feel my heart beating faster.

'Do you know who it is, the Sikh teacher?' I asked Veerji.

'Not yet. I will call you back. Let me call someone to confirm,' he replied.

In the back of my mind, I was trying to make sense of what Veerji just told me. Targeted killing? No. What would they get by killing a Sikh teacher? I could not wait for Veerji to confirm it. I checked the *QNS* news channel on Facebook. It reported two people being shot. Nothing more. Both had died on the spot. Three people were shot dead the previous day as well—a prominent Kashmiri Pandit, a pharmacist by profession, who had never left Kashmir; a Hindu street vendor who had come to Kashmir from some other part of India; and a Kashmiri Muslim living in some far-flung area of Kashmir. That was five, but Veerji said seven. I hadn't read about the others.

I checked online and found that two more civilians were killed in separate incidents, both Muslims. So, it was not a matter of Sikh or Hindu; they were killing civilians now.

Nobody called me yesterday. Nobody told me to go home. Nobody cared about those killings. Now that a Sikh was killed, everyone was panicking. In Kashmir, we stopped treating humans like humans long ago. They were Muslims, Sikhs, Pandits, militants, army walas, mukhbirs, and so on.

Civilian killings were a thing of the past. In the initial years of Kashmir militancy, they were targeted and killed. But as a general notion, we believed that civilians were never targeted directly in Kashmir; they mostly died in cross-firing, caught between the conflict, accidental bomb blasts, so on and so forth. We, in Kashmir, believed that we were safe as a civilian if we were not on the wrong side of the freedom movement. Though more than 15,000 civilians had been killed during the militancy era, we termed those killings primarily of people who were in the 'wrong place at the wrong time'.

During the last three decades, the militants had been fighting a war against the Indian army, which for them, represented the Indian government or the occupying forces. We, Kashmiris, termed any civilian death as collateral damage. Those targeted by the militants were informants, government stooges, collaborators, or people who said something against the independence of Kashmir. In contrast, those who died at the hands of the army were militants, aides, sympathisers, or those who were anti-India.

I was still confused about taking half a day off when Gurmeet ma'am came to me.

'Bupinder sir, did you hear they killed a Sikhni and a Pandit?'

She was from Jammu, had got married in Kashmir, and was living here for the last two and a half decades. Theirs was the only Sikh family living in a Muslim-majority locality. And she never felt unsafe.

'Yes, I heard. Did you say Sikhni? They killed a woman?' I was confused. Veerji did not mention that.

'So should we go home?' she asked.

'You are safer in the school than you would be at your home,' I joked. Gurmeet ma'am was a tiny lady, no more than 5 feet in height and underweight for her frame. She treated me like her younger brother and would bring me lunch and tea from home. Her house was only a mile from the school, and I usually dropped her home in my car after school.

'Let us see. Let's tell the headmistress and see what she says. By the way, is the name or photograph of the teacher out yet?' I asked her. She checked her WhatsApp and found a picture that was circulated. A lady was lying on the ground, face down, and there was a bullet entry on her back. We could not identify who she was.

Both of us went to the headmistress's office and told her about the incident.

I called Veerji as I started my car. 'Give me some details. I heard it was a lady teacher. I am leaving for home now,' I told him.

'Two teachers in some school at Souvra. It's a targeted kill, meaning they are going to kill non-Muslims and non-Kashmiris,' he said. Souvra. Someone I knew worked there. But, who?

'First, tell me who was killed. It can be a personal vendetta as well,' I replied. I could feel the tremor in his voice and the anger in his tone.

'Stop being your optimistic ass. Can't you see? They are making a statement. They killed three people yesterday and two today; four are non-Muslims, and the Muslim was an informant. This is the Azaadi movement all over again.'

'Calm down. First, tell me, who was this Sikh teacher?' I asked.

'The one whose kids you tutored,' he replied. Supinder ma'am. Damn.

I clutched the steering wheel of my car harder. My hands felt cold and stiff like they were drained of blood. I had to stop my car on the side.

'Supinder ma'am? But, why, why would they kill her?' I was too confused. Damn, why? My legs were trembling. Her face flashed in front of my eyes. Till a few months back I had been tutoring her two children. Every day she would bring me tea and snacks or fruits. She would talk to me about her children's future, about her own education, and her being a working lady. She wanted the best for her daughter. She was coping with her extra energetic son. All the images flashed in front of me. I could see the faces of her children. Her daughter would be broken; she loved her so much. Her son, who was too young to grasp the enormity of what happened but intelligent enough to know that it happened, would go berserk. Her husband worked in a bank and would come late, mostly after I left. I had never met him. I wondered how he would manage taking care of the children and his job without her.

All reason and logic seemed to fail me. Knowing her, a humble lady, who was not involved in politics in any way, I wondered what her killing would achieve. Why, why would anyone want to kill her? She meant no harm to anyone.

'What happened? Who is it?' Gurmeet ma'am asked. Her voice brought me out of my trance. I had forgotten I was talking to Veerji. I did not know when and how the call got disconnected. I gathered my strength to drive again.

I called him again. By that time, new pictures of Supinder ma'am were being circulated, and some more information about the incident had come out.

'They lined up the school teachers first, checked their IDs, and then singled out the non-Muslims,' Veerji told me over the phone. I had kept his call on speaker, so Gurmeet ma'am could also listen in.

'Then, it could be a personal vendetta?' I inquired.

'You say whatever you want, but you too know what it is,' he replied.

What? Minority killing? Targeted killing? Bullshit?

'Let's not jump to conclusions. I'll call you once I reach home, or I'll come to your office after some time,' I replied.

'They checked their IDs and then shot them?' Gurmeet ma'am repeated. Her forehead had a wrinkle, and a 'w' formed between her eyebrows. She was clutching her phone so hard that her knuckles had turned white. 'Don't know what will happen? Are they after Sikhs now?'

'Don't worry. Stay at home tomorrow. I'll call you in the evening.'

By the time I ended the call with Veerji, we had already reached her house. She was still sitting inside as if she had forgotten to get out. I told her to go home and relax. It was nothing serious, not until we knew the full details.

I was still unable to grasp it fully. Why would they kill Supinder, of all people? I could not find a reason or logic behind her killing. If they wanted to kill a Sikh, they could have killed anyone anywhere. Why go to a school and check the ID and then kill? There was a reason behind it all. I decided to go and see Veerji directly.

During my ride back home, I got several calls from different people, asking me where I was and whether I had heard the news, telling me to be careful, and speculating why and how it happened. I was in a daze. In the back of my mind, there was one constant question. Why her? Why so much effort?

I had heard about targeted killings in the 1990s, during the peak of militancy when fear and paranoia prevailed. But I was too young to witness and remember it. But the target was specific: the Kashmiri Pandits. If they wanted to target Kashmiri Pandits, or Sikhs, as people were speculating, they could have done that with anyone. This was more than that. More than what had happened in the 1990s.

The Kashmir freedom movement, or the militancy, started in 1989 with the formation of the Jammu Kashmir Liberation Front (JKLF), whose mission was to liberate Kashmir from India and merge it with Pakistan. The insurgency began with the targeted killings of Kashmiri Hindus. Militants identified them and their houses, and killed them mercilessly, leaving behind a warning to others to leave Kashmir. Posters and pamphlets were pasted throughout Kashmir saying, '*Musalmano Jago, Kafiro Bhago, Jihad aa raha hai.* (Muslims awake, infidels leave, jihad is coming.)'

Hizbul Mujahadeen released a full press release in a major newspaper, warning Kashmiri Pandits, in particular, and infidels, in general, to leave Kashmir within two days or die.

Around 70 per cent (1,00,000 out of 1,40,000) of Kashmiri Pandits left behind their homes, properties and belongings and moved to the adjoining Hindu majority province of Jammu or Delhi. Within weeks they went from being a well-established community to becoming migrants and refugees within their own country. But that was in the 1990s, and this was 2021. Whatever discrimination, injustices and atrocities happened, the Sikhs were seldom targeted.

There were only three episodes of Sikhs being targeted directly during the last thirty-two years of militancy in Kashmir. They were the Chithisinghpora massacre in 2000, the Push Kriri killings in 2000, and the Mehjoor Nagar incident in 2001. Around 120 Sikhs were killed in this period, including the above three major incidents. That was a handful when compared to the entire data on Kashmir killings.

I wanted to go to Veerji and find out the whole news and the motives behind the killings. On the other hand, I was expecting a call from home as well. And praying that they hadn't come to know about it, especially my wife. I wanted to reach home and tell her the news myself before she heard it from anyone else and panicked.

For us born and raised in Kashmir, this news of violence, killings and blasts were an everyday occurrence. But I wondered what my wife was thinking. This was her first long stay in Kashmir after all.

2

Kerala to Kashmir

Srinagar, Kashmir
7 October 2021, Thursday
Afternoon

Indu was on the veranda, waiting for me, while my parents were sitting in the garden. Her eyes were a bit swollen, and a trail of tears had left a mark on her cheeks. She had come to know about the incident from somewhere, my guess was through the internet.

Before I could go hug her and tell her what was happening, I was stopped by my father in the garden.

'Do you know who was killed?' Papa asked me. 'It is a woman, the principal of Idgah Higher Secondary School,' he added. Indu also came to the garden and sat on the small wooden box that my mother used to keep her vegetable basket.

'Supinder ma'am. I used to teach her kids,' I said.

'*Haaye, haaye*, I guessed it was her. Who told you?' Without waiting for my answer, he handed me his phone. 'Here, see this. Some organisation has come forward and taken responsibility for yesterday's killing.'

The Resistance Front (TRF) had claimed responsibility for the three killings that happened recently. First, the Kashmiri Pandit Makhan Lal Bindroo, who had not left Kashmir in the 1990 pandit exodus and flourished as an eminent pharmacist; his shop Bindroo Pharmacy was also a multi-doctor clinic, in the centre of Srinagar city, where several doctors did visiting consultancy on different days of the week, mainly in the evenings. Within half a kilometre of his pharmacy was the biggest police station of Srinagar, Sher Gadhi. There were multiple CRPF bunkers in the vicinity, and despite all that, he was shot in broad daylight. The TRF accused him of being an RSS stooge, an Indian agent.

Second, the poor street vendor, probably from Bihar or UP, who sold gol-gappas on a handcart. He was accused of being an informant to the Indian government. Third, a Muslim villager was accused of being an informer, a mukhbir, to the army. In Kashmir, these are the reasons to be murdered.

We expected TRF or some other similar militant outfit to come forward and take responsibility for today's killings as well.

'But why would they kill a school teacher, that too, a woman? What could she have done?' Indu kept rubbing her neck. She would sit and then stand and then sit again, unable to decide what to do.

'Who knows? This is the cost of living in Kashmir. It asks for a sacrifice now and then,' Papa said.

'We will find out by tomorrow anyway,' I said.

'You are not going to school tomorrow,' Indu replied standing up again.

'No, I am not going to school till Monday. Someone will claim responsibility for the killings or the news channels will dissect what has happened by tomorrow.'

'What if they had come to your school?' she asked.

'Then it would be me you would be reading about,' I replied calmly and regretted it immediately. 'I am done now.' Saying this she stood up and walked inside. After a few minutes, I went to her.

She was still standing in the room, resting her weight against the wardrobe, glued to her phone. Before she could say anything, I hugged her and said, 'Love, I am sorry. I was just kidding.'

'How can you say that?' She pushed me away and sat on the edge of the bed, drooping, staring at the leg of the study table, avoiding my gaze.

'It was just a joke and I said sorry.'

'I missed you,' I added. The problem with my face is that half the emotions are lost in the beard, and the other half hides behind the specs. The Howard puppy face I was trying to make had no effect on her.

'What's happening? It's big news. Everyone is calling me, asking questions for which I don't have answers,' she said.

We did not have a cable TV connection at our home. My mother and father were least interested in watching it, and Ramneek only watched Netflix and YouTube. So I bought a smart Android TV for him. He had cerebral palsy and spent his time at home watching TV, using his smartphone, and laptop, mostly viewing anime like *Dragon Ball Z*, *Naruto*, and *One Piece*.

Ever since I heard the news, I was so busy that I did not get time to see the news on YouTube. The big news was already on TV, and I was blissfully ignorant about it.

'What are they asking you, baby? Tell me?' I asked Indu.

'They are saying it's seven people in the last week alone, and civilians are being killed, especially the non-Muslims. They are asking me why I am still here and not leaving Kashmir,' she said.

'Slow down, baby. First, relax. Give me your hands.'

Her fists were clenched hard, so I took her hands in mine and added, 'We are not some tourists, that we just pack up and leave Kashmir. We live here. This is our home and I work here. Even if we have to leave, we cannot do that overnight. The people who are questioning you are scared because they only know what the media are saying. It's fear psychosis. Things will settle down soon.'

'How do you know they will settle down? What if there are more killings?' she asked. I did not know, I just wanted to console her, calm her down. I hoped they would settle down.

I was sure we would see a lot of hate-spewing and fear-mongering and not just simple reporting in the media.

'Come, sit here. Let's see what is happening, and what the media channels are showing.'

I pulled her into my embrace.

***

Indu grew up in Kerala, God's Own Country, where she had the Arabian Sea on its west which brought a cool breeze and truckloads of fish and seafood for them. In Kashmir, we had Pakistan, which brought a hot temper and a truckload of guns and ammunition to us. Whenever she talked about her childhood, she painted a vivid and colourful picture of it. Especially, when she spoke of her vacations and stay with her grandmother, her voice exuded excitement and happiness.

Her grandmother's house was on the banks of a river tributary, Meenachil, situated in such a way that access to the river was through the backyard of their house. Indu's grandfather, a homoeopathy doctor by profession, was a comrade and a village hero. After his death at the age of sixty-four, her grandmother lived alone. She was in her eighties. Their house had a constant flow of people who came to the river for bathing and washing. With every group came gossip and local stories. Indu's knack for narration and storytelling had developed in that house. Indu recollected that she and her childhood friends spent most of their afternoons in the river, so much so that her grandmother had to come with a stick to fetch her back and send the others home. No wonder, the proverb, 'It takes a village to raise a child,' came to be.

There was a small temple atop a hillock located next to her grandmother's home. People woke up to the sound of M.S. Subbulakshmi's rendition of 'Suprabhatham': '*Kowsalya supraja rama poorva sandhya pravarthathe. Uthishta narasardula karthavyam daivam ahnikam* (Sri Rama! Kausalya's endearing son! Wake up, dear, you have to do your day-to-day duties; do wake up please.)' The temple festival was organised once a year and lasted for eight days. There were processions every day, with lots of exuberant music and rhythms. Deities were put on an elephant which accompanied the procession. On the eighth day, in the final procession, thousands of people would join. The sounds from instruments like Maddalam, Idakka, Kombu, etc., would reverberate through the whole village, and fireworks would light up the sky. It was an enthralling experience. At the end of the eighth day, all those festivities would end, and visiting relatives would leave. Indu used to feel sad. But then she and her friend would go treasure hunting, searching for the fallen hair from the elephant. It was considered auspicious. According to urban legend, if you wore a bracelet made of elephant hair, it guaranteed prosperity, health and good luck. Nobody was worried about where the children were or what were they up to. Why would they be worried? There was peace and harmony all around.

Whenever she narrated it, I could see the collective experiences of brotherhood in that temple festival. In India, we celebrated many cultures and festivals. Diversity enriched us. These festivals, cultural and community-level activities held people together and gave them a sense of rootedness and belonging to a place.

What was my childhood like? I too had many memories with my grandparents but most of them were overshadowed by the grim memories of *hartals* and strikes, of deaths and sorrows, of gunshots and bomb blasts.

For me, a crowd of people meant a mob protesting. It meant I had to run to take shelter before things would escalate. I never felt attached to the identity of a Kashmiri. Maybe that was why I never resonated with the way Indu was proud of being a Keralite, a Malayali. I felt closer to my religious identity. I could proudly say, 'I am a Sikh'. But I would not add Kashmiri to it. I never felt I belonged wholeheartedly. I had always been confused about it.

Whatever conflict she had seen was minuscule compared to what we had grown up with. Our tolerance and understanding of violence were different. For her, the picture of Supinder and Deepak, the other person who was killed, was like scenes from the movies where bodies lay sprawled, tattered, and bloodied. For us, it was our history, our folklore.

It took me years of conversations with her to break the image of Kashmir she had. Unsafe, terrorism, daily encounters and killings, an eternal war between the army and the terrorists. Add to that the whole Kashmiri population supporting Pakistan and hating India. That was her image of Kashmir before meeting me. It had slowly changed. During her stay with me after marriage, Kashmir had been very peaceful. There was not much news of killings or blasts or any other incidents. Only two civilians were killed in September, a sarpanch on the sixth of the month and a non-local vendor on the seventeenth. Both incidents happened in faraway places. And the death of the non-local vendor was overshadowed by the shooting of a railway constable on the same day. In two months of her stay here, she had a better understanding of life in Kashmir.

Some days, we went for late-night drives around Dal Lake. I like it during the night. On one side, the glowing houseboats, with their fancy names lit in different colours, created a perfect reflection on the water, only disturbed by the ripples in between. On the other side, the busy banks which were overflowing with tourists during the day were in deep slumber, the big hotels across the road lit only by the neons and streetlights. There was no nightlife, clubbing, or partying in Kashmir. But the serenity and calmness you got on these deserted roads was quite the experience. She liked it too.

Many a time we would park our car somewhere and take long strolls on the banks of the lake. Often we would drive further to the outskirts, where children would be fishing in the backwaters. She liked one of the cafes there, which had an open terrace and overlooked the whole of Dal Lake under the clear blue sky, with the Zabarwan Hills as the backdrop. The view was surreal. At least for the first few visits.

I had taken her to some of the most famous cafes of Srinagar, to give her a semblance of liveliness. Cafes like Books and Bricks Cafe, Parsa's Food for All and Winterfell Cafe hosted a vibrant crowd. Cafes in Kashmir are known not only for their cosy ambiences but for the large collection of books they keep on their shelves.

After visiting the Books and Bricks Cafe, Indu told me that it had a personality of its own, giving rise to intense feelings which called for introspection. It was not just a place to sit and drink coffee. She liked the creative interiors, how they had used pages from old novels as wallpapers and wooden crates as ceilings. The small bookshelves hosted a nice collection of books. The aroma of freshly ground coffee beans, clubbed with the nice music they played made the cafe ooze warmth. After visiting them, she realised why I liked the cafes so much. They were perfect places for writing and reading. She had told me many times that I was a cafe person.

On one such outing she told me Kashmir was too laid-back and slow, calm and peaceful, so much so that she felt depressed looking at the snow-capped mountains as they towered over the lake, creating a shiny dark-blue background in the moonlight. The vibrant city life she was accustomed to in Bengaluru was in complete contrast to Kashmir. She had started missing it. Once she told me, 'We will buy a house here someday, and you can open your own cafe and do your poetry and writing events there.'

'You are liking it here, then?' I had asked her.

'It's very slow, but calm and peaceful. Maybe after retirement, we can settle down here. And isn't this what a writer wants?'

But all that had changed now. I wondered if she would still want to live here. Would she still call it calm and peaceful? It was a long day, and I was scared about how things were turning out and what more changes it was going to bring in our lives.

***

In the first week of October 2018, Ranvir called me out of the blue, 'Bupi, *jaaneman*, how are you and where are you?'

'Bro, bro, bro, I am great! Chilling. You say, how's life in Gujarat?'

He called me after several months, but that was how it was. We did not talk often. Ranvir was my close friend, working in Gujarat.

After a few pleasantries and catching up, he told me, '*Achha sun*, two of my friends are coming to Kashmir. Can you help them and show them around the Valley for a week or so?'

'If they pay for my food and fuel, why not? I am game,' I replied. No way was I missing out on free travel.

'They are on a budget trip. But yes, that much they will do,' he replied.

After making a few plans, I called him again.

'I can take them camping to Sonamarg and Pahalgam, but then, you know Kashmir is expensive as hell,' I said, and then gambled on, 'But, if you can order a Coleman tent, then it would be free night stays, and they would experience Kashmir like proper travellers and backpackers. And when you come here during summer, we can use it. It will be an investment.'

I knew he was earning well and ordering a tent would not be a big issue for him. He agreed to it. My old tent, which had I bought second-hand from a French tourist in Himachal Pradesh, was already tattered. It was a win-win situation for me. I got a free tent, got to host two girls and guide and travel with them at zero expense. What more could one ask for?

What I did not know then was I would later marry one of them.

When I first saw Indu at the airport, she was shivering in a brown fleece jacket and blue jeans, her arms around herself to keep the warmth in. The transition from Delhi's heat, where she had stayed for a night, before coming to Srinagar's cold weather, was abrupt. Most probably, she wore the jacket at the airport.

She had an aura of somebody who was unapproachable. Something told me not to take this woman lightly. Perhaps it was the way she carried herself. She had a wheat-almond complexion and a round face, with shoulder-length hair neatly tied in a ponytail. She stood a little below my shoulder. We still spoke to each other about our first meeting, about what impression we had of the other then. Indu described everything in detail, thanks to her excellent memory and great observational skills. The only vivid memory that I had was that of lemon grass oil which had leaked into her backpack, giving a nice fragrance.

But one thing we both know was that ours was not a love at first sight. Meeting Indu was my very first close interaction with a girl from far south. I was born and brought up in Jammu and Kashmir and had been working in Kashmir for the last eleven years. I was acclimatised to it, but for her, the pleasant autumn was like a severe winter. I did not know what to expect from someone who had never seen a winter in her life. She was holding on to her habits strongly, and wanted to take a bath every time we went out, and before and after every trip. In Kashmir, we didn't sweat much, and frequent bathing was not required. Much later, when I travelled to Kerala to visit her family, I realised where that habit came from.

She struggled with layers and layers of clothing she had to wear to protect herself from the cold, when we went to the mountains. I was amused looking at her small hands, like those of a child, unable to close the zipper of her jacket. When I moved in to close it, I felt I was overstepping. But soon, Indu adapted well and was flexible and open to new learning, an essential quality for a traveller.

October in Kashmir was the peak of autumn. The weather was pleasant. The sun was soft, and people usually sat outside, warming themselves in the sunlight. It was cold if you were in the shade, and so was the morning and evening breeze. The sky was a perfect spotless blue and the clean pollution-free environment let you see the snow-capped mountains in the distance, in all directions. The leaves of the mighty chinar trees turned yellow and orange, and some fell to the ground, carpeting their surroundings. If you clicked a picture in any direction without even looking, you would end up getting an amazing wallpaper.

We had already planned the itinerary before she came to Kashmir. And after a few hours of rest at home, we were supposed to leave for Sonamarg on the same day. She was so mesmerised by the picturesque landscapes for the first two days of our trips, that she kept quietly looking out the car window wherever we went, and whenever she said anything, it was, 'Wow, it's so beautiful.' In that week, we travelled to the major tourist destinations of Kashmir; Sonamarg, Pahalgam, Doodpathri, Gulmarg and Mughal Gardens. We stayed in tents and camped in the most mesmerising places, where the moonlight illuminated the snow-clad peaks in the background.

We lay stargazing at the clear skies for hours, shivering. The only thing keeping us warm was our conversations and the hot Kashmiri Kahwa. She told me she preferred black coffee with a hint of pepper.

On the long drives, we listened to each other's music playlists and talked on and on about everything and anything. She liked Piyush Misra and I liked those old Malayalam songs she played. Our conversations shifted from philosophy to psychology to books and travel to war and peace and so on. We were a group of three, in their late twenties with an inquisitive mind and lots of questions. We shared a passion for travel and reading but were different in many ways. We knew that we may not see each other ever again and that gave us a space to talk without being judged. I had a lot of hitchhiking and travelling stories to share. We laughed and argued, explored places and connected unconditionally. When I look back, I can see that I might have started falling for her at some point without consciously being aware of it.

It was the first time in her life that she was seeing autumn. I knew the seasons. Within a month, winter would knock on our doors, and with every passing day, the colour was going to fade, leaving everything black and white. For her, the four seasons were scenes in poetry. In Kerala, there was consistent weather punctuated by a monsoon. For us in Kashmir, it was a completely different story. We had four clearly defined seasons. Our winter was snowy white and our autumn hosted a canvas of orange and yellow chinars. The spring bloom of tulips and roses painted Kashmir in all the bright colours one could imagine while the flush green returned in summer and the streams flowed white with the ice-cold rapid waters coming from the Himalayas.

'You are so lucky that you live here,' she had said to me. She was in a dreamland. The moment she set foot in Sonamarg and saw the snow-capped mountains up close, close enough to grab a handful of snow and feel it, she jumped in excitement.

'I challenge you to live here for a month, then tell me the same thing later. It tends to become monotonous after a point of time,' I told her.

'I want to live in a hustling bustling city, with cafes and theatres and clubs, full of nightlife and parties.'

'And I came here to escape from that,' she smiled and added, 'You know, in the plains, in whatever direction you see, we have an open sky.

But here, there are mountains everywhere, like the way we used to draw in our childhood, a half sun peeking out of a mountain pass and a river flowing down from it. This is exactly like that, in all its glory.'

And I used to draw a beach line with coconut trees and a sailing boat.

As humans, we did not value what we had. What seemed beautiful to her was boring and unexciting to me. The mountains and valleys she found grandiose were just an everyday sight. The Dal Lake become a common mass of water. The clear sky felt like a permanently painted ceiling and the mountains curtailed the view beyond them. It was not the scenery or the view, that connected us to a place. It was the life we lived there, the liveliness of it, the meaning of it and the contentment we derive from living that life. And importantly, how secure we felt living in that place.

She was interested and excited by everything Kashmiri. She kept pointing with awe at any new thing she encountered—phiran, kangdi, wazwaan, houses, orchards, and so on. While answering her questions, I realised how little I knew about Kashmir.

When I told her it snowed above eight to ten feet in winter, she asked me, 'If it snows heavily, how do people live here in extreme winter?'

'Most of them shift to the lower valley where it snows less, and those who stay here keep a ration of stock for at least three months,' I told her.

'And what if there is a medical emergency?' she asked. 'If it is eight feet, they wouldn't be even able to open their doors for months.'

I was too ignorant to answer her questions.

'We will ask some local people here. They will give a better answer, and you can have an interaction with them as well,' I replied, saving myself from shelving a half-baked answer. We found that the state government and Indian army helped them clear the snow during extreme winters, keeping their roads accessible, and also provided medical aid if required. And most of the people moved to the lower valley for the one month of excessive snow, as I had told.

She was warned by her friends and family to be cautious in Kashmir. In those ten days, she only witnessed normalcy and peace like everywhere else. Kashmiris were the most hospitable people. They would go out of their way for their guests. There were no incidents of violence, and in the city, people were full of life and vigour. The markets were bustling, overflowing, in fact, with tourists.

'I don't know why people say Kashmir is not safe, I do not feel unsafe here,' she told me. 'But that feeling of uncertainty that anytime anything can happen remains all the time, I guess because of all the news we see about Kashmir,' she added.

'Yes, it is perfectly safe,' I told her. At least for tourists. Only if you had come in 2016 would you know how safe it was, I said to myself.

Indu had come into Kashmir, and into my life when it was very peaceful and quiet.

3

Sacrificial Lambs

Srinagar, Kashmir
7 October 2021, Thursday
Evening

Raman called me around 4 p.m. '*Bro, momos cancel Bhabhi ke.*'

'Bhai, leave the momos. I guess she won't even be having dinner at home today,' I replied. Indu looked at me, realising that I was talking about her.

'Didn't you know Supinderji personally? It is so unfortunate. I am thinking about her children, orphaned for no fault of theirs,' Raman said.

'Yeah. That's the curse of living in Kashmir. Where are you?' I asked him.

'Still at the bank, leaving within an hour, I guess,' he replied.

'Call me once you reach home,' I said.

I had no clue the day was going to be like this. Just the night before, Indu and I went to Winterfell for a coffee. I wanted coffee, but she wanted momos at Everest Kitchen, a Tibetan restaurant. I was all game for coffee, pizza, pasta, or even burgers. But momos? No, not at all, because I loved mutton or chicken momos, and not being able to eat them would be heartbreaking. And who eats veg momos anyway? Being Sikhs, we eat only jhatka meat, which was not available at Everest. There were only three shops in the whole of Srinagar which served jhatka. Our coffee date at Winterfell went on for so long that when we reached Everest, it was closed. I could see the disappointment on Indu's face.

'I'll take you out tomorrow. Promise. We'll come here directly,' I said. I had invited Raman to come with us.

'And what will we eat? Veg momos?' he asked me.

'No, we will wait for her to finish eating mutton momos, then we will go for fried chicken at our place,' I told him. The jhatka shops served only the main course. All three shops had minimal seating and were not family or couple friendly. Most people opted for takeaway. Taking Indu to those shops was not an option.

For vegetarian food though, we had all the freedom. Raman and I visited almost all the major cafes and restaurants in Srinagar, especially for pizzas, pasta and beverages. We had singled out the best ones and Indu reaped the benefit of it. Some Sikhs would not even eat at a place where halaal was served, not even a cup of tea. They would not enter such cafes and restaurants. But we did not mind.

'I have seen people who either eat or don't eat non-veg. But this selective eating of jhatka meat, I haven't seen much. In Kerala, we also have different shops for jhatka and halaal, but only a few people bother about it,' Indu had told me the first time I told her about my food restrictions.

What happened just yesterday seemed long ago. With every passing hour, the day was turning grim. When I read that TRF had again posted a media release taking responsibility for the two killings, thereby, taking the score to five killings in two days, I was angry. It was not a personal vendetta. Veerji was right. It was a targeted killing. I had been debating with him otherwise. But if TRF was involved, it was definitely a targeted killing. The Resistance Front was believed to be a shadow faction of Lashkar-e-Taiba, a prominent terrorist organisation. When they claimed the three killings, they must have had reasons for it. What would they say about Supinder? Stooge? RSS? Collaborator? No, if they said so, it would be a blatant lie.

Raman lived in the same neighbourhood as Supinder. He called me again the moment he reached home around 5 p.m. Indu and I were still in our room, listening to YouTube live updates from different news channels.

'Bro, it looks like the whole of Kashmir has come here. There are people everywhere. I don't think I would be able to take the car home. I think I'll have to park it somewhere else.'

'Yeah. I heard that. Veerji called. Everyone is assembling outside her house. They have delayed the cremation also. It will happen tomorrow. Everyone is angry,' I replied.

'Do you know anything about the other person killed? The Pandit guy?' he asked.

'Not much. His name is Deepak Chand, a PM package employee, I guess. Hey, I heard, it's the TRF again. Some poster has come out. I haven't seen it yet, but they claimed responsibility.'

'Ya, I got it. I will forward it to you. They accused both of them of hoisting the Indian Flag on Independence Day.'

'Then, they will have to kill every school principal. Everyone hoisted it. We also did it in our school. That's ridiculous.'

The day we got the government order to hoist the flag at school, with a proper parade, signing of the National Anthem, and a proper flag code, we too were speculating some unrest. We were ordered to ask all the students to attend school and take part in the ceremony on the morning of 15 August.

'They will burn us along with the school and the flag,' a colleague had said while we all sat debating the motive behind the order.

'Kashmir is a union territory now. Not a state anymore. We have to do what the Centre says,' another one had said. The headmistress kept quiet for some time before speaking.

'Government order. We will have to do it. The question is how. We will have to find out some way because we have to send the video as proof of the ceremony.'

She kept jiggling her left leg so vigorously that her whole body was shaking. I decided I was not going to school that day and no way was I was going to ask any student to go, I thought to myself. Our school, Government Boys High School, was in Kralpora, which people used to call mini-Islamabad, for the number of encounters, stone-pelting episodes, and other anti-India incidents that happened there. Once in a while, the police would round up teenagers and young adults and pick them up for questioning about such incidents. A few times, some of them were beaten up if found guilty. Hoisting a flag in such an area was inviting trouble.

But on 14 August evening, the day before the hoisting ceremony, the SHO of our area called the headmistress and told her that there was some input and asked us to cancel the ceremony. By the time we had done a full dress rehearsal with a few students. We were told to send those videos to the higher-ups.

But for Supinder, I guess, that was not the case.

'In that case,' I told Raman, 'there can be more killings. Hundreds of people followed the order.'

'Then you don't go to school for some days,' he said.

'Yeah. Let's see, anyway. I don't think we will meet today or tomorrow as well. Keep me posted if you hear anything. And yes, forward me the poster.'

The poster Raman sent openly declared that more such killings would take place, and anyone who was siding with India or following government orders like hoisting the national flag would be targeted.

My first instinct was to show it to Indu, but then I wanted to talk about it to someone who understood the Kashmiri situation more. So I called a friend, Sadaam, who was a student of politics and an active participant in such debates. He taught political science to civil service aspirants at a coaching institute.

'I was just thinking about you,' he said the moment he answered the call.

'Yeah. You were about to call me, alright. These excuses have grown old. You need to be more creative now,' I replied. 'Anyway, did you see the poster and the reason they gave for killing Supinder?' I added.

'Yes, yes. I saw it earlier. That was why I was thinking about you. Remember we were having this discussion when the order had come to hoist the flag in the schools and other government offices?'

'I remember telling you that if these things are done forcibly there would be repercussions. But I never thought that it would be against specific people,' I replied.

'We were worried that there would be burning of schools or stone pelting but nothing happened at that time. But everything was just quiet before the storm, these killings are the vengeance for 370,' Sadaam said. There were rumours everywhere that the revenge for Art. 370 would be taken. People felt that the government was oppressing them. Covid acted as a buffer for some time. Otherwise, there would have been implications in 2020,' he replied, his voice changing from pensive to energetic suddenly.

'Are you justifying these killings?' I felt irritated at his mention of vengeance. 'Killing innocent people who are equally oppressed? Really?'

'There would be implications. That's what I meant. I am not justifying the killings, but we knew it was bound to happen. In the last thirty years, we have understood that much at least,' he said.

'But why Supinder and Deepak? Why a Sikh and a Hindu? There were thousands of Muslims who followed government orders. Why not kill any one of them? If it was meant as an example, that explanation would have been more plausible,' I replied.

'Just because it is a Sikh this time, you are talking about justice? All these years, such killings have been happening. We, Muslims, have borne the maximum brunt. Fifty pandits died and they packed their *boriya-bistara* and left Kashmir. Tell me how many Sikhs have been killed? Hundred, two hundred? Not even those many. Thousands of us are killed every year. Another thousand blinded and disabled and then there are those who never returned. We have read more *gayabana-janazahs* than you have attended funerals,' he sounded angry and irritated.

'This is your fight. You want Pakistan, you pay for it. Why do we have to be a part of the slaughter? We don't want that,' I replied in an equally angry tone.

'Leave it. There is no point talking about it,' he said. 'You take care of yourself and don't go to school for some days. Nobody knows what is going to happen in the next few days,' he added.

'Yeah. I will do that. You take care of yourself,' I replied before disconnecting the call.

He was one of the people with whom I have had such discussions multiple times. He was a soft-core sympathiser to the Kashmir freedom cause and had always felt that India was oppressing the Kashmiris and that the only way out for Kashmir was to align with Pakistan or to become an independent country. As for the question of how and what would happen after such allegiance or independence, he had no answers.

I felt a sudden uneasiness and went out to have a glass of water. The poster that Raman sent me was on the phone screen.

When I returned to the bedroom, I was still processing the discussion. Was Supinder killed because she followed a government order? Or because she was a Sikh who followed the order? The moment I showed the poster to Indu I realised ignorance was bliss. Until now, she was sad and depressed by the killings, worried and anxious about answering to the people who called her, but after seeing the poster, her anxiety swelled up. She had seen the video of our school's flag hoisting event. I was there instructing students how to do the march past.

'You also hoisted the flag in your school,' Indu asked me, her words filled with worry.

'I did not. I mean, the whole school did. The principal had to hoist it. The teachers just stood there at the ceremony,' I replied.

'Would it be safe for you to go to school like this?' she rested her head on my shoulder and kept smoothing her pants.

'I will not go tomorrow,' I held her hand and caressed it with my thumb.

'And then, the day after tomorrow, and after that?' she asked.

'I don't know, baby. It will be alright, don't worry,' I replied. The reality was I doubted I knew the answer myself.

'How do you take all this so calmly?' she sat up and faced me.

'Take what?' I asked.

'These killings, encounters, the bomb blasts, the shootings, the deaths, all of this.'

For her, the conflict was horrible, and the violence was unreasonable and illogical. For me, it was everyday life. Growing up in Kashmir did that to you. We talked about these events daily as if they were everyday things. As Sikhs, we were seldom part of these encounters or deaths, or killings. In the three decades of unrest, during which time some Kashmiri Muslims seeking azaadi and the Indian Army were in an unending conflict, we thought of our deaths as sacrifices in order to be allowed to live in Kashmir. Sikhs were mere spectators and sometimes collateral damage, nothing more.

'It is what I have grown up with, baby. It is just another day in Kashmir. The last few years have been quiet, but this was what it used to be like. It is a cycle, years of peace, and then years of unrest.'

'Isn't that sad, unfortunate?' she asked, sighing slowly.

I wanted to avoid the subject, and it was difficult to answer her questions. Every answer would give birth to a new question. So, I just nodded.

'Let's go and have some tea,' I got up from the bed. I'll make one for everyone. Come out for some time,' I said to Indu.

'Ok. I'll call my brother in the meantime. He had called many times, but I didn't pick up his call,' she replied.

Deep down, I was still trying to make sense of it all. I read the TRF poster once again. Why was it wrong for her to hoist the flag and right for others? Because she was a Sikh? Because they were Muslims? Do they think she wanted to hoist it? Was she happily hoisting it? And the Muslim teachers, did they feel forced, too?

By the time we had our dinner, graphical details of the killings were being shown on a media channel. Supinder and Deepak could be seen sitting on chairs in the school garden. Two armed men were shown coming through the gate and shooting them. The news person gave a narrative of the terrorists trying to create unrest and break the peace that had been established after the revocation of Article 370 and Article 35(a) in the year 2019. Another media channel showed a picture of Supinder and Deepak and then interviewed the staff members of the school, who narrated their eyewitness accounts. A debate on one channel was dissecting the incident, terming them as minority killings, and predicting more such events in the future if the situation was not contained.

The TRF, on the other hand, had warned the people that there would be more such attacks. They had a clear vision and mission, which was by now understandable to everyone. Scare non-Kashmiris out of Kashmir. Tell non-locals that they were not welcome as settlers or employees but only as tourists and travellers. Tell Kashmiri Pandits that returning to Kashmir would have consequences for them.

Indu talked to her brother, who, I guessed, would be providing his analysis of the event, like everyone else who called her. For outsiders and non-Kashmiris, it had a clear and transparent motive, killing of non-Muslims by Muslim terrorists, and labelling it as jihad. The Kashmiris, on the other hand, knew it was a warning to everyone, not just to non-Muslims, to dissociate themselves from the Indian administration. More than a communal killing, it was an ideological killing, sending a message to those who side with India. Those who followed government orders and sympathised with India would face the same fate.

It was just after dinner when Snowber called.

'Bupi Bhaiyya, are you in Kashmir?' she asked.

'Yes, where else would I be,' I replied.

'I thought you also got scared and left. I heard some people have come to Jammu already.'

Snowber lived in Jammu and worked in a hospital. She was a poet by passion, and I met her some years back at a poetry open-mic event I organised in Jammu. Ever since we had become good friends.

'Did you know them? They were also school teachers,' she asked.

'Yes. Not that I have worked with her. But I used to tutor her children, a boy and a girl,' I replied.

'And the other one?' she probed further.

'No, just the name. Deepak Chand,' I replied.

'What do you think is happening? Tell me your own opinion of it, not the news.'

I knew she would be asking something like this.

'It's too soon to have an opinion. Yesterday, two Hindus were killed. Today a Sikh and a Hindu. It is clearly targeted at non-Muslims right now. But if there are more killings of Indian sympathisers as they are calling them, or collaborators who are Muslims, and not just Sikhs and Hindus, things might look different. But we don't know that yet,' I replied.

'Do you also see the killings as Sikhs and Hindus and not as human beings?' she asked.

'They are human beings. There is no doubt about it. But you cannot rip them off of their identities, can you?' I asked.

'Tell me about the three Hindus killed,' she asked.

'Bindroo was a pharmacist, very famous. The other was some golgappa wala. And today's Deepak Chand was a Pandit government employee.'

'Any more details?' she inquired.

'No. What is your point?' I was getting a little irritated. In the middle of all the mess, she wanted to talk. Our conversations were centred around the craft of writing, books that she read, and some philosophical debates. She was a staunch feminist and believed that I was too. Mostly, she wanted my personal opinion on things as if she was assessing my views and principles.

'My point is you don't care about the Hindus or Muslims. You did not even bother to check who they were, their families, their names, where they were from, and other things. But you were able to tell everything about the Sikh lady when I asked,' she replied.

I could not answer her. I had no answer. I guess as human beings, we have an 'our' and an 'other'. We associate more with 'our', empathise and sympathise more with 'our' than we do with the 'other'. This duality has been defining us always. Every one of us. Our identity, our pride, our respect. We associate with our 'our'.

Maybe she was telling the truth, and even if it was not the whole truth, her point was still valid. I had not checked about the others. Not because I was not bothered about them but maybe because I was distant from their pain and suffering. But I could feel more for Supinder, not because she was a Sikh, but because I knew her personally.

'If it was not Supinder, if I did not know her personally, I would not have known about the person even if he or she was a Sikh,' I defended myself.

'So you don't bother to check about anyone, even Sikhs?'

'I care for everyone equally. Every life lost in these killings adds to the misery, is a terrible loss for all of us. You know, you have the privilege to ask these questions because you are safe in Jammu. People sitting comfortably can ask questions. But those in the heart of the matter are just trying to survive.'

Indu looked at me astonished. 'All well?' she asked softly. 'Nothing,' I mouthed and nodded back at her. 'Can we talk about it some other time? I am exhausted and cannot have a feature-length debate right now,' I tried to calm myself while replying to Snowber.

'Arre, Bupi Bhaiyya, I was just asking. Don't get irritated,' she said. Her questions, whenever we talked, were not to get answers but to get insights and ideas about how I perceived things.

'What happened? Why were you angry at her,' Indu asked when I disconnected the call. I was not angry at her. I was angry at myself. Snowber's question had left me dumbfounded. I had to justify myself, and justification was always a sign of covering up. Was I so inconsiderate? I actually did not read anything about anyone else.

It was very difficult to answer her questions. In the age of cancel-culture and intolerance, anything and everything can be taken otherwise. One had to be politically correct, and sensitive to burning issues, gender, religion, and whatnot. You could be easily labelled as racial, Islamophobic or homophobic by just stating the facts. I wonder how people would have treated Dickens, Austen and Hardy in these times. Would Dickens be called out for promoting child labour, and Austen be called a chauvinist and Hardy be hated for portraying weak women?

I have always believed a writer shows us what is happening in society by presenting its real picture, and not just creating a paradise or a utopia that shows us what the world and society should be. In this age of cancel-culture and censorship, it is becoming increasingly difficult for writers to speak the naked truth and portray the reality. The characters are now considered mouthpieces of the author, and any stance and stand of the character belongs to the writer. The correctness, as in political and social, and the recent hypercritical obsession with isms and biases, like feminism, veganism, the gender identity, and a growing discord between telling the truth as opposed to sugar-coating it has weakened the said faculty of the writer to bring out the reality onto the pages.

And when I talked to Snowber, it was all of these considerations that defined our conversation.

Indu kept staring at me, waiting for my answer.

'Nothing, dear. Just some futile debates,' I told her. 'Do you know more about the Pandit guy who was killed?' I asked Indu.

'Yes, I read about him. He dropped his three-year-old daughter and his wife in Jammu just a few days ago. He was just thirty-eight years old.'

When did she read that? I wondered. Am I actually prejudiced?

'Why are you asking this now? You already knew about him. He was a teacher too,' she said.

'Yes. Just asking. Why are you looking so grim? What did your brother ask?' I asked.

'The usual, like this is a minority killing, you should not stay in Kashmir, plan something. Everyone is saying and asking the same thing,' she replied and asked, 'You look irritated. What did Snowber ask you to make you lose it?'

Indu and I had a pact. We would voice our emotions aloud to each other, always tell what we felt to avoid miscommunication, and if we ever fought, we were to solve the issue before sleeping. We had never broken the pact. But to tell the other person how we felt, we first had to recognise the emotion ourselves. And most of the time, we were confused about our feelings.

'No, it's not about what she asked. I am just tired of the same conversations. I simply want to sleep now. I want the day to end.'

Even at the dinner table, we talked about the killing. It got too depressing for me. How our pleasant conversation all of a sudden turned into these heavy and anxious ones. Indu did not even open her laptop the whole day. It was a working day, and usually, she was busy reading research papers or seeing patients for her study.

Just a few days ago, Indu and I made a new blog titled, *The Critique Couple*, where we were going to review movies and books. She had an extensive collection of movies on her hard drive. She had watched most of them, especially the classics. I had an extensive collection of books and was proud of my reading portfolio. I had read a majority of the classics, from Chaucer to Spencer and Shakespeare to Milton, Dickens and Hardy.

Her movie collections were arranged by directors, alphabetically. Whenever she talked about a movie, she knew the names of the directors and the cast. I would not even know the name of the movie, and even if I had already watched one, I seldom knew the names of anyone except the leading actors. We recently watched *My Fair Lady*, an old classic of 1964. It was an adaptation of George Bernard Shaw's *Pygmalion*, a play that I had already read and of which I remembered every single detail. We had a list of another twenty movies and ten books that we planned to review over the next six months. I knew how Indu's taste in movies and books had developed when I visited her house. She had already told me once that her father was a voracious reader. 'Not only novels and non-fiction, but he also loves to read a variety of newspapers once he returns from his morning walk.' They had a veranda in their house in Kerala, where all of them would sit in the morning, sip their teas and read the dailies and the weekly magazines. They would discuss the news and politics and other things they read. And not only in the morning, but most of the time their dinner conversations would extend for hours discussing things and sharing perspectives and opinions. When I visited her house, the thing that I liked the most was their home library, which had tons of books from different genres. And in Kashmir, I did not even subscribe to a newspaper. She asked me to get a subscription to the *Hindu* for her when she came to stay. The irony was that in Kashmir we got the paper on the next day of its publication. The current affair was not so current in Kashmir, despite what was going on.

I lay in bed, introspecting how I did not even look at the details pertaining to the other people. I slowly bought out my phone to check the details of the people killed in the last few days. All of them had a name, Mohd Shafi Dar, Majid Ahmad Gojri, Mohd Shafi Lone, Virender Paswan, Makhan Lal Bindroo and Deepak Chand. Anxious about the next day, I put the phone down and tried to empty all the thoughts brewing in my mind. Kashmir was turning me into this. All we did here was talk about killings and deaths, about violence and politics. In the last two years of peace, Covid and non-violence, I had forgotten that it used to be like this always, a never-ending loop of quiet and violence. I was only two years old when we migrated out of Kashmir for the first time. My father told me that those were the years of chaos, deaths and killings.

I wondered what we would do if there were more killings. But then, I knew we would move on, as we always did. My family had seen such killings in close quarters when they migrated out of Kashmir. This never-ending loop started when I was born. Was I the Saleem Sinai of my story, I asked myself.

4

From Landlords to Tenants

Kashmir, 1989–1991

On the evening of 30 October 1989, as the nurse delivered me, she said, '*Ik aur ugarwadi agaya* (one more extremist has come).' She said this because I had cried so loud and held the nurse's finger so tight, my mother recollected. Then, the nurse covered it up with laughter. She was a Kashmiri Pandit.

That was the year when Kashmir saw its first civilian killing. We officially mark the year 1989 as the start of Kashmir militancy. Seventy-nine civilians and thirteen security personnel were killed that year. It was the first time that civilians were killed, and the city was reverberating with bomb blasts, shootouts and targeted killings. But it was only the beginning, just a trailer.

The year 1990 showed what Kashmir was going through. Bloody and violent, that year, 862 civilians were killed and hundreds of encounters between the army and militants resulted in the killing of 183 militants and 132 security personnel. A total of 1177 killings in a year, an average of three people every day. Widespread sloganeering against non-Muslims, the targeted killings of some high-ranking Kashmiri Hindus, and an ultimatum issued by the militants to leave Kashmir compelled the Hindus to leave the state. By March of the year, almost 70 per cent of the Hindus had already left the state.

At that time, we lived as a joint family at my paternal grandfather's house in a picturesque village called Kundi, some thirty kilometres from the capital city. The family consisted of my grandparents, my parents and me, my father's two elder brothers, who were both married and their two children. My father's three sisters lived with their husbands at their in-laws' houses in other villages in Kashmir.

Kundi was a small Sikh village comprising thirteen households situated on an ascending hill. The villagers had cleared the land into steps and built their houses. On one side of the village was the main transportation road, which connected it with Srinagar. On the other two sides were hundreds of acres of farms and orchards owned by the villagers. Almost everyone in the village had a minimum of 40 acres of land. The southern side of the village was bordered by the adjacent Muslim village.

Most of the Sikhs used to be just overseers and did not till their own farms or tend to the orchards. Instead, they hired a workforce from the neighbouring villages.

But that was in the past. Now, the village was empty, with barren lands and empty houses and not a single person living there anymore. The adjacent lands all had been sold off to the nearby villagers, and the Sikhs who lived there had either migrated from the village to the city or out of Kashmir.

'We had acres and acres of apple orchards and walnut trees and cherry plantations,' my mother told me whenever I asked her how rich we were. 'Your grandfather was the village leader, a very respected man. And your grandmother, oh! She was one hell of a lady. The whole village respected her. Nobody would look her in the eye. She was the strength of the family, the wisest and the most learned woman in the whole village.'

I accepted the grandfather part without question, but grandmother, Beji, at least for me was a loving motherly figure who made delicious food, told me stories, and taught me how to eat a ripe pear without spilling the juice on my clothes. No way could she be so strict.

We had a big house, which, unlike all other things I had been told, was verified, for its skeleton still stood sans windows and doors. I visited it sometimes. In the thirty years of my life, I had seen that house wither away bit by bit. I loved its architecture so much that I decided wherever I settled down, I would build a similar house, if not the exact copy.

The main gate of the house opened into a mosaic pathway made of stone, which divided the large garden into two halves, and led directly to the main door of the house. Once you entered the main door, a corridor again divided the house into two rows. One part had two bedrooms and a bathroom, while the other one had a large living room, a bedroom, and a kitchen. The corridor itself led to the other end of the house, and a door opened into a small veranda, whose stairway led into an open expanse of a three-tiered area. The first tier had a large pear tree and an open area, the second tier had apple trees, while the third and the largest tier was used as a kitchen garden and was lined with cherry plantation. On both sides of the house were small passageways that connected the front lawns with the orchards at the back.

I took my mother to the house after two decades of abandoning it. 'Once when you were a year old, you crawled through the corridor to the veranda and tumbled and rolled down the staircase. You bumped your head, and had a big blue *anda* here,' Maa said touching my forehead. 'Everybody scolded me for being a careless mother.'

'Beji and I would cook inside while your father and Pitaji, would wait in the living room, calling us, saying that the aroma of chicken was making them hungry. Look at this house now. It breaks my heart.' Mother became teary-eyed whenever she spoke of the house.

My grandfather, Pitaji, was a person with a vision who believed in education when everyone in his village thought farming was more prosperous and better. For a decade, he remained a visitor in his own village because he rented a small two-room house in the city to educate his children. He gave up the comfortable, laid-back life with a good income and other luxuries for the sake of his children's education.

My father's eldest brother went on to become a colonel in the Indian army and the other elder brother became a reputed dental surgeon, the first Sikh from Kashmir who went to Mumbai for his education and won a gold medal during his college years. As for the three sisters, all of them graduated and got married into families of repute. My father, the youngest brother in the family, did his post-graduation and eventually became a lecturer in a college.

The first one to migrate was my doctor uncle, who shifted his family to Chandigarh in mid-1990 but came back to join as a dental surgeon at Anantnag District Hospital. The colonel uncle was posted in Jammu as a commanding officer and lived there with his family, which left my grandparents and the three of us—me, my father and my mother—at the village house.

During 1990, many Sikhs were also targeted, but the number of Sikh families that migrated from Kashmir was negligible, and unlike Hindus, they did not migrate en masse but as individual families scattered over the next decade.

In 1991 the fatalities rose to 1393, with 594 civilians, 185 security personnel and 614 militants. The increase in the number of militants created an atmosphere of fear, leading to a slow and silent migration of more families, including some Muslim families.

It was that year, in September, when we felt the sting personally.

My uncle, the doctor, went to visit his family in Chandigarh and met with an accident there and died. The other uncle, the colonel, brought his dead body back for cremation to our native place, Kundi, the next day. Within an hour of cremation, our house was attacked by militants who abducted him and his cousin. The next day their bodies were recovered.

When I asked him about the incident, Papa told me, 'It was so sudden that we did not know how to react. Beji and Pitaji were distraught with grief. Both aunts were broken, the children too young to comprehend that they had suddenly become fatherless. I didn't even remember how I felt emotionally. I loved them.' Papa was visibly upset when he narrated everything to me. He said, 'We were broken, scared and angry, cursing and blaming ourselves for what had happened. Why did colonel sahab have to come to Kashmir? Why didn't we do the funeral of doctor sahab in Jammu? But I guess colonel sahab was also too emotional and grief-stricken to take any decision at that time. People around him counselled that doctor sahab should be cremated at his ancestral land, and he had let his guard down.

'In two days we had lost three family members. Within ten days we had lost our home as both the widowed aunts moved out of Kashmir, and we moved to Srinagar city and eventually to Jammu. The once prosperous home became an empty house.'

When I asked Maa how Papa was before the incident, she said, 'Both his brothers loved him a lot. They spoiled him with their love and affection. His elder brothers had taken the family responsibility, which allowed him to be carefree. He had no obligations. When I got married to him, he was financially independent, but his brothers would still help him with his indulgences. We had been married for four years when it happened. You were only two, too young to remember much.

'It changed him. All of a sudden, he became responsible for his family. He had to take care of his parents and his own family. Things happened so fast that it took him a while to take control of his life,' Maa told me.

During the next three years, of which I had little memory, we lived in Jammu and Kathua. My father, despite his education, was not able to secure any permanent or worthwhile job and had to juggle various menial ones. All I remembered of those days were through the photographs in our family album. Only small snippets and fragments from the time remained in my memory along with the stories that I heard repeatedly from my parents while I ask them to explain those photographs to me. Picnics at a park, taking an oil massage on the open terrace, visiting my cousins in Chandigarh, and being covered in colours during the Holi festival.

During the years we spent in Jammu, between 1991 and 1994, Kashmir boiled with militancy. Of more than seven thousand people who were killed, half of them were militants fighting for Kashmir's freedom. Pandits as a community had already migrated to Jammu, but the clashes between the militia and army were numerous. The Kashmir freedom movement was said to have been at its peak at that time.

Unlike Pandits, who chose to migrate, Sikhs stayed on in Kashmir. Only a few hundred families, who felt fearful or who believed that there could be reasons for the militants to target them, left Kashmir. And out of those few hundred, a majority came back to Kashmir over the next few years.

I asked my parents several times what made them come back to Kashmir, and each time they gave me different answers. In every answer, the underlying emotion was alienation. While my father said it was not possible to survive in a new place without any proper source of income, my mother believed that it was the loneliness and longing that brought them back. She said, 'We were clueless about those we left behind in Kashmir. Were they alive or dead? Were they well or not? All my family was in Kashmir, while your father's family had broken away and spread to different places. But all his life he had lived in Kashmir, his friend circle, his social structure, everything was missing in Jammu. We both wanted an excuse to go back while we both pretended to be strong. None of us wanted to say out loud that we wanted to go back.

'We went back when it became too difficult for us to adjust. Your father was getting irritable and angry at small things. He missed Kashmir. In Jammu, he felt like an alien, everything was so different in Jammu, the food, the weather, the people, the houses, everything.'

My mother made it sound like they came back because of my father's adjustment and alienation issues.

According to Papa's version, we came back because of my mother. 'She was becoming depressed. She kept thinking about her family, her father, her brothers and sisters, who were still in Kashmir.'

But whatever happened, the excuse they were looking for came in the shape of my mother's pregnancy with Ramneek, my younger brother. She was alone and I was only four years old, too wild to be contained and disciplined. Father was the sole breadwinner, so she had to take care of herself and me without anyone's help. There was only one option. Return to Kashmir for proper care and rest, return to her family, to her roots.

Eventually, in the summer of 1994, we came back to Kashmir, though not as landlords but as tenants.

5

Home and Homeland

Srinagar, Kashmir
8 October 2021, Friday

I woke up late, around 11 a.m., unaware of how the world around me would have changed overnight. However, such days brought some certainties. Today, like me, thousands of Sikhs and Pandits would have taken the day off. In Kashmir, it was common knowledge that if there was a civilian killing that made it to the news, the next day, there would be protests throughout, and most areas would see curfew impositions and internet blockage. The markets, business avenues and offices would be closed down. But if the civilian belonged to the minority community, the reaction would be different. The minorities would simply stay home for a few days for things to settle down, and then they would go back to work.

That was what I thought would happen. And I was so wrong. Two things had happened even before I got out of bed.

First, a mob of thousands of people, both Sikhs and Muslims, gathered outside Supinder's house, not just to pay their condolences but to also express solidarity and demand justice. Major political and bureaucratic figures condemned the killing. Everyone cautioned not to give this killing a religious colour and avoid any riots.

'What happened is very unfortunate. We are with our Sikh brothers. We demand justice,' I could hear a news snippet playing in the other room.

'We are in it together. This killing was a warning to the government employees who participate in activities and enforce the dictates of the Indian government. We request the government to bring the culprits to the law and punish them,' another voice spoke.

Everyone was glued to my father's phone on which this WhatsApp forward was sent.

The second thing that happened was that hundreds of Kashmiri Pandits employed under the Prime Minister Relief Package (PM Package) left Kashmir in the early morning.

In 2010, the UPA Government, headed by Dr Manmohan Singh, initiated a relief and rehabilitation package for Kashmiri migrants, under which several thousand jobs were offered to those who wanted to return to the Valley. As a result, around 3000 Kashmiri Pandits and over a hundred Sikhs, including me, came back to the Valley.

Indu had woken up earlier than me and was in the living room talking to my father and my mother. There was something amiss about the way they were replying to my good-morning greeting. They were barely nodding. I had an intuition that the day was not going to be easy.

'All well?' I asked everybody.

'Yes, yes, all well. We were just talking about Supinder. News is that she had adopted some Muslim girl and took care of her financial responsibility,' Papa replied.

'They killed such a good lady,' Maa added.

'Oh! I did not know that. She never talked about it,' I said.

I was sceptical of this new information. Posters of her social endeavour were floated around her house and social media, and everyone was shaming her killers for murdering a noble person. It was a hot topic in the whole of Kashmir.

'People are saying it is not a religious or minority killing, but a warning to the government collaborators,' Indu told me as she stepped in to hug me, but then decided not to, realising my parents were there. I could see a sense of relief in her body language.

What Indu said felt more placating and self-comforting than just a fact. We, humans, tend to find solace in whatever we could hold onto. The killings were stifling only if the guns were pointed toward our people. The moment they were trained on someone else—the other—it became okay. We sympathised, condemned and showed our disgust, called it out and then went back to living our lives like nothing happened.

'Whatever it is, innocent humans are being killed and families are bereaved for no reason.'

I was still thinking about her children. I wanted to go and meet them and talk to them, but then I could not think of what I would say to them. What could one say anyway?

While everyone discussed whether to proclaim the killing as a religious one or not, very few people saw what was actually happening. Targeted or not, a killing was a killing. Sikh or Hindi or Muslim, a killing was a killing. The people left behind should feel the same pain.

I went out to the garden to soak in the sunlight, to soak in my contemplations. I called a friend, Harshdeep, who was also employed under the same PM Package employment scheme as I was, to check what he knew. He was more active in the employee association than I was.

'Pandits ran away again,' he told me immediately. 'You see, they will not come back till March, till the next session starts,' he added. Most of the Pandits were employed as teachers.

'Nothing like that, bhai. Within a week the offices will call us back to join the duties. These one-off incidents won't instigate a full-fledged migration again.'

I was aghast at his opportunism. He did not talk about the killings at all but was eager to jump to conclusions about Pandits' fear and migration so that he could enjoy some paid vacations.

'Come over tomorrow. We will talk in detail,' I told him. I realised calling him was a mistake. He only increased my stress and anxiety beyond measure.

'Okay. I will come tomorrow evening. Do you want to go to Supinder's funeral? A lot of people are going there today,' he said.

'No, Papa is going there. I'll stay home today. I will go to her house after some days to meet the children,' I told him.

'You see, we should also stay home until the Pandits join back. *Asi kay mufta de aye de aa* (Do our lives cost nothing)?' he said.

'You come tomorrow. We will talk about it,' I repeated myself.

By the time I came back inside, my father was getting ready to go to Supinder's funeral. Two of my uncles had called and told me that they would pick him up and then go to the funeral together. My mother was in the bedroom watching TV. Indu was speaking in Malayalam, her mother tongue, to someone on the phone and I did not understand a single word of it. All I could guess was she was angry at whoever was on the other side.

Meanwhile, news channels and social media erupted into a frenzy of debates. Some labelled the killings as minority killings and proclaimed that Kashmir was unsafe for Hindus and other non-Muslims. Others called it the return of terrorism in Kashmir, while some others said it was the work of agencies to bring unrest to Kashmir again. While we who lived in Kashmir ignored such news, those in other states shaped their idea of Kashmir by such news.

'Why does everyone want to hear it from me when they have already seen the news or read about it? It is so frustrating, what do they want me to say?' Indu shouted after disconnecting her call.

'They are calling because they are worried about you. By the way, who was it?'

Indu was too anxious to answer my question, and continued, 'But I don't know if I can take it anymore. I can't even switch off my phone,' she said, throwing her phone on the bed. She was incessantly consuming every drop of news and their dissection the channels poured out, in their typical dramatic anger and shouting against Pakistan and Muslims.

'You need to stop watching the news,' I said as I took the phone when she leaned in to reach for it.

Our phones kept ringing all day. My friends from other states called to check up on me. But more than me, it was Indu who was at the centre of all attention. Her family and friends, who had come across those debates and news, called her to say it was no longer safe for non-Muslims to stay in Kashmir and asked her what she had decided regarding that. They came to know that some terrorist groups had proclaimed that they would kill all outsiders who wanted to sully their beloved motherland.

News panellists and anchors labelled Kashmiri Muslims as jihadis, terrorists and Islamic radicals, and pointed out their love towards Pakistan and intense hatred towards India. They claimed that the killing of non-Muslims was to create fear and panic, to make them leave Kashmir. They said that the Kashmir freedom movement would again gain momentum, and such killings would be widespread. With all this information thrown at them, Indu's parents and relatives, who had never bothered about Kashmir until now, had suddenly become obsessed with it.

But that was human. Around a thousand people die every year in Kashmir due to insurgency. Some die as militants, some as part of the armed forces fighting them, and some as civilians caught in the crossfire. Most of the time, we did not give a damn about them. They were just numbers in a newspaper. If at all, we might sympathise with the bereaved members of their families. But that was it.

Indu curled up into a ball, spinning the *kada* on her wrist, which she had started to wear at home these days. My mother had given it to her as a mark of the Sikh faith. When we got married, we were clear about our religious choices. We would not convert. We were not even following our own religions earnestly. We were the new-generation liberals. She kept rocking slowly and spinning the *kada*, lost in thought. Looking at her made me sad. That was the cost of loving a Kashmiri.

'Come. Let's go out and sit with parents. It will change your mood a little.'

She avoided my gaze and turned to the other side.

'I will sleep for some time,' she said and pulled up the blanket to cover herself. I could see her nails unevenly bitten.

'You take some rest. I'll see what the parents are doing,' I replied.

I kept her phone beside her pillow. The more you think, the more you would suffer, I thought as I left the room silently. I called up Raman and told him to come over the next evening. It was a second Saturday, a bank holiday. He added Veerji to the conference call, and he also agreed to meet the next day. They were the only people in Kashmir with whom I could have some meaningful conversations. I was eager to know what news and information my father and uncles would bring back when they came home from the funeral. The opinions and the predictions of the locals would be very different from the TV news. People often say the one inside the box could not see the whole problem, while the one who looked at the event from an outsider's perspective had a bird's eye view and could comment more on it. But with Kashmir, the problem was that those outside the box did not see the box with their own eye. Their image of the box was curated for them, and they were shown what the curator wanted them to see. But the ones inside the box had entirely different perspectives that came with their biases and prejudices.

While my father had gone to the funeral, one of his close friends, Ali uncle, visited us. Ali uncle was an amusing person and I liked his company. Whenever he visited us he would bring fruits, a crate of tinned juice and other confectionary for Ramneek. And the best thing was he would not talk about what everyone else was talking about. If the common topic was politics he would talk about religion, if it was religion he would talk about education, and so on. He would tell me stories of the times when he and my father were together. He had come to check on us and to find out whether we were feeling unsafe or worried about what was happening around us.

'I thought you might be scared,' he teased in his usual tone. A small smirk, which made it evident that he was joking, but a serious face that commented on the situation transpiring around us.

'Our daughter,' he referred to Indu, 'has not seen such things ever. Is she fine?' He asked.

'Yes. She is holding up good, more than I expected,' I settled on the sofa next to him expecting him, sooner or later, to brew up an interesting conversation. But he was in a hurry and told me that he would come again when my father was home.

'Oh! Yes. You have things to talk about only with Papa. Why will you sit with us?' I also wanted to tease him a little.

'Then make me a cup of tea,' he pulled up his legs to sit cross-legged on the sofa, assuring me that now he was comfortable and would be sitting for a long time.

'So how come these two three killings made you think that we would be scared?' I asked him.

'After the revocation of 370, this is the first time anything like this has happened. We were living in an illusion that everything was fine. That there would be no more violence and killings and bad times. But this incident has brought us back to reality,' he added.

'That's Kashmir for you,' I replied.

'You know when your father left Kashmir back then, I was both happy and sad for him. I thought that he finally will be able to live a peaceful life in Jammu,' Ali uncle said with sadness and added, 'There he would have different problems, but unlike in Kashmir, he would be mentally and emotionally peaceful. He has seen a lot in these times of militancy. And now again he is here, again in all this violence and trauma and turmoil.'

'What to do, uncle? This is our fate. He does not like it here anyway, but because of me he had to come back.' I told him. I knew, given a chance, Papa would not want to live in Kashmir, but because my job was in Srinagar, he had to. He was fed up with all the issues and dramas that unfolded when he was in Kashmir.

'Yes, this is our fate. Every Kashmiri has the same fate. Pandits, Sikhs, Muslims, everyone has suffered here. Just because we Muslims are in the majority, our suffering seems minuscule, and nobody cares about it.'

What Ali uncle said was true, Kashmiri Muslims had the highest number of casualties in the three decades of militancy. But the other communities justified it by saying that it was their fight. So they had to sacrifice.

I was waiting for the other two uncles, Bikram Singh and Manjit Singh, and the tons of rumours, opinions and prophecies they would bring once they come back after attending Supinder's funeral.

Ali uncle sat for another twenty minutes talking about how he had seen Kashmir change in front of his eyes. As a kid, he told me, he never thought about religion and community the way he thought of it now. Some of his best friends were Hindus—Kashmiri Pandits—who never tried to contact him once they left Kashmir. 'What did I do to them?' he asked rhetorically. My father had told me the same thing many times whenever he felt disgusted about the way things had turned out in Kashmir.

When my father came back along with the uncles in the evening, all of us sat in the living room to hear what they learned at the funeral.

Bikram uncle said, 'We heard she was sitting in her office when the gunmen came. The militants first shot the Hindu teacher, and when she ran, they shot her in the back. This is new. First time going to schools and killing teachers. Disgusting.'

Bikram uncle was my mother's youngest brother and by far the most conversational and happy-go-lucky uncle in our family. He was friendly with me.

'You don't go to school for some days now,' Manjit uncle said. 'We heard a lot of Pandits have left Srinagar early this morning. You are also a PM Package employee. So, you should also stay home until things become normal again.'

Manjit uncle was the eldest brother in the family and he had an aura of respect around him. He was the philosophical type and a storyteller. I loved talking to him.

'I won't go for the next few days until things settle down,' I told him. Harshdeep also said the same thing. In my school, there were twenty-two teachers, out of which only three were Sikhs. There was no Hindu teacher in our school. Nobody from the school had called to check on me. It was obvious to them that for the next few days, other Sikh teachers and I would not be coming to the school.

'Things will not settle down. This will only get messier. The TRF released a new poster claiming the killings. They've said anyone who is a government collaborator will be killed, and so will anyone who speaks against them,' Manjit uncle said and added, 'The freedom movement will now grow more than ever. Who knows, even the Taliban might be supporting them.'

'Did you also host the National Flag in your school?' Bikram uncle asked. I nodded in the affirmative.

'You should go to Jammu. All the Pandits have already left. You have a house there too. It is better if you leave. Government officials will be the first targets,' he added.

'Even if we leave, all of you will still be here. Our other relatives will also be here. So we will still be under stress,' Papa said.

They were already talking like something big had happened. Like an exodus was underway for Sikhs as well. Like it would be 1990 again, but this time for Sikhs instead of Pandits. Was I being too optimistic or too naive, I was not able to decide.

'What about you? When will you return to your shop?' I asked Manjit uncle, who owns a TV repair shop near the city centre. The gol-gappa seller who was killed two days ago was only a mile away from his shop.

'We will do what we have been doing all these years,' he replied calmly. 'We have learned to do business in these tough times. The shop will be closed for a few days, then we will resume. What options do we have?'

In the thirty years of turmoil in Kashmir, Sikhs were the most affected economically and financially. Their establishments were the first to be damaged in any protest if they did not adhere to the popular public sentiment of keeping the businesses shut and closed. Though majority-community establishments could function with half-shutters or back-doors, Sikhs were threatened to close down businesses to support the protests. As a closed community, Muslims helped each other out. What could be bought from a Muslim shop was seldom bought from a Sikh shop, even if they had to pay a higher amount for the same product. It was their way of supporting the *ummah* or community. Another fear at such times was for your life. When a Muslim can simply close the shop and join the protest, and play pretend, a Sikh cannot even do that. The State was either under lockdown or under hartals for extended periods, which made it even harder to recover from business losses. Then, there were calls for shutdown and government-imposed curfews.

'We have grown in this chaos. We are used to it now,' Bikram uncle added.

Although Indu did not understand the entire conversation, she knew the grimness of the situation. She was fluent in English, Malayalam, Tamil and Kannada, but when it came to Hindi, she needed subtitles. And Sikhs of Kashmir were further removed from Hindi as their mother tongue was Hindoo, a dialect of Punjabi, borrowing some words from Pahadi and Gojri.

After the dinner, she asked me to explain everything in detail.

'They are right in suggesting you move to Jammu,' she said.

'It's not that simple. I have a job, and Pandits have the Central Government to help them out. If I go, no one will help me when I return.'

'Don't you think I am also a target? After all, I am a Hindu who has come from another state to Kashmir. If they want non-locals and non-Muslims out of here, I would also qualify as a soft target.'

'Nobody even knows you exist here.'

'I feel like I'm living in a cage. Do you think we can go to Dal Lake again in such a situation? If you want to live inside the home forever and not go out, then it is fine,' she said, clenching her fists. Her voice was tremendously loud, unlike in the morning when she spoke so softly that I had to strain my ears to understand her. I held her hands to calm her down.

That much was true. Everyone had told me not to step out of the house. Although I did not want to go out at all, I felt like my freedom had already been taken away. I told her, 'I wish you would understand. It is easy to move out. We just have to pack and drive. You have been doing that ever since, from Kerala to Bangalore then Delhi and now you will be going to Australia. But wherever you go you keep a part of Kerala with you and keep going back to it whenever you can. You have a homeland to go back to, physically and emotionally. Moving out can be adventurous and positive. But do you understand migrating out is different?'

The only semblance of home and homeland we had was here, in Kashmir, even though we are minorities. The non-locals who were moving out were going back to their homes. They were the majorities back there.

With every sentence, my voice rose.

'You are hurting me,' she said as she freed her hands from mine. I grabbed them back and rubbed them. 'I... Sorry, I did not...' I was at a loss for words.

Indu was determined to get her answers. 'So tell me this. If you will be a minority wherever you go whether it is Kashmir or Jammu or any other place in the world, then how does it matter? And after all, what is wrong in being a minority in any place.'

I felt a sudden soreness in my throat and a tightness in my chest. I wanted to be alone and to be with her at the same time. I wanted to escape the conversation.

6

Invisible

Srinagar, Kashmir
9 October 2021, Saturday
Morning

Harshdeep came around 11.30 a.m. His son, Vanshu, who studied in Class III, accompanied him. He had not sent him to school. I guess nobody would have. That day, no Sikh would have gone to their offices, and no Sikh children to schools or coaching classes.

Harshdeep was only two years older than me, but he had found love and got married when he was 25. I met him for the first time during a teacher-training workshop. He was employed in 2010, the first batch of teachers under the PM Package.

Unlike me, he learned the Kashmiri language and adopted the Kashmiri lifestyle very quickly, which in turn facilitated his liaising with the local population. He ended up working in the district office on deputation rather than in schools and garnered a lot of influence amongst teachers of the district. His connections and good repute enabled him to help other teachers who needed any help in the district office.

'I went to her funeral yesterday. There were thousands and thousands of people,' he told me while having afternoon tea.

'Yeah. Papa was also there. He was telling me about that.'

'They should have not killed her. People say it is a minority killing. But then, why would they zero in on a Sikh teacher and kill her when thousands of other school heads also hoisted the flag? Even Burhan Wani's father hoisted the flag,' he added. Wani was the commander of the Hizbul Mujahideen.

'Sacrificial lambs. That's what we are,' I told him. I did not want to be in a conversation with anyone. I did not want to answer anything. But I was the one who invited him, so I had to indulge. When Harshdeep arrived, I was already in a grumpy mood from yesterday's conversation with Indu about leaving Kashmir. With every word he said, I felt like fighting with him, or ignoring him or not replying at all. I asked my father to join us in the living room. But talking to Harshdeep's son made me feel a little better. He was like his father, talkative. Over the last few years, I had met him several times and developed a good relationship with him. Indu made tea for the three of us and then went back to her room. Later along with my father, she also joined us in the conversation.

After greeting my father and Indu, Harshdeep said, 'We will stay at home the next week. I called the office people in the morning and they said, the Sikhs and Pandits will not be asked to join their duties until the conditions are better. An unofficial direction has been given to all the office in-charges in our district telling them not to ask minority employees to come to offices for some days. And I called the Pandits also. They are going to Jammu.'

I had not called my school yet, and they had not called me either, so I had no idea what was going on. One thing Harshdeep was very good at was talking to people and winning their confidence. He knew all the Pandit teachers in our district and had a good relationship with most of them. I was always happy teaching, but going to the office for administrative work was repulsive to me. Working in an office as a clerk on deputation was the last thing I would do. He loved the importance and influence he could exert on others, while I loved to interact with students.

'Any news from those living in the camp?' Papa asked Harshdeep.

'A lot of them had gone to Jammu yesterday morning. Some are still going. One of my friends was saying that not everyone is willing to go. They have children studying in school and coaching classes,' he replied.

At the time of appointment under the PM Package, the government had promised accommodation to all the employees under the Relief and Rehabilitation clause as a safety measure for those employees. The government feared that the locals and the militants would not like the return of Kashmiri Pandits to the Valley. But not everyone got accommodation in those camps, or rather colonies, as promised. A lot of us rented out houses in areas closers to our place of posting. And at such times of unrest and protest, the people in rented accommodations felt unsafe. Harshdeep and I lived in a rented accommodation.

'What are you going to do?' Papa asked him again.

'I am also planning to go for a few weeks until we are forced to return to our duties,' Harshdeep replied.

'If you go to Jammu, what will happen to his schooling?' I asked Harshdeep pointing at his son.

'His mother is asking the same question. He is just in third standard. We can cover up for a week or two of absence once we come back,' Harshdeep replied.

Harshdeep, by nature, was a cool person who never took things seriously and went with the flow. A true opportunist. In this tragedy, he found a way to spend some time with his parents in Jammu.

'So within two weeks, you will come back? Is that your plan?'

'Yes. We are allowed only that much leeway from the government. After that, we will have to join our duties once the issue is resolved,' he replied. 'And even if we don't join, we will have to resume schooling. Exams are around the corner.'

Though it sounded like a good plan, it was only a temporary solution like all other things.

'I don't want to go to Jammu,' his son replied. 'Our exams are starting next week.'

'They will get postponed,' Harshdeep told him, predicting the course of the conversation.

'You overestimate it. Nothing will be postponed. No schools will be closed. From Monday things will resume as usual,' Papa told him and added, 'Only those who truly want to settle in Jammu will go. People like you and me will talk about it and come back here again.'

'But uncle, his academic year will go to waste, if we go to Jammu,' Harshdeep responded. He just wanted to go back to Jammu for a week and return to Kashmir.

Papa asked him right away. 'If you are going to come back to Kashmir anyway, then stay here. Nobody will kill you at your home. But what schooling and what education are you talking about? What opportunities do you think Sikh students have here in Kashmir? Without mental peace and freedom, without free will and choice, do you think education will help them prosper? They will pass and get marks, but the mental development? Do you think that will happen?'

'We also studied here and have become employed. You also studied here and became a lecturer. The one who knows how to study can study anywhere,' he countered.

To which Papa replied. 'Yes, that is true. But education and schooling are two different things. Education is not only about studying. That he can do at home as well, through open schooling. Why do you put him in a good school and not a government school? Why do people want to put their children in DPS and Goenka and Biscoe? It is not just for studies. It is for all-round development, which for Sikhs was never possible here. And those who actually got it had to fight for it, fight for what should be given as a regular convenience.'

Harshdeep looked at me for support, but I shared the same opinion and feeling as my father. Mine would perhaps be harsher. I was feeling a stiffness in my neck, and the talking was making my head throb.

'School life for every Sikh kid in Kashmir has been fraught with issues, at least it has been for me,' I replied.

Indu looked at me in disbelief. I had told her about my school life, boasting about my childhood pranks and incidents of heroism, but never mentioned that I had a miserable time in school. For me, my school life was like a sports injury. It did not pain while playing, but once you slept over it, the next day, it turned green and I felt excruciating pain. Now when I looked back at my schooling, I knew how much I missed out because of being a Sikh. I studied in Kashmir up to class VIII, and in those eight years, I changed five schools.

When we came back from Jammu in 1994, I was old enough to be put in a school. My first school was a newly opened Christian missionary school in our vicinity, St Paul's Academy. I was among the first dozen students to be enrolled. The number of students never exceeded forty in those first two years, and we had a very low student-teacher ratio. In my class, there were only five students. I studied there for two years. Eventually, the school was shifted to another location. So, I was enrolled in another school near our house.

It was in this new school that I experienced how difficult it was to be a Sikh student. The number of students in my class alone was more than the total number of students in my previous school. And in the whole school, there were no more than ten Sikh students.

I shared my experiences. 'Think about it. For me, the morning assembly was my first challenge. For any Sikh student in Kashmir, that was a problem. A typical morning assembly in any school starts with a verse from Holy Quran and is followed by a beautiful *naat* in praise of Prophet Mohammad. When the whole school sang along, the Sikh students would keep their heads down and keep mum, because reciting something from another religion was considered blasphemous. I guess they still do this in Vanshu's school. In government schools, I know it is there.'

I remember that when I sit to pray with my parents in the evening after school, I would also keep my hands open like praying in the Islamic way. My mother would then hold my hands and close them.

Indu intervened, 'But that happens everywhere. If you go to a Christian missionary school, you have to recite some prayers, while in some others you will have to recite slokas, or Sanskrit prayers. Then, why is it so different here?'

I replied. 'When one lives in a microscopic minority, surrounded by a majority that holds their religious belief in everything they do, the minorities also try to measure up to it. The insecurity among minorities creeps in so hideously that they also start bringing their religion into everything they do.

'If you look at the Sikhs in Punjab, they don't feel insecure about their identity and as a result, they don't cling to it with all their might. In Kashmir, we have raised huge walls to keep our identity from becoming diluted, and ritualistic and religious beliefs have become our means of reinforcing those walls. That coping mechanism has made our boundaries of food, friendships, community bonding, and even everyday living stricter. Moreover, when you say the same thing happens in other schools, you have to see that those students have the option of changing the school and taking admission in one of their liking. But in Kashmir wherever we go, it is the same thing.'

My father also added to it, 'Even in colleges where I used to teach, most functions would start like that, and every speaker starts with an Islamic greeting instead of a general greeting for everyone.'

I continued. 'Yeah. And once the assembly was over, the classroom was another issue. In a mixed secular classroom, kids did not know their boundaries. For us, it was fun to tease each other, fight with each other and play with each other. But teasing would easily turn into communal slurs thrown at each other. The first target was our *jooda* or hair bun, and if God-forbid anyone got hold of it, it was taken as the biggest disrespect leading to an all-out attack on the other party. Another way to bully a Sikh kid was the *barah baj gaye* joke that was so prevalent in our times. And, every time barah was mentioned we, Sikh kids, would become uneasy and start looking around in apprehension expecting someone to blurt out a joke or make some gestures that would signal twelve. The kids would ask me, what is four into three, or six plus six, or something which would have twelve as its answer. Sometimes I would fall for it and answer, and then they will erupt into peals of laughter.'

Barah baj gaye was a handed-down joke, the meaning of which nobody knew. My classmates would say, *Sikhon ke barah bajtey hain* (When the clock strikes 12 for Sikhs), and they would do funny, idiotic things. And if I did something stupid, the first thing they would say was, 'What happened? Is it twelve, already?' I did not know how to respond to it other than fighting back with abuses and sometimes punches. Years later when I came to know the story behind it, I wanted to tell them all, 'Yes, it is twelve. So you better be careful.' I felt a sense of pride after listening to the story.

During the Mughal rule when soldiers abducted the local women and abused the public, Sikhs would fight back, and mostly it was at the stroke of midnight. They would launch surprise attacks on the Mughal camps, rescue the women, kill the Mughal soldiers and ransack their camps. After I heard the reasons behind it, the statement turned from a joke into a story of bravery and pride. The Mughals were so afraid that they would not sleep at night, and would say, be cautious, Sikhon ke barah baj gaye.

Vanshu validated my claim, 'Yes, yes. Students in my class also say that sometimes.'

But I had more to share. 'As we grew up, we outgrew these silly jokes. The students we fought with became the best of our friends, who would then become our shield in case anyone joked about our faith. With time, our Muslim friends valued our faith and would do everything possible to accommodate us. The jokes disappeared and so did the fights and communal slurs and abuses. But new issues reared their heads.

'The other problem was the language, while most schools claim to be English medium, the primary language in the schools was Kashmiri, which was the mother tongue of Kashmiri Muslims. Most instructions and lectures were given in Kashmiri which we never understood. Still, in my school, most of the teachers use Kashmiri. But I guess in private schools, now English and Urdu are used.

'In one school, where I went for my upper primary education, I was the only Sikh student in the entire school. There the administration was a little considerate towards me and allowed me to sit in the classroom during the morning assembly. But subject choices, especially languages, were always a problem. Most of the schools had only Kashmiri and Urdu as a language. Choosing Hindi or Punjabi was never an option. For me, personally, it was a bigger problem than other Sikh students, for they have always studied Urdu as a language, and they never thought of choosing Hindi. While I have been in Jammu in my formative years and during my homeschooling, I was familiar with the Hindi alphabet rather than Urdu. Then, when I was put in the Christian missionary school, they also taught me Hindi as the teachers, who we called Sisters, were from south India and knew Hindi.'

My head was still throbbing. It was the onset of a migraine.

Harshdeep remained quiet. He knew that he, too, had faced all these problems like every Sikh student had and was still facing.

'Why didn't you complain to the principal or the headmaster of the school about it?' Indu asked me. 'And now, you are a teacher. Why don't you change it in your own school?'

She was ignorant about the intricacies of Kashmir. But I could not blame her. She was raised in a completely different environment, and I had never told her about these challenges in detail.

'It doesn't work like that, and even if you complain, nobody is going to do anything about it. The only outcome would be me getting on the wrong side of everyone else. Moreover, in the school I teach, there are only Muslim students. So it doesn't matter what they recite,' I replied and added, 'Had there been a Sikh or a Hindu student, then I might have actually objected to it.'

'And this is just the tip of the iceberg, there are tons of other things as well. Food, style of dressing, social belonging, grievance redresses, and many more. The more you scratch the surface, the uglier it gets,' Papa added.

'But uncle, we cannot change these things. So, we…we have to accept them, and if we keep crying over these things, it will only make us angry and depressed. It won't help in any way,' Harshdeep said, sulking.

'You cannot change these things. That is why you need to change the place. I have always said this and will always stand with it. Kashmir is not a place for Sikhs, for education, for business, for jobs, or living,' Papa announced as he got up from the sofa. 'We will have to always accept all these things, and many more if we wish to stay here.'

My father began walking towards the kitchen. 'You people talk. I'll go check what's cooking in the kitchen. You will have your lunch here, right?' he asked Harshdeep.

'No, no. I will be leaving in a while. Param has asked me to come back for lunch,' he replied. Meanwhile, I kept thinking about my school days. One major problem that I faced, and every Sikh student in Kashmir still faced, involved food. We had completely different food habits from the Muslims, and that was an issue in common food canteens and messes. In Kashmir, Sikhs would not eat food prepared by the Muslims, and Muslims would not eat food prepared by the Sikhs. It was so imbibed into our way of life that, when we went to a Muslim friend's house, they served us packaged food like cold drinks and chips rather than homemade tea or food. When in school, even if someone touched our food, we would have to throw it out. We would not share our food with our Muslim friends, and neither would they. Our eating spaces were different.

It would be a problem during camps, picnics and treks. If it was a day picnic, we would bring our food from home. But if it was an overnight camp where food was to be prepared by the school administration, the Sikhs students would prefer not to go. I, myself, had skipped several such events, like sports tournaments and camps, only because of the dilemma of what I would eat. Even when we went to sports matches, the common food served to the players would be biryani or some other preparation that we would not be able to eat. Instead, we would be given a packet of juice and two bananas as a replacement. We would not even yearn for the food served to them as proof of our resolve. It was much later, during my college years, that I realised that those things should not have happened, and then during my years as a teacher in Kashmir, I was a part of the administration that could do nothing against those things.

Our major problem is the problem of not even realising that it is a problem. That was what made it a silent torture. A Muslim prayer, or naat or a verse from the Holy Quran being made part of the assembly, or the Islamic greeting whenever anyone started a lecture, event or address to the public was so normal that no one realised that it could affect the student from minority households. When I read about it, the Constitution mandated that government schools or schools run with government aid could not inculcate any religious element in the daily curriculum, be it assembly, sports or classroom transactions unless specified as a minority-run school.

Cultural functions in Kashmiri schools followed the same programme—they started with an Islamic greeting, then hadith, naat, and other socio-religious aspects follow. If a Sikh student participated, he either sang a Punjabi song or danced to one. It would not appear weird to anybody if a Sikh student was present without participating in such events.

School life was not our only misery. We faced serious challenges even outside of the school premises. In the playgrounds, we were less in number, and if ever, any fight broke out during playtime, people would gang up against us. After the play, if the team decided to go and celebrate at a cafe or restaurant, we would again be left out, or most of the time, we would choose to go home instead of going with the team. The lack of Sikh eateries in Kashmir has rendered the foodie inside us salivating,' I realised I was venting.

Harshdeep replied to my outpourings, 'I agree. What you are saying is true. It is obvious that during winters when we Sikhs visit Jammu, all our food issues would be resolved as we share the same food habits as Hindus who also own a majority of the eateries and cafes in Jammu. From December to February, you can see Sikhs flocking together at momo shops and chicken shops in Jammu city, trying to eat everything and anything they can get their hands on, without the fear that it might be halaal meat.'

This otherness Kashmiri Sikhs faced was not something directed against Sikhs. It was more of a consequence of living as a micro minority, for no one was actively discriminating against us. But still, we found ourselves at the receiving end. If I asked any Kashmiri Sikh, I could expect the answer, 'Some compromises are to be made everywhere. At least we are getting an education.' Living as a minority meant the Kashmiri Sikhs had to settle for the bare minimum. You did not demand your rights but were thankful for whatever was being given to you. The purpose of education was an all-round development of mind, body and soul. But we settled for just a certificate proclaiming that we had passed the class with good marks.

Like me, thousands of Sikh students settled for less and never realised their true potential, not because they were discriminated against but because they simply never knew what they could have done if they were not bound by the everyday compromises they had to make.

'Isn't it better for our children to be raised in Jammu or anywhere else than in Kashmir, at least they will live life to the fullest, eat what they want, go where they want, participate in whatever events they can, without thinking about other things?' Indu said in a low voice.

'And how much schooling does actually happen in Kashmir?' My question was, of course, rhetorical. I continued, 'In the last decade, students have got mass promotions at least five times without sitting for exams. Every year half the session is wasted in strikes and protests. The point is, why do we have to suffer all this? Do we want azaadi from India, or join with Pakistan, or want Kashmir as a separate country? No, we don't want that. Then why do we suffer if it is not even our agenda? If the Muslims are suffering it is a sacrifice they are making for their freedom movement. Our suffering is just collateral damage, and we keep smiling like fools.'

Harshdeep was silent but you could make out that he was in agreement with what I said. He asked, 'Do you think we can leave Kashmir? You told me you migrated when you were a child, but then you returned. My parents also migrated in 1992. But they come back every summer and stay in their native place for at least five to seven months every year. That is the way every Sikh family is. We are seasonal migrants, summers here and winters there.'

'We were born here, and so were our fathers and forefathers. So leaving Kashmir is not easy for us. But because of that stubbornness, we have suffered a lot as well,' Papa replied as he came back from the kitchen.

Our kitchen was directly across the living room, and our conversation was easily audible to him. My mother accompanied him.

'My brothers and their families live here. They never migrated out. Their children studied and grew up here. They have their business and livelihood here. For them leaving Kashmir is unimaginable. If they do, they will have to start everything from scratch,' she said.

Papa replied to my mother. 'But why don't they allow their children to go out? And like them, why doesn't any other Kashmiri Sikh let their children go out? Most of our children have got their college education from outside. They would find a job outside Kashmir easily, though not a very good one. But at least they would be out of here and start their lives there, which will give a different and better future to the next generations. Most of those who have come back are doing menial jobs here. It is better to do the same job outside Kashmir and suffer a little for the sake of the future than to perish here.'

'I don't want to raise my children in Kashmir,' I said. I could see Indu's face brighten up. Though she already knew that, and so did my parents, as I have always been talking about leaving Kashmir. But saying it aloud now was so reassuring to Indu.

'You have the option. You should,' Harshdeep said.

Papa continued. 'When we went out, we had an emotional bond with Kashmir. You people, on the other hand, do not have such attachment issues to the place. The shift in social structure will also favour you. We were strongly connected with the people around us, deeply invested in relatives and neighbours and villagers. We felt too drained to leave all that behind. And when we went out, we felt like aliens in Jammu, strangers to everyone around us. Our adjustment issues were acute. You are independent and have spent most of your time out of Kashmir. It's a good choice to leave. If not your generation, then nobody can leave from here.'

In his voice, I could hear the dejection of his first migration and the failure of his second when he tried to start afresh in Jammu.

7

A Red Winter

Kashmir
December 2000–March 2001

It was an unusually dry and cold winter. We lived in a small, two-room, rented apartment on the outskirts of Srinagar called Wanbal. From early December to the middle of March, schools in Kashmir were given a winter vacation, which the global warming had considerably reduced to less than seventy-five days now. Those three months of no school every year were the dullest days for me. The excitement of vacation would fade away after the initial week when the weather would restrict us from indulging in any outdoor activities.

And if we, the already bored children, were too unlucky and it snowed heavily, the electric poles would give away and fall, taking away from us the only source of our entertainment which was television. Though our school teachers gave us enough homework to last the whole winter, it did not work for me. Every year during the first week of vacation, I would not even look at the books, and then for the next two weeks, I would sit and finish everything so I did not have to worry about it during the rest of the vacation. By the end of those three weeks, the severe winter, locally called Chilla-i-Kalan, would take over. We would be completely homebound unless it snowed. The snow would bring the temperature up a little and we would go out covered in layers upon layers of woollens to make our snowmen or go down on sledges on the inclined roads and small hills.

While the whole month of December and the first half of January of the year 2001 passed uneventfully, the last two weeks were particularly terrifying. Grenade attacks, army-militant encounters, strikes and curfews, protests and stone pelting, made it to the news every day.

But it was on 3 February 2001, that everything came crashing around us.

It was around seven in the evening. The sun had already set. My mother, my younger brother, and I were tucked in our quilt watching TV while my father returned from the gurdwara after the evening prayer congregation.

He turned off the TV and looked at my mother in silence.

'What? Everything alright?' she asked as she got out of the quilt and left the bed letting the cold air into the quilt and taking away her warmth from us. 'Shall I make tea? You look worried,' she said as she passed by him. She turned the TV on again and gestured at my father to come to the kitchen.

I could sense some discomfort in his gait and his quietness. But for me, TV was more important at that point in time, and I concentrated on it rather than following them to the kitchen. They sat there for quite a long time before coming back to the bedroom. I could make out they were speaking but the TV was too loud to many any if it comprehensible.

It was during dinner that I came to know that there was an armed attack on the Sikhs living in Mehjoor Nagar, just a few miles from us. At least one person had died on the spot, and over a dozen were severely injured.

Around 6.30 p.m., three people carrying automatic machine guns came riding a motorcycle on the main street of Mehjoor Nagar, which at that time was quite busy with people coming back after the day's work. Some elderly people with their grandkids were returning from the gurdwara. It was a melee attack. They drove by firing bullets at everyone along the way. Before people could comprehend what was happening, the attackers fled, leaving behind a trail of blood on the street from killing people and injuring many. People were traumatised for the rest of their lives.

Years later, for a story I wrote to a local newspaper on the incident's fifteenth anniversary, I interviewed a few survivors about what exactly happened that day. One such survivor and eyewitness was a friend of mine who was seventeen years old when it happened.

He said,

> My cousin and I had gone there to buy chicken for some guests at our home. The chicken shop was already closed, so we had to come back. The moment we came down our street from the main

one I heard shots, three at a time. We ran further down and ducked behind a wall. We knew it was firing. Then, there were three more shots, a small pause and a shot and a pause and then shots again. I had closed my eyes, and all my concentration was on the sounds. The shots were moving further away from us. After sitting there for five more minutes, we ran home. When we came back to the main street, there were ambulances and police sirens all over the place. Just outside the chicken shop, someone had been shot dead. I was thinking what if the shop was open? It would have been me instead of that person. Or what if we had stayed there, or met somebody and were talking to them? A dozen such situations played in my mind in which I would have been dead if I had taken a single different step at the time.

The rumours were already in the air that something was going to happen to Sikhs soon. But like always, we were blindly optimistic that they were just rumours and that we were safe in Kashmir. A few days back an auto-rickshaw driver's dead body was recovered from the highway in his auto. People had seen two Sikh personnel of the Special Operations Group of Police (SOG) board his auto a day before his killing. Suspecting it to be a custodial killing, a state-wide protest erupted when his body was recovered. Already a few had happened that year, but this time it did not end with protests alone.

Another person I interviewed, lovingly called Haji sahab by the locals of the area, who had lived in Mehjoor Nagar all his life and owned a small grocery store on the road where the shooting happened, told me about how confused and terrified he was.

He pointed towards the road and said,

I was in the shop when two people drove from there, carrying guns, and then I heard the shots, *tha tha tha*, then a pause and then again, *tha tha tha*. Those days my shop counter was small, so I ducked under it to hide. I thought they would now throw a grenade inside the shop, or something like that. I was clueless, about who they were and why they were shooting. There was no army wala outside to shoot at. So who were they trying to kill? After ten minutes when I came out, I found they had come to kill Sikhs. What did the

Sikhs do? Auto wala was killed by the police or Allah knows who. Why kill Sikhs? I ask them, are there not any Muslim police walas and army walas who have killed locals and *shaheeds*. Then, why don't you go killing every Musalman in Kashmir?'

'It was wrong. They did wrong,' he said lowering his voice. '*Zehr dala Kashmir mein* (They poisoned Kashmir), otherwise when did we think that Sikhs are different from us? They have equal rights in Kashmir as we do. Pandits as well. They left themselves. Otherwise, why would we tell them to go? They were like our brothers,' he rubbed his face with his palms and then caressed his long beard. 'Son, these circumstances ruined us, Kashmiris, like this, otherwise all of us were one. Sikh, Musalman, Bhat (Pandits).

Haji sahab was not the only one, but anyone from his generation would say the same thing. They lived in an era of peace and tranquillity in their youth. The 1990s changed everything for them. They still reminisced about the past, about the times when Sikhs and Pandits and Muslims all were on cordial terms.

Those who were born in the 1970s and 1980s and who were young adults or teenagers when the Kashmir Freedom Movement started, had a completely different perspective of the situation. They were the most traumatised generation, more than those born after 1990. Their childhood was peaceful, but the moment they began to spread their wings and enjoy their lives, their wings were clipped and they were put in an eternal cage. Their youth was spent in curfews and strikes, their education wasted, and an everlasting trauma carved in their souls. These were the people who picked up the guns and blamed everything on the Indian Government and politics. The 1990s kids were born when Kashmir was already consumed by the flames of militancy and hatred, and the army was at every nook and corner. They never knew of the good times, and for them, talks of peace and quiet, of non-violence and communal harmony looked like scenes out of a utopian novel.

When the Mehjoor Nagar incident happened, there was a mixed response from the Muslim community. Some condemned it for disrupting the peace. Some appreciated it for the warning it was sending out so as not to mess with them, and some did not care about it.

Though the shooting was in response to the killing of the auto driver, the aggression, instead of being directed at the organisation, in this case, the police, it was aimed towards the religious community of those police officers. That night my parents spoke in muffled tones.

Following the shooting, a curfew was imposed throughout Kashmir. The localities where the Sikhs lived were being patrolled by the police, and several high-ranking army and Border Security Force (BSF) officers came forward to assure our safety.

Also, the next day, the full extent of the shooting was reported in the news. Six Sikhs were killed and five were severely injured, the news read. There was nothing about the families who lost their loved ones, a community which lost its safety and hope, and the people who lost confidence and were traumatised. They never made it into the news.

Sikhs had broken the curfew and reached Mehjoor Nagar, where the then chief minister, Farooq Abdullah, had come to address the community. So enraged were the Sikhs that a young man in his early twenties attempted to breach the chief minister's security to attack him with a knife. The promises of safety, year after year, were just hollow. Several families decided to move to Jammu the very next day and loaded their households into trucks. The local government and the political and community leaders from Punjab came in, requesting the ailing people to stay, like they had done every time, telling them that they would make sure no such thing happened in the future. That they would provide security to the Sikh-populated areas.

Like always, the wailing turned to sobs, and only a dry trail of tears was left on the faces of orphans and widows. When the mothers could not cry any more tears for their lost sons, and when the fathers could not shout any more profanities at the murderers, when the community felt tired again, everything went back to being as it was, cursed to oblivion. Everybody continued with their sorry lives, awaiting another such incident, so that the whole cycle could be repeated.

Kashmir was uncertain. No one could guarantee your safety. Not the chief minister, not the Prime Minister. It was too volatile and instinctive to know what would happen, where, and when. And the promises of keeping the Sikhs safe were nobody's to make. Everyone knew that. Whoever stayed in Kashmir stayed at their own risk. Some called it courage, some foolishness, some helplessness.

The next few days were all alike. When our neighbours came, there was nothing new in the conversation. When our relatives came, they repeated the same questions and gave the same answers as the neighbours. When we went to my grandparent's home, the same conversations took place with everyone. It felt like I was stuck in a repetitive illusion. Just the background and people changed, but the words and emotions did not.

'What will happen now? You know they (some name or another) moved to Jammu! We don't think we have a future here. But what can we do? We are not afraid of these things. This is our homeland. We will live with courage. We are not Pandits. We are Sikhs. These small skirmishes won't budge us. If we move to Jammu, we won't get any benefits like the Pandits.'

The same dialogue over and over again, in different tones from different people.

My father was at the forefront, urging people to assemble and move to Jammu, mass migrate, for it was not safe for the next generations to come. He told them that Kashmir would never know peace, at least in the foreseeable future. A few families joined him, but a majority called him out. How could one leave Kashmir? These were their roots. He said that he would move out of Kashmir, with or without them.

By the end of the month, our family had already decided that we would move to Jammu. My father was determined to leave. He had seen enough to overlook it again. The previous year, when the Chithisinghpora massacre happened, where thirty-five Sikhs were killed, my father thought that it was the first and last massacre of the Sikhs. But with this incident, he was certain that many more were to come. He was frustrated at how the people around him could not see the implications of what was happening, how they were ignoring what the future held for them, and how they were sabotaging the futures of the generations to come.

I was awaiting the reopening of schools, which was supposed to happen in the first week of March. When my father decided to move to Jammu, I was the most distraught one. I had to leave behind my friends and the school and go to a new one, make new friends and settle down in a new social circle. I was currently studying at New Caset School since the last two years. I was the only Sikh student in the whole school. But I made some very close friends. Mushtaq, Qayoom, Fazil, Rameez and many more. When I asked my father about it, he told me that we would be moving in April or May when the new admissions start in Jammu. I would be put in a good school there, and for the time being, I could go and study in the school for those two months.

When the schools reopened after the winter vacation and I told my classmates that I would be leaving because the Sikhs were being killed in Kashmir, there was mixed reactions. A few of them had heard their parents talking about it.

'Abbaji was talking to someone about it. He said that like Pandits, now Sikhs are the targets, and once all the Sikhs leave Kashmir, then there would only be Muslims. Then Nizam-e-Mustafa can be brought about,' one of my classmates told me.

'No. Once all the Sikhs leave, then the army will throw bombs everywhere and kill us all. They are not doing it so far because Sikhs live here and they don't want to kill the Sikhs,' said another.

'So, you will never come back to Kashmir then? Where will you go to school? Where will you live?' my bench mate asked me. I had no answers to any of his questions, and no reaction to anyone else's statement.

'You will go back to where you came from?' one of the girls asked me. I had no idea where I came from. But it was clear that I was not from Kashmir. I had never thought about it, but when she asked me the question, I wanted to know. When I returned home that day, I asked my mother the question the girl asked me. I was thinking it would be Punjab, for all Sikhs came from Punjab.

'We were born here. Our parents and grandparents and their parents were all born here. We did not come from anywhere else,' my mother told me. The next day I told that to the girl, reinforcing my claim on Kashmir. But when she asked me, 'Then where will you go back to if you did not come from anywhere else?' I had no answers. Nor did my mother and my father. Years later, I still don't have an answer; neither does any other Sikh.

We moved to Jammu that year for the second time, leaving Kashmir behind forever. Years after the migration, I asked my father what made him decide to leave his home and roots and come to a place where he had previously migrated but had not succeeded in settling down. Where did he get the courage to take such a step? My father said: 'When the Chithisinghpora massacre happened in March 2000, I too was one among such people, optimistic and hopeful, saying and believing that it was a one-time occurrence. Moreover, Chithisinghpora was, and is to this day, an ambiguous incident. We were sceptical about it. But in 2001, when the Mehjoor Nagar incident happened, I realised one thing. It is not the events that prompted me to move. It is the daily living conditions and the prospect of the future that pushed me. I knew even if such an event was never going to be repeated in future, the daily lives, the uncertainty, and the mental pressure alone would kill us slowly.'

Those who stayed behind, like always, told themselves that this was the last event. And then in November again, three young Sikh girls were killed in Push Kriri. They were sitting inside their home, doing their evening prayer when militants came barging in and fired at them.

For the next ten years, Papa tried his best to settle in Jammu, and he did succeed, until in 2011, I got this job and had to come back to Kashmir.

8

Aspirations and Options

Srinagar, Kashmir
9 October 2021, Saturday
Evening

After Harshdeep left in the afternoon, Indu asked me if Harshdeep would ever be able to move out of Kashmir. When someone justified staying back in Kashmir, and they wanted and supported it like Harshdeep, it was clear that he would be another Kashmiri Sikh who sat and grieved and wailed about leaving Kashmir but ended up living in it. I told her, 'Love, I think aspirations play a major part in one's life. We, in Kashmir, are raised without dreams and aspirations. From a very young age, we are taught to be mediocre, to be average and live life happily as an average nine-to-five person. Though there is nothing wrong with that, it limits our goal of aspiring for anything above that. Once we get it, we don't want to aim higher.'

After lunch, we went to bed and watched a few episodes of F.R.I.E.N.D.S. The whole day had been a long boring conversation. I felt comforted and relieved now while sitting next to Indu, watching Netflix. That was all I wanted.

After watching a few episodes, we reassessed our life goals and spoke about all the travelling we wanted to do. Like me, she also considered travelling an investment rather than an expenditure. In fact, she liked to explore more than I did. I wanted to take her to Ladakh on a bike ride, and she wanted to take me to the northeastern states. We wanted to go on a foreign trip as well.

We had talked about it in detail many times already. Her brother had given me a *Lonely Planet* guide to Europe as one of the wedding gifts and we had loved it ever since. I wanted to write a similar book on Kashmir, especially about its treks and trails. Though the anxiety about the situation always crept in, those talks made us forget what was happening around us for a few hours.

The conversation with Harshdeep was unsettling for Indu. The discussions about my childhood issues, resentments, followed by suggestions from my father about moving out of Kashmir, clubbed with the conversation with the two uncles the day before, had made her uneasy. She was, before this incident, never exposed to such serious conversations. Time and again, she came back with some questions about the current scenario.

I wanted the time to speed up to the evening, so I could meet with Veerji and Raman. I told her that we watch something to divert our attention from the depressing things around us. But it was not working at all.

'Kashmiri people are very laid-back and relaxed. At least the ones I have met so far. Most of them are content and happy with whatever they have. How do you live such a life?' she asked. I gave her a truthful reply. I said, 'There are only two options for a middle-class family in Kashmir. First, you get a government job, and then you spend your entire life comfortably there. The yearly increments in salary, the hike in dearness allowance, a promotion once in a decade, with these promises and a foreseeable comfortable living, no one wants to achieve anything higher. Once the job is secured, marriage is on the cards. After that, life will start with sacrifices for the upbringing of your children, who will again be thrown into the same mediocrity. Even though dull and average, this is the ideal life, the life of a laid-back government employee.

'The second option is a private job or it is unemployment. Kashmiris don't have the time for aspirations and dreams. They are fighting for survival. Hobbies and leisure are not something they can afford, mentally and economically. For them, the highest dream is to either get a government job, if eligible, or to find a semblance of it in a private company that won't throw them out for non-performance. A stable job even if it is not appreciating financially. And between these two is sandwiched the future of our youth.'

Harshdeep was more than comfortable in his office job. A stable salary, an affectionate wife and an active kid. With a typical Kashmiri attitude and having no hobbies and leisurely activities, he felt Kashmir was the best he could want. What else would you need from life? Good weather, good salary, good family, an easy job.

'If you still wanted more, then you are an unsatisfied soul, my friend,' he would say whenever I told him to aspire for more, to read, to travel, or to play.

Indu understood the outlook better than I did, and I was surrounded by such people. 'Don't settle into such a lifestyle. It's dangerous more than just being boring,' she told me.

'Do you think I would? I have always wanted to go out to a place where I can utilise my creativity fully,' I replied.

I wanted a cityscape, a place full of theatres and cafes. I wanted to write for the theatres, read poetry at the cafes, join an intellectual community, go once a month to a book club reading, organise *nukkad-nataks* and street plays, mentor children, be part of the creative community and much more. And none of those things were available to me in Kashmir.

When we were dating, we talked about our plans in detail, not the colour of the curtains and baby names, but our career trajectories and financial choices in detail. Our plan was to move to Bangalore once Indu finished her studies. That would be in 2023. She would find a stable job, and I would experiment with my writing and freelancing jobs. With her credentials and degrees, it would be easy for her to get a well-paying job. And the worst-case scenario would be me taking up a teaching job or starting a tuition centre. With twelve years of teaching experience, it wouldn't be difficult, we figured. So, Bangalore was our city.

But that was still a distant dream, which now seemed more distant to her than it actually was. Her family and friends were still worried about her and kept sending her new videos about the incident whenever anybody shared them. They kept her anxiety wet. And in all this anxiety, I wasn't sure what she was thinking about anymore. In her eyes, all I could find was a quiet calmness like the one we had before a storm.

On a usual day, from 2.30 p.m. to 3.00 p.m., I would still be in school, preparing to come home. Indu would be researching, while my parents would be taking a siesta after lunch. Once I came back, I would talk to Indu if she was free or work on some of my writing projects until she was free. Most evenings, we would go for a drive or read something or watch some movies.

'Do you think, we should move out of Kashmir before I finish my studies?' she asked me.

'Baby, let's not talk about it anymore. This is just a passing moment. In a week, everything will be alright. Just trust me, and you need to focus on your work,' I replied. 'And I have to go to Veerji's house. Raman is also coming. Meanwhile, you read one paper, at least.'

'Ok,' she nodded. 'You come back then. I want to talk about it. It is making me anxious and I am not able to study.'

I knew how crucial it was for her to be at the peak of her performance as her mid-term candidature was coming up in a month. Ideally, she should be working a minimum of sixteen hours a day.

'Ok, baby. We will talk about it. You rest or read. I'll come back in two hours,' I said.

Though I had been living in Kashmir for more than ten years by then, my close friends were only two people, Veerji and Raman. I had seasons of activity and inactivity, and my circles widened or shrunk accordingly. At times I organised events, met with new and emerging artists, poets and writers, and went to different cafes and event venues. During these times, I made good friends with cafe owners of Kashmir and a ton of literary people. At other times, I concentrated on writing projects, staying home for months, and cutting off my social interactions. Whatever it was, only Raman and Veerji were the two constant people.

Veerji, who was over ten years older than me, was my go-to person for everything. Discussing my ideas, planning something for the community, going for brainstorming rides around the Dal Lake, borrowing money, and so on. He was a towering figure in our community working tirelessly for the youth. He was in charge of the only Sikh Community Library, the Komal Library, in Srinagar and had mentored hundreds of Sikh students. From his own salary, he subscribed to dozens of magazines, periodicals and newspapers, bought hundreds of books and study materials for the library, and sometimes even gave out money to needy students. He did all this despite being a paraplegic. He had a customised Activa Scooty, modified to be a trike by adding a set of side-support tires in the rear. We used to travel most evenings around the Dal Lake using his scooty. The other benefit of this scooty was that during strikes and curfews, we were allowed to pass when everyone else was detained. The police, army or the protesters allowed him to pass. When most people had to sit at home during strikes, we travelled around the city.

He was already on a call with someone when I entered his room.

'My dear, I told you Kashmir would be affected after the Taliban ousted America,' he shouted at whoever he was talking to. He signalled me to sit down. He was waist-deep in his blanket with a book open in his lap. His one hand kept tracing the outer edge of a book while he spoke on the phone.

'Minorities aren't safe here now,' he declared.

He threw the phone on the blanket, '*Murakh!* cannot understand even the simplest things. By closing your eyes, the darkness won't go away.'

'They have always been considerate of Sikhs. There is this unsigned, untold pact. You know that. They haven't harmed Sikhs. We do not matter at all,' I reminded him. His bedroom was a small room measuring ten-by-ten feet, with big almirahs covering the walls, end to end, on the two sides. A bed covered the rest of the floor, leaving space only to walk to the bed. Wherever you see, you will find books, stacks of them, mostly thrillers—Agatha Christie, Dan Brown, David Baldacci and Robert Ludlum.

'They haven't. But that does not mean they won't. And that is a lie we tell ourselves every time someone is killed. My dear, we justify the killings every time for one reason or another,' he said.

Kashmiri Sikhs believed that the militants didn't want to kill them. They believed that Muslims feel closer to Sikhs than Hindus, as both of them were minorities in India. One reason was that the armed rebellion in 1984 was the first large-level armed movement in Independent India by a minority seeking a separate country, Khalistan. Kashmiri Muslims felt that both communities were suffering at the hands of India, and both had similar goals—azaadi or freedom from India.

And then, there were so many examples of communal solidarity and brotherhood between the two communities. During the 2014 Kashmir floods, the gurdwaras were open for relief and rehabilitation. Thousands took shelter. After the 2019 Pulwama attack—a suicide bomber targeting the armed forces—Kashmiri Muslim students were targeted across Northern India, and were forced to vacate schools and colleges, and rented accommodations. The backlash was severe, but the Sikhs took it upon themselves to evacuate them, guarantee their safety and fight for them in Chandigarh, Haryana and Delhi. Muslims came in large numbers to thank Sikhs on social media for the same. During the 2019 protest against the Citizenship Amendment Act and the National Register of Citizens (CAA-NRC), Sikhs supported Muslims.

During the last five years, as a token of their appreciation, many Kashmiri Muslims joined Khalsa Aid, a Sikh organisation accused by the Bharatiya Janata Party (BJP) and Rashtriya Swayamsevak Sangh (RSS) of primarily aiding Muslims worldwide. This Sikh-Muslim soft spot was something that the armed militants had a clear understanding of, giving hope to the Sikhs living in Kashmir that they were safe.

'Don't judge the situation too quickly. This could be entirely something else,' I added. Perhaps I was not willing to accept that the murder was a targeted killing. It could be accidental. Or she might have been killed after saying something or trying to protect the Hindu teacher.

I said, 'You don't know her. I know her personally. If she has been killed, there would be some reason behind it. It can be a targeted killing, but the target is her, her as a person, her as Supinder, not a Sikh person, not because of the religious identity.'

'We will know,' Veerji sighed.

'With these new organisations like TRF, the scenario is changing. Everything will be clear within a few weeks. But as of now, one thing is pretty clear. They don't want non-Muslims and non-Kashmiris to come and settle in Kashmir,' Veerji replied after some time. I grabbed the book open in his lap. He was reading *Atomic Habits*.

In the Kashmir freedom movement, killing Hindus and other non-locals did make some sense—as they were seen as the majority community meting out discrimination toward Muslims. With the rise of Hindu nationalism, Muslims felt unsafe in the country. The migrants were considered outsiders who had come to Kashmir as part of what Kashmiris thought was a planned move to change Kashmir's demography. Kashmiris considered that most Hindus were Indian sympathisers and conspirators against the Muslims of Kashmir.

But what would be accomplished by killing the Sikhs? And whenever there was any local incident against the Sikhs, videos of militants telling the locals not to harm the Sikhs were circulated. Sikhs also believed that their existence did not bother the militants. Firstly, Sikhs were just one per cent of the total population. Second, they did not have a political or bureaucratic say, and third, they did not pose any challenge to the Kashmir freedom movement in any way. So, there was no point in trying to scare the Sikhs. Also, it would take them a few hours to kill all the Sikhs, if the militants ever wanted it seriously.

'Time will tell, and then I will remind you,' he left it at that. That was the best way to conclude when you were out of reason and logic. Time will tell, I told myself too. There was a long silence.

'Did you call Raman?' I asked him, 'He said he would come by four-thirty. It's already five.'

'If he comes on time, who will call him Raman?' Veerji replied. He called again to check on him. 'He won't be coming. He's stuck with something. He said he will call later.'

'If these militants are from Pakistan or Afghanistan, they won't even know the social dynamics of Kashmir. They will not differentiate between a Hindu and a Sikh. A Kafir is a Kafir. For them, it is either Muslims or non-Muslims,' Veerji sounded agitated.

What was worrying to me was that all of it sounded correct. Kashmiri Muslims made up most of my professional circles, friends and acquaintances. I spent my time at with them, and this was how it had been all my life. They knew us, and we knew them. But if the militants did not come from Kashmir, they wouldn't consider this delicate relationship and would kill mercilessly.

'Let us wait and watch for a few days if there are more killings. Only then can we say anything,' I said. There was a larger plan at work, and we were not able to see it yet. We decided to wait and watch.

9

Nada

Srinagar, Kashmir
10 October 2021

What would you do when you have nothing to do? Getting up without a plan, without a schedule or a goal, was contentment. A blank mind, no deadlines, no rushing, nothing. But that satisfactory feeling could be ruined if someone interrupted it and reminded you that doing nothing was a wastage of time, that it was the mark of an unsuccessful person.

My nothingness was broken, when I was laying in my bed, relaxing, staring at the ceiling with a wide smile, by Indu.

'What are you smiling at?' she walked into the room with a black coffee.

'Thanks for the coffee. I was just smiling. Not thinking anything,' I said as I reclined against the headboard.

'No thanks. This is mine. I thought you were sleeping and I didn't make any for you,' she replied as she took a sip and passed the cup to me. 'Take two sips only, and give it back.' 'Small sips,' she added immediately as I took a deep breath before bringing the cup to my mouth.

'Why are you so smug early in the morning?' she settled into the study chair. Her laptop was already open.

'Nothing. It's Sunday. What are you working on so early?' I asked her and passed the cup back. It's black coffee with pepper. Every time she made it, it felt tastier than before, and every time I made it, it was flushed down the kitchen sink. I never got the proportions right.

'What Sunday? You have been home for the last three days, and I don't think you will be going for the next three. It has been all Sundays for you. I don't have the time. I already lost three days. I need to catch up before I get scolded,' she replied. 'And don't you have anything to do? Like reading a novel, or writing the story you were working on?'

'Let me have some breakfast. I'll write today,' I said feeling energetic seeing her work. I checked the e-paper to get an idea of what was happening around the city.

It was distressful from page one. 'Two Cops injured in Kulgam Militant Attack', read the major headline. Next to it was a report that claimed that more than thirty per cent of families living in the Sheikhpora Migrant colony had left Kashmir. A silent departure was already on its way. And then, the Sikh community body, GPC, Gurdwara Parbandhak Committee, held a press conference saying that Sikh employees would not attend duties until the government ensured security. I could see what would happen next. Incidents of attacks on police parties, like the Kulgam Militant attack, would result in tighter security. A lot of police nakas would be set up, and frisking and checking of random cars, bikes and people would be conducted throughout Kashmir. That would anger the citizens, and the vicious cycle of hate would begin afresh.

Facebook and Twitter broke out more news than traditional newspapers. There was an encounter that happened in a nearby area called Chanapora, not even a mile away from our home. One militant was killed, and a lot of gunfire was heard, it reported. That was yesterday when we were deeply engrossed in the conversation with Harshdeep. We did not even hear the shots. And I was glad that we didn't. Otherwise, Indu who was already frightened, would have become more afraid. In the past, several small incidents happened in the vicinity, and whenever she asked me about them, I could easily tell her that they were very far away. She had no idea of the geography of Kashmir, and she did not know the names of the surrounding area. It was easier to place the area away if she ever asked. But if she heard the gunshots herself, I could not have done anything about it.

The day before, I had dodged the conversation she wanted to have about leaving Kashmir. With this firing and shooting in close vicinity, she would have been terrified, and I, speechless. I went out to tell my parents, to caution them against telling any such thing to her. I knew she would come to know somehow. But I wanted to guard her as much as I could from such news, and the anxieties and anguish that would follow. In the hope that she would not read the news on her own, I went back to her, with the proposal to visit the library in the evening.

'We can go to the library. Raman could not meet yesterday. He will come there today. What do you say?' I asked.

'You go. I have some work,' she said without even looking at me.

'Okay, I will ask you again in the evening. You focus right now,' I said before leaving her to work undisturbed.

It was a good thing that she was working with a full focus keeping away from the news and toxicity.

'You people will go blah blah blah in your language and then I have to keep looking at your faces. What will I do there? If it was only Raman and you, that was fine. He talks in English. But with Veerji and others in the mix, you just forget about me.'

'Okay,' I said feeling like being scolded by my principal from high school. 'I thought it will lighten up your mood. We cannot go to Dal Lake for a few days. That's why I asked,' I said in as low a voice as I could.

'Don't,' she said. I usually use this low voice to emotionally win her over, but ever since she figured it out, it did not work on her. 'Let me study. We will talk about it after lunch. You go out, take a book or write. I need to focus. Please,' she said again, looking into her laptop.

I took my laptop to the living room and thought about continuing my adventure with nothingness from the morning. I fell asleep on the sofa, and when I woke up two hours later, I had a quilt on me, probably my mother's handiwork. Indu was still in the room. She had come out in between to make another cup of coffee for herself. Father had gone out somewhere before I woke up the first time in the morning, while Ramneek was glued to Netflix in the bedroom. Mother was making some dishes in the kitchen. The quiet of the house was broken when Indu came out again and sat in front of me.

'What?' I asked her anxiously.

'Why are you pale?' she asked.

'No. I mean, yes. First, you tell me. All well? You look irritated and… tell me.'

'I was conducting a session. I am annoyed because of that. I can't tell you more,' she replied.

'Don't scare me like that,' for a moment, I thought she heard some news or something else had happened while I slept.

'Why are you scared? Do I look so annoyed?' she asked, trying to force a smile.

'No, I was just…nothing. So, what's the plan? I am going to the library in the evening, around five. If you change your mind before that, you are welcome,' I told her. It was already lunchtime.

'And what are you going to do till five? Sleep somewhere else? That's all you are doing these days.'

'What else should I do?' I asked in my defence.

'Do something. Anything. Read, write, play, watch TV, anything but sleeping.'

'What's wrong with sleeping?'

'What happened to you? What happened to the Bupi I met when I came to Kashmir, that creative, social, extremely extroverted, hyperactive Bupi?' she asked.

'He's sleeping,' I replied, attempting the widest smile I could while baring my teeth and raising my eyebrows as high as I could, to lighten the serious mood she had so easily created with a single question. Before she came to Kashmir for the first time, I was actively involved in many social activities. One of the most creative things I did in Kashmir over the years was to establish Unfound Creativity Club. Actually, it started in Jammu during my winter vacation in 2017. My best friend, Bhanu, suggested we organise an open-mic event in cafes where poets and spoken word artists could come together and read in front of an audience. When I came back to Kashmir after the winter vacation, I replicated the same here. It was a success. A lot of people followed the trail and started their own clubs and organisations. Through Unfound, we organised more than a dozen such events and found hundreds of writers, poets and performers. Bhanu kept doing the same in Jammu.

When Indu and I started dating towards the end of 2018, I was already conducting such events across the state and made friends with a lot of creative people. What I worked for so hard in Kashmir was a prominent culture in Bangalore, the place where Indu lived at that time. In December 2018, when I visited her, she took me to several such places, most notably to Ranga Shankara, a drama theatre.

That was the first time I watched a play. I remember in that play titled *Room*, there were only three actors in conversation with each other. It was a very engaging play but all I could think was what I and other people in Kashmir were missing. We wanted more art; we wanted more life. My creative zeal was reinvigorated. I wanted to create a similar culture in Jammu and Kashmir. And I was successful to an extent.

By the start of 2019, several people started organising similar events. The literary scene of Jammu and Kashmir changed for young people. In July 2019, we launched a book club as well and collaborated with major cafes and bookshops in Kashmir. Cafe owners like Javid Parsa of Parsa's food chain, Kamran Nissar of Winterfell, Danish, Anam and Krushna of Books and Bricks came forward, allowing me to host my events free of charge at their cafes. They even volunteered to give out their books to the members of the Unfound Book Club. The biggest bookshop in Kashmir, Gulshan Bookshop, volunteered and promised a ten per cent discount to our members. I was super active and happy that things were working as I had planned. But that looked like in the past now.

Everything came crumbling down when in August 2019, a month after the launch of our book club. Kashmir was shut down for over three months as Article 370 was revoked. Kashmiris were already in lockdown when Covid-19 came and extended it for another year.

The book club, the creativity club, and all my other endeavours were flushed down the drain.

Now when I looked back at those days, I felt numb. Numb because all my social life ceased, no more events, no more interactions with such creative people. I was a different person altogether during those two years of active social life.

The last three years in Kashmir made me a dull, boring person, who sat home after his day job, ended up scrolling through Instagram and Facebook, and awaited the night to sleep. The aspirations and dreams of a better tomorrow were all pinned on Indu completing her studies. That would be the day I would leave Kashmir and settle in Bangalore or somewhere abroad where I could again ignite the creative flame in me. The dream of the future made me work on my writing profile. I kept writing and submitting and getting published so I could have a good portfolio when I started my writing career. Now, Indu reminded me about my active times. She pointed out, 'You should wake up the active Bupi. I am not asking you to go out and socialise or start your events again. But at least cater to your own hobbies. When we first met, you were reading a whole novel in a week, and now in this whole year, you haven't even read five. Or you could write. You always complain that you don't have time, and when you get time like this, you waste it sleeping. Call Bhanu at least. He will drill some sense into you.'

'Whose anger are you venting on me?' I asked her. I hadn't called Bhanu in a month or so, but that was how we were. We would call when we wanted, no formalities, no obligations. We were best friends, though we never acknowledged it because that term could not define our relationship. Indu said, 'I am not angry. I am just worried about what you are doing. I won't say it again if you say so. But you need to introspect about it. Look at the conditions here in Kashmir. This is not a place where we would want to settle down. So you need to work on your writing career, and when you have the time to do it, just think about that.'

She walked to the kitchen to check on my mother.

In the first six months of our dating, there had been around 142 terrorism-related incidents and 318 killings before the major Article 370 and Article 35(a) lockdown hit us. Overnight there was a complete blackout, phone and internet were cut off. Indu and I were cut off from each other. For a month, we could not even talk to each other.

When I called her from a police station where they provided a calling facility after a month of lockdown, all she could do was cry. Later she told me she tried calling me every day, wishing the call would somehow get through. That was the only time during our relationship when we had not talked to each other. Before that lockdown, she could not relate to our problems as she was not at the suffering end. But with the blackout, she came to know how inaccessible I had become to her overnight. For her, earlier, the news was not something relatable. The killings and terrorist encounters, the bomb blasts, everything was just ink on paper, some happenings somewhere so far from her that she did not even bother about it.

During the lockdown, she obsessively read about Kashmir, its problems and history, the dynamics and political turmoil, and when it was over, she found herself in a mess. Loving a Kashmiri was so hard.

We had several debates about whether Kashmir was a place where we saw our future. Her one question always troubled me, 'Would you like our children to grow up in such a place?' And I never had a satisfactory answer for that. What kind of a future would they have in a place like Kashmir, like me trying to hide the news from their spouses, trying to escape from every troubling conversation, and trying to run away from Kashmir while living in Kashmir? All their life they would be trying to set up a living, creating a dream home, and then out of the blue, questioning all their efforts and decision of living in Kashmir or leaving it.

It was not a place I wanted my children to grow up in.

10

Azaadi

Jammu
2001–2010

Sometimes I think I should have never returned to Kashmir, never taken that job. I would have been in a much better place. After my graduation, I would have certainly gone for a master's in chemistry. I would have gone to Uttarakhand's Kumaon University from where my friend Jatin later completed his MSc. He was my college mate and we had a chemistry class together. Sometime during the beginning of my second year at college, I became good friends with him. Like him, I would have pursued a PhD. He went to an IIT. I would have at least made it to some reputable institute if not an IIT. By this time in my life, I would have finished my doctorate and would be doing a job or a postdoc somewhere. I would have never actually thought of coming to Kashmir. Maybe Delhi or Bangalore, working like an IT guy, but never Kashmir.

In 2001, after the Mehjoor Nagar incident, my family did not move to Jammu immediately. It took my father about two months to figure out everything before moving out. It was in April that we migrated out. I had passed my class VI in October of the preceding year. By April, I was halfway through class VII. Being in the summer zone, the schools in Jammu started their session in April, so I was admitted as a new student in class VII. More than six months of my schooling were lost with the shift of sessions from the winter zone to the summer zone. Just a month ago, I had come out of a three-month-long vacation, and in another two months, a one-and-a-half-month-long summer vacation awaited me. That initial year in Jammu took a toll on my education.

I was a bright student in Kashmir, where I studied in a state board curriculum. The transition to the Central Board of Secondary Education (CBSE) was hard for me. We were used to learning the questions and answers by rote learning. In Kashmir, fifty per cent of our education was rote learning, and fifty per cent went missing with school closures due to strikes, encounters and protests. CBSE was anything but rote. By the end of the year, students had to appear for the exam, where they would be asked questions not only from the whole book but also questions based on the other texts and concepts. In the state board exams, the chapters for which we had already written exams were not included in the portions for the finals. The final exam was conducted for less than forty per cent of the textbook, and only the questions in the exercises at the end of the chapters were asked. The CBSE curriculum was very hard for me to cope with.

The rest of the transition into school life was easy or rather pleasant for me. From being the only Sikh student in my school in Kashmir, I was one among the four in my class. There were Hindus and Muslims in my class. In the whole school, there were more than fifty Sikh students. It was something that amazed me and confused me at the same time, for most of them were not friends with each other. For me making friends within my own community was the most logical and rational thought. In Kashmir, it mattered a lot. But once I realised that the reason for that line of thought did not exist in Jammu, it all made sense to me.

First, the common language was Hindi, which I was far more comfortable with than Kashmiri. Whatever religion or community one belonged to did not matter here, for everyone communicated in Hindi. Nobody felt left out. Second, everybody ate together, or at least in a group with their friends. They shared lunch and ate from each other's boxes and tiffins. In Kashmir, being the only Sikh, I had to sit away from everyone to eat. Nobody would eat from mine, and I could not eat from anyone because of the jhatka-halaal difference. In Jammu, the only divide was being a vegetarian or a non-vegetarian, and that too only on those days when somebody brought non-vegetarian food. The canteen served only vegetarian and as such was accessible to me. I could order whatever I wanted without thinking about jhatka and halaal. And as it was often said, people who ate together stayed together. I developed close friendships in Jammu, lifelong friendships. Over time I realised how the food restriction that was there in Kashmir affected my social life. I had never shared food even with my closest friends in Kashmir, never gone to their house for a sleepover or for a night out. In Jammu, when I wanted to go for a sleepover at a friend's house, my mother allowed me without any apprehension, for I could easily eat food at their place. And it was not only at a Hindu or a Sikh friend's home, I could easily go to a Muslim friend's home because everywhere in Jammu, jhatka and vegetarian food was easily available, almost in every locality.

And it was not only my school life that changed. After school hours, in the evenings, I could go to any food shop and eat hotdogs and momos, sandwiches and burgers to my fill, dishes I did not even know existed. I had seen them only on TV. This newfound freedom to go wherever and eat from wherever was what was missing in Kashmir.

In the colony we stayed for the first two years, Channi Himmat, I made a lot of friends. It was a colony of mixed cultures and people. There was a big gurdwara, a bigger temple, and several small mosques in the colony. The only thing I was actually missing from Kashmir was the long melodious azaan from the mosques I had been hearing all my life, five times a day, without fail. The azaan was so subconsciously embedded into me that its absence made me wonder why I missed it. In Kashmir, for every few hundred meters, you will find a mosque, and when it is time for the prayer, all the mosques will simultaneously give out the azaan so loud that it can be heard from a mile. At my masi's place, in Batmaloo, Kashmir, there were four mosques, one on each side of their small Sikh colony comprising a dozen or so houses. During azaan, the sound was blasted at them from all sides, and my young cousins had grown so accustomed to it that they would know when it was time for the next azaan. Their body clocks had been tuned to it. We sometimes made fun of them, saying that though a Sikh, they remembered the whole namaaz instead of the paath. In Jammu, you could not hear that, at least not in the place where I lived. There were occasional jagratas when the bhajans were loud, but no azaans.

There were two major things I found difficult to cope with in Jammu. One was the weather. I had been to Jammu during winter vacations as a visitor for a month a few times. My paternal aunts lived in Jammu. Compared to the extreme winter in Kashmir, Jammu used to be all warm and cosy. It was cold for Jammuites but not for us Kashmiris. To us, it was pleasant, like our Octobers, the onset of winters. But I had never come to Jammu in the summer. In Kashmir, the maximum temperature would not go beyond thirty-five in the summer. In Jammu, it would not come below forty during the three summer months. The spring and autumn in Jammu were hotter than our summers in Kashmir. I was always sweating.

The other thing was the sound of crackers at the marriage parties. In Jammu, most of the marriage parties hosted dinner, and there were always very loud firecrackers for the celebration. For almost a year, I would shiver at the sound of it as it felt like a grenade blast or an encounter between the army and militants. Not only I, but my parents also had the same reaction, and then we would all laugh about it. The association of the sound with grenade blasts was so ingrained that even if the firecracker was lit in front of my eyes, I would still be scared, identifying it with a grenade or a gunshot. It went away with time.

By the time I passed class X, the internet had become a fad. Every weekend we would go to internet cafes to chat in the Yahoo rooms, asking ASL to foreigners. Orkut and Myspace social media platforms had just arrived on the scene, and we were showcasing our lives, interests and orientations out in the open.

I had heard of theatres and movie halls in Kashmir. When militancy started, there were around a dozen movie screens in Kashmir, all of which were burned downed or closed. My mother would tell me that she had seen *Betaab, Kati Patang* and *Ram Teri Ganga Maili* in theatres. In Kashmir, I had heard bus conductors yelling the names like Sheeraz, Khayyam, Neelam, Shah, Regal, Firdous, Palladium, Naaz and Broadway cinema hall as bus stops. They had become mere landmarks. My mother had promised me that I could watch a movie in the theatre after I passed my class X exams. The results were out by May. The songs of the movie *Bunty Aur Babli* were famous, and the movie was going to be released by the end of the month. I was waiting for it. During our summer vacations, from May to July, I would be visiting Kashmir, my maternal home. So it was a perfect movie for my first silver screen experience. That summer vacation in Kashmir, I told everyone what it was to be inside the theatre, with a very big screen, with the lights turned off, and people going crazy with hooting and clapping, hundreds of them at the same time. I was too shy to whistle or hoot, while for all my friends in Jammu, it was quite the usual thing. From seeing theatres in movies, I was now seeing movies in theatres.

In Jammu, my school years were very stable. For five years, I was in the same school, Maharishi Vidya Mandir, Sainik Colony. In Kashmir, I had changed at least six schools in seven years. By the time I made friends, I would shift to a new school. Thanks to this, I had no school friends from Kashmir. In Jammu, friendships were more meaningful because they developed and grew over the years. We went through thick and thin, through successes and failures, through romances and heartbreaks, shoulder to shoulder. Some of these friends are still close to me. Rishi, Neeraj, Rankush and Anubhav have been in constant touch over the years, even though all of us went in different directions after our schooling.

In 2008, when I joined college for my BSc in chemistry, botany and zoology, I forged new friendships. That was the age of mobile phones, and it gave us the ability to plan things. If any of us had a thought, an uncooked plan of a trip, or bunking the college or likewise, we could call each other and decide what to do the next day, where to meet and what to bring from home. I explored Jammu in its true sense only after I joined the college. I was financially independent as I earned enough money from my web designing projects, a skill I picked up in Kashmir when my father put me in a computer institute. One of my friends, Imran, bought a bike, a Pulsar 135 cc, with which we used to visit far-flung areas of Jammu. I sometimes took my father's old scooter to college, but it was more of an embarrassment as it would not start with the first kick, and sometimes we had to push-start it. Jatin, another close friend, used to mock me that the scooter was possessed, for in the presence of girls, it would always embarrass us, while in the presence of boys, it would start with a mere touch of a foot. Jatin and Imran were the closest friends I made in college.

Seven years of living in Jammu changed me a lot. From someone who stayed away from fights and feared bullying, I had become a fearless boy, who participated in college elections, led students for protests, and did not shy away from fistfights when needed. The first year of college passed by in a blink.

During that year, there was a Jammu vs Kashmir protest going on in the whole state. It was for the first time the people of Jammu had come to the streets to protest. In Kashmir, it was a common occurrence, but for Jammu, it was not even heard of. It started in May 2008, when the

Government of India and the state government of Jammu and Kashmir decided to transfer some ninety-nine acres of forest land in the Baltal region of Kashmir to the Shri Amarnathji Shrine Board. It was for setting up temporary shelters and facilities for the pilgrims who visited the holy cave of Amarnath every summer. This grant of land became the bone of contention later. The pilgrims were Hindus, and the land belonged to Kashmir, which the local Muslims thought of as their property. Initially, the environmentalists protested the clearing of forest land. But soon, huge protests erupted in Kashmir against the land transfer as it was seen as favouritism towards Hindus. Hundreds of protesters were injured, and at least six died. The whole of Kashmir retaliated with a full-blown protest, with all the major organisations and leaders coming forward to support the protest. Schools, colleges and businesses were shut down and there were strikes. Counter-protest rallies were organised in Jammu against the then government of Jammu and Kashmir People's Democratic Party (PDP)-Congress.

With every passing day, the protests intensified in Kashmir and finally, the government had to give in to the pressure and revoked this transfer—Land Grant—which resulted in another wave of counter-protests in Jammu. When Kashmir calmed down, Jammu started to boil. It had become a Hindu vs Muslim protest rather than a land allotment one. Soon it turned political, with major political figures playing to their interests. The alliance government of PDP-Congress was threatened when the PDP leader, Mehbooba Mufti, withdrew support in protest to the revocation of land allotment. The chief minister had to eventually step down. The void created as such catapulted into a further political war when Omar Abdullah, leader of the National Conference played down the incident. Hindus of Jammu went to protest against the protest in Kashmir. But it all went out of control when a few young people committed suicide by ingesting poison during the protest in Jammu. The rage and anger consumed the state for two months. Public properties, schools, buses, shops and government offices were burned down.

Within no time, the protests turned into communal riots. The army was called in, and the state was put under curfew. Our college was shut down for at least two months as a result of this. Whenever we went to college, the students also came to the roads with stones and sticks to protest in favour of the Shri Amarnathji Shrine Board. That year, I felt like I was somehow again transported to Kashmir.

In Jammu, the Muslims were in the minority, and as a result of the protests, they were the ones who suffered the most. At least seventy-two Muslim houses were burned in those two months, and a lot of their properties were destroyed and ransacked. It was a complete reversal of events as compared to Kashmir. As a minority who has lived in Kashmir, I could understand the fear the Muslims of Jammu faced now. They were more patriotic and nationalist than the Hindus but still had to face the brunt of the mob.

That year, the college announced a fifty per cent relaxation in the syllabus for the final exams, and we were the happiest people. We did not care the least about what happened in the state for whatever reasons. For us, mass promotion or syllabus reduction was more important than land allotment. Over forty people were killed and thousands injured during the agitation, and we protested for mass promotion or syllabus reduction in our college—the two months of missed class work and another month of protest to get justice for those two months made it feel like three months went down the drain. And when college finally started in September, Jammu's first shopping mall had just begun its operation, and some of the best eateries opened on its top floor. It was our doom. Both financially and educationally. Domino's pizzas were our lunchtime snack. We spent most of our time in the mall, window shopping, eating, and just loitering on the stairways and corridors.

In 2009, during my second year in college, I spent most of my time in the table tennis room and National Service Scheme (NSS) camps and workshops. Due to the Amarnath Shrine board controversy in the previous year, most of the college activities were suspended. We had to catch up with all of those, camps, workshops, debate competitions, seminars, academic events and sports events. The year was a very busy one for the students. But it was different for me. That year, my childhood friend, Sarabjeet Singh, migrated to Jammu for his engineering degree. We spent the whole year together, so much so that sometimes he would bunk his classes and come to my college and sit in our botany and zoology classes. Even the professors knew about him. He either stayed at my house, or I stayed at his. Our neighbours thought of him as my elder brother, who had just returned from his boarding school.

During that one-and-a-half year of togetherness with him, I did the most adventurous things. We went on unplanned trips out of the blue. We would be sitting at home watching TV, and suddenly would tell each other, 'Let's go to Amritsar or Simla or McLeodganj,' and by evening we would be on our way. In the middle of the night, we would search for coffee shops and, at last, go to the hospital cafeterias. When we went to the university dosa shop, we would eat at least three dosas each. We would pick unnecessary fights with the representatives of college politics. It was utter madness.

On the socio-religious part, we mobilised the Sikh youth of our respective colleges and started a Khalsa Youth Club, which gave free tuition to poor kids, free books and literature material, both religious and educational. We organised rallies against eve-teasing and women's harassment, and we sensitised the public about disabled people, their plights, and their rights.

Despite all that, I did score a good percentage in the second year. It was at the end of my second year that my father applied for the job vacancy on my behalf without even asking or informing me. One fine day, he just took me along and told me to appear for the interview at the Service Selection Board's office. And when the results came, somehow, I was selected for the job despite being nonchalant and chilled during the interview. I scored in the interview, which gave me the edge over people who were more qualified than me.

As I had a job, I could not attend college as a regular student anymore. So, in my third year of college, I enrolled as a private student which meant that I needn't attend classes but had to come for practicals and appear for the internal as well as the external exams like regular students. I was supposed to go, first in December, to join the chief education officer's office and then in March 2011, to join my place of posting. Sarabjeet was still in his second year of BTech, while I had to go to Kashmir.

That year again, Kashmir saw a lot of unrest, wherein the famous *ragdo-ragdo* protest and dance were born. Three Pakistani infiltrators were killed by the Indian army in June 2010. The people of Kashmir called it a staged encounter, and as a result, a movement to completely demilitarise the State of Jammu and Kashmir was launched by Hurriyat Conference, which was led by Syed Ali Shah Geelani and Mirwaiz Umar Farooq. In Kashmir, there were around 70,000 to 1,00,000 Indian troops and paramilitaries stationed. The protestors sought to reduce this number to the minimum possible. But during the protests, some 112 protesters were killed, which included a number of students, teenagers, and an eleven-year-old child as well. Things escalated when a seventeen-year-old student, Tufail Matto, was killed while returning from school.

The Armed Forces Special Powers Act (AFSPA) allowed the army to have absolute power to maintain public order and peace in a disturbed area. The act was considered draconian by the local Kashmiri population and has been held responsible for several Human Rights violations in such disturbed areas. In Kashmir, over the years, this law has been seen as the harshest and most deceptive measure to harass civilians. And in the same year, those who were selected for jobs under the Prime Minister's Package for Relief and Rehabilitation were told to go to Kashmir and join the duties. This package was debated and dissected by the local population and was seen as a measure to bring back the Pandits to Kashmir and that meant taking away the already scarce jobs available to Kashmiri locals. Another major concern was that Pandits were considered Indian sympathisers by the Muslims, and their presence in Kashmir was viewed as one that would weaken the freedom movement.

The Kashmiri Pandits in Jammu staged a sit-in protest, a dharna, asking the Central Government not to remove or dilute the AFSPA as it provided the security forces with constitutional protection for preserving the country's sovereignty. For Pandits in particular and migrants in general, the presence of the army in Kashmir was seen as a reassurance of safety and peace.

That year was very violent with one exception. The main tool used by protesters other than the usual stones, was a dance called *ragdo-ragdo* dance. The people would come together and shout and sing and dance.

Hum kya chahte? Azaadi
Zara zor se bolo – Azaadi
Hai hak hamara – Azaadi

Hum chheen ke lenge – Azaadi
Khushboo wali – Azaadi
Hai jaan se pyari – Azaadi
Aye moula dede – Azaadi
Shodah ke sadkey – Azaadi
Agar shaheed huwa toh, mera kafan pe likhna – Azaadi
Aayee, aayee – Azaadi

What do we want? Azaadi!
Say it loudly – Azaadi!
It is our right – Azaadi!
We will snatch it for ourselves – Azaadi!
The fragrant one – Azaadi!
More precious than life – Azaadi!
Oh! Almighty grant us – Azaadi!
For the sacrifices of martyrs – Azaadi!
If I become a martyr, write on my shroud – Azaadi!
Here comes, here comes – Azaadi!

And the other one was.

Girti deewar ko,
Ik dhakka aur do.
Bharat ki sarkar ko
Ik dhakka aur do.
Aa, ragda-ragda,
Dey ragda,
Bharat ko ragda,
De ragda,
Ragda-ragda,
Bharat ko ragdo.

To the falling wall,
Let us give one more push.

To the Indian government,
Let us give one more push.
Come, stomp, stomp,
Stomp on India,
Stomp more,
Stomp, stomp,
Stomp on India.

Not only would they dance and sing these resistance anthems, but every other shop shutter and wall was also painted with '*Hum kya chahte – Azaadi*' and '*Ragdo-ragdo, Bharat ragdo*'.

For those living in Jammu, it was scary going to Kashmir for jobs already, and if the AFSPA was to be removed, the last vestiges of peace would go with it and it would become impossible to go there. The protests simmered down by October, and we received instructions to join our Kashmir offices.

Had I not taken that offer, I wouldn't be writing this story or, for that matter, all the others which I had written during the last decade. A tiny shift in the decisions taken would have taken me somewhere entirely different. For good or for worse, I would never know. The financial stability I had with this job let me explore and travel more and gave me the liberty to experiment with my passions and hobbies. And at that point in time, when the job was announced, financial stability was all we wanted.

When we moved to Jammu in 2001, for the first three years, my father couldn't find a stable source of income. Our household ran on his minuscule earnings from the shop in Kashmir and a meagre stipend given by the government to all Kashmir migrants. Before coming to Jammu, my father used to run a wholesale shop for rice, wheat flour, cold drinks and some spices. When we shifted to Jammu, he did not shut it but instead hired a salesman to run the shop. So for two years, he had to take several trips back to Kashmir to manage the shop, restock it and get the money. Eventually, due to losses, mismanagement and a dishonest salesman, he had to shut the shop down. That was in the latter half of 2003. For the rest of the years, he kept trying to find some other source of income while our savings eroded slowly.

My mother and Ramneek, on the other hand, were homebound most of the time. None of my mother's relatives lived in Jammu, and she did not have any friends either. So, she had nowhere to go until her sister's family came to Jammu in 2004 as her husband got his job posting there. But every year during the winters, our relatives from Kashmir visited us frequently. With us being here, they had a home to stay in Jammu.

In 2004, my father found a job as a bursar with a business tycoon in Ludhiana, who owned many schools, colleges, theatres and clubs. He had to manage two of the schools, one in Ludhiana and another in Dehradun. We moved into a bigger house, for which the rent was considerably more than the previous one. I had a room of my own there. We were financially stable for two years when my father was holding that job. Those were my crucial school years, classes X and XI and I needed the money. The school canteen bills and cafeteria treats became an everyday thing. Though I did not go to any tuition or coaching institute, I went out in the evenings to meet my friends.

In 2006, my father left that job and came back to Jammu permanently and planned to start his own school, a school for mentally and physically challenged children. He named it Aasra Special School. Aasra meant a homely shelter. Being a father of a child with cerebral palsy, he asked himself, and sometimes the parents of such children, an important question. 'What will happen to these children when we die?' It was a very scary question. No one wanted to answer it, even if they knew the answer. Children who had mental or physical disabilities and were completely dependent on their parents had nowhere to go after the death of their parents. Siblings seldom take care of them. They were either put in orphanages for special children or in special boarding schools. Both such facilities were absent in our state.

My father had a single objective. To create a place where such children could live after their parents. His first step was the school, a day boarding one, where he could train such children to be as independent as they could be. He faced a lot of challenges in his mission. Some parents of such children did not want to spend money on them, for they knew their education would not have any returns. Their logic was such kids would not be able to get jobs. So why waste money on their schooling? Some cursed their fates for having such children and had a firm belief that these were their punishment for some past life misdeeds and sins, while some others had complete devotion towards them but believed that the schooling would not be able to help them. So my father decided not to charge the parents anything, neither for schooling and vocational training nor for meals and transportation. Instead, he requested donations from established businessmen, government employees, and others to run the school. He asked special educators, speech therapists and physiotherapists to visit the school whenever they could, and he asked the doctors and medical officers to lend their help as well. Many of them came forward, and he ran the school for twelve years. He put multiple proposals to the government for full-fledged funding assistance so that he could convert it into a residential school. But all his attempts failed.

Sometimes I felt that the school was his way of providing for Ramneek after all of us were gone. Initially, he was uncertain whether I would look after Ramneek. What about him after I got married? Would my wife be kind? Would she be interested in taking care of Ramneek? Some of the students who came to our school were orphans. Their extended families were looking after them, and they were certainly not doing a good job of it. They had tried to put them in schools and orphanages outside the state. Like the Pingalwara in Punjab which was run by the Sikh Community, on a very large scale, and sheltered more than a thousand mentally and physically challenged people. My father's ambition in Jammu, unfortunately, did not succeed. After the school closed down at the end of 2018, my parents and Ramneek shifted to a government accommodation in a colony specially designed for migrants in the Nagrota region of Jammu. He had his stipend, and I had secured a job by then. My salary and his stipend were more than enough to support the family. So I told him to sit back and relax and stop looking for a job. Ever since then, my parents would come to Kashmir to live with me during six to eight months of harsh Jammu summers. When it started to get cold in Kashmir, they would again go to Jammu for the winter.

Father loved his time in Jammu. Due to the school, he became a noted social worker. He was known throughout Jammu as the sardarji who works for the disabled. He sensitised the people, conducted mass awareness drives, and met every government delegation to put forward the cause of such people. Even after the school closed down, he continues to be socially active. And for that very reason, he never wanted to stay in Kashmir. He felt isolated and suffocated in Kashmir. Jammu is his home ground.

He keeps telling me to quit the job and move out of such a negative and mentally stifling place. The money and comfort from the job keep telling me otherwise. But whichever way we look at it, both his and my time in Jammu was far better than it was and is in Kashmir.

11

Daydreams

Srinagar, Kashmir
11–16 October 2021

The first thing I did on Monday morning was to call my school and see what was happening. To ascertain if I had to come in on that day or if I could continue my love affair with being unoccupied for another couple of days. But the day brought a sense of foreboding. The newspaper headlines were a mix of emotions for us, individually. The headline that triggered such perplexion was, 'No leave granted to minority employees after civilian killings, govt clarifies.' That meant I had to go to school officially. Unofficially nobody knew what to do. Another headline read, 'National Investigative Agency (NIA) arrests three Islamic State of Iraq and Syria (ISIS) and two Resistance Front (TRF) operatives,' and just next to this one was another news item saying that four over-ground workers (OGWs) of TRF were arrested somewhere in Kashmir. Also, a gunfight between the army and militants was underway in Poonch, a remote area in the Jammu province, separated from Kashmir by mountains and dense jungles.

But that was stale news. Monday newspapers brought news that had happened the day before. So I went to check the official websites of Greater Kashmir, while Indu scrolled through her own sources on her phone. And both of us looked at each other at the same time with our jaws dropped. Five soldiers of the Indian army were killed in the encounter that was underway in Poonch. Though Poonch was not a part of the Kashmir province, it was connected through a dense jungle, which was a perfect hideout for militants. Through the same jungle, arms and ammunition also found their way into Kashmir.

'What's happening? How long are these killings going to happen?' Indu sighed and asked 'How far is Poonch from here?'

'It is very far, not a part of Kashmir. It's a border area in Jammu. And these arrests and killings mean the government and the army and the police are acting efficiently,' I replied as I scrolled further down.

'So, the government wants you back in school? They are not giving any leaves to minority employees?'

'Why do they have to? It is not a minority killing. It was a civilian killing. By that standard, they will have to grant leaves to all the civilians, and that means closing down everything.'

'You are not going to school,' she ordered.

'I'll apply for casual leave for a few days,' I replied.

'You apply for a longer leave. We will go to Jammu, or you can come to stay with me in Delhi,' she said.

'Baby, I have already told you that running away is not the solution. How many leaves can I take? And what next? This is Kashmir. Such things will never stop.' Saying this I put my phone down and took her hands in mine. 'Anyway, you will have to join your institute in November. So it's fine. Twenty more days,' I said as softly as I could.

'And what about you and your parents?' she asked.

'We will be fine here. We are used to this,' Discussing this again and again was irritating me. I wanted to stop.

'This is what Supinder and Deepak and all others were telling themselves and their families. We will be fine here. This is a lie you tell yourself. You know it. What if something happens to you or your father? You cannot stay inside the house always,' her voice was getting louder with every word. She withdrew her hands from mine.

'If I was in such a situation, would you leave me and go to Delhi, and be happy there, knowing that I am in danger?'

'Stop playing UNO. What is surprising is if I say something, you try to make it sound as if it is my responsibility, my problem. It's not like that, and these kinds of killings are going on since the 1990s. The army and militants are in an eternal gunfight. This is not towards civilians.'

'I cannot go to Delhi like this. I will always be thinking about you people,' she said and slumped into a chair. I began to massage her shoulder.

'I will check about the leave. Anyway, winter vacations are in December. I'll see if I can take November off. Then I can come with you to Delhi or stay with my parents in Jammu.'

I applied a little more pressure to her neck. 'Now don't sulk and continue to work. Yesterday you were scolding me for wasting time, and today I haven't seen you open your laptop even once. Get up, baby.'

'A little more massage and then I'll go,' she said. I couldn't say no.

The same day two militants were killed, one each in Anantnag and Bandipora, and a new encounter started in the Tulran area of Shopian, where three militants were allegedly engaged in a gunfight with the army.

The next day, three militants were killed in the Tulran encounter, along with two more in a separate incident in Shopian. The Poonch encounter spread to Rajouri, an adjacent area thickly forested with more difficult terrain. It continued the whole week and spilled over to the weekend as well. On Wednesday, the thirteenth, a separate gunfight erupted in the Tral region, where one militant was killed. On the same day, NIA raided more than thirty-one locations and arrested fourteen terrorists. On 14 October, a junior commissioned officer and a soldier were killed while trying to force out militants. On 16 October, two more soldiers were killed, taking the toll to nine. The paratroopers, an elite section of the Indian Army, had joined the hunt to kill the militants. That was not a relief at all, for it meant that a lot more were there and the troopers had to be called in to flush them out. My father said this was what happened in the mid-90s as well when militancy was at its peak. Wherever the police went to search, they would find militants or arms and ammunition. They mingled so well with the civilians that it was hard to figure out who was a militant and who was not. That uncertainty propagated fear.

Though these encounters and killings happened quite far from where we lived, I was still made to sit inside. It was boring, dull and suffocating. Veerji and Raman, on the other hand, attended their offices. Every day we would hear more and more Kashmiri Pandit employees leaving the Valley. On the one hand, all these encounters and militants being killed meant that the security forces were doing their job in keeping the city safe for minorities and other non-locals. It also meant that more and more people were picking up arms and joining the movement.

On the evening of 16 October, in a press conference, the divisional commissioner of Kashmir said that it was their foremost duty to provide security to the minorities. All the PM Package colonies where the employees lived were being monitored, and police vehicles and Central

Reserve Police Force (CRPF) personnel were stationed, securing every entry and exit point. In areas where the Sikhs lived, we could see constant patrolling of police cars and paramilitary personnel.

My only personal interaction with the outside world was through phone calls, and that too was limited to Raman, Snowber and Sadaam.

Veerji had come to my house on Wednesday evening, telling me that he had gone to different Sikh localities and seen what the administration had claimed. There was a security upgrade to all such areas. He also told me to stay home, for I was not just a Sikh but also a PM Package employee, which made me a soft target.

I called Sadaam later that evening, to check on what rumours were rife in Kashmir. He was good at gathering them, and would always give prophecies of things much before they happened. Once in 2019, when the state was unaware of what was happening, he had told me, 'Buy food stocks and groceries for a minimum of three months. You will thank me later.' I asked him the basis of his nonsensical foretelling. He just smiled at me and told me to believe whatever I wanted. But his warning was not unwarranted. Something big did happen in 2019.

Regarding my present query, he told me that people thought of these killings as a warning to all the Kashmiris, irrespective of their religion, to stay away from the Indian government. The attacks were in response to Article 370 and other government policies.

'They will kill more people like these, to set an example. I don't think this is going to stop anytime soon unless the government takes strict action,' he said.

'What do they want now? To exile Sikhs as well?' I asked him.

'No. It's not about Sikhs. The Kashmiris think that the Pandits were coming from Jammu and taking away their jobs, and then they cry that they don't feel safe here. They think that the Pandits should not come here if they did not feel safe here. They think new posts are created every year to draw Pandits slowly back to Kashmir. In this turmoil, the Pandits got the most benefit. What do you think the unemployed, frustrated youth of Kashmir would do? Welcome them with garlands? And after 370, more and more outsiders will be coming. The people think that it is the government's ploy to change the demographics of Kashmir. These killings and the ones to come after this are a response to all that,' he replied.

It was a widespread mindset in Kashmir, and I had come across it in various places. Even one of my school teachers had once told me, that I was way under-qualified than a vast majority of the Kashmiri locals, who were sitting unemployed at home because the government decided to give us special consideration and jobs.

What Sadaam said was a local sentiment. 'But what do Sikhs have to do with it? Why target them?' I asked him, and he responded with, 'The Sikhs don't behave like the Pandits. You are much more aware than that. Even in the 1990s, it was not the Pandits who were targeted, but the people at higher posts and important positions. It so happened that all of them were Pandits because that was how Kashmir was back then. Pandits had a monopoly everywhere. In every government office, you will only find Pandits. It was a fight against the government and the government employees in Kashmir, and most of the government employees were Pandits.'

'You might remember there were a few Sikhs who were killed during that time. They were high-ranking officials. But, did you people also run away? No, because very few of you people were in the government services. So, not many Sikhs were killed,' he added.

'Whatever you say, you cannot justify the killing of people, just because they represent a government. They are not the policymakers, just policy followers,' I said and added, 'Give them a livelihood, money and security as the government does, and they will follow whoever pays them. Why is being employed by the government to raise your family a crime?'

I could not follow his logic, nor did I know what I was saying. I just felt irritated at the whole conversation.

'Ok. Chill, bro. Nobody is killing you Sikhs. I bet there won't be another Sikh killing now. There might be some Pandit or Bihari killings but not Sikhs,' he said in his confident tone. I wanted to believe him this time. But I also realised that a human killed, be it a Sikh or a Hindu or an outsider, whatever label you give, is a human life lost.

The other thing that amused me was his use of the term Bihari, which did not mean people from Bihar, but anyone who lived outside Kashmir. It was a common racial slur in Kashmir, pronounced in a typical Kashmiri way, *Behaer*. I wondered how much of what he told me was going to be true. Would there be more killings, but not of Sikhs? Would it create the 1990s-like conditions again?

What soothed my nerves after the conversation was a call from Bhanu. He called after a long time, almost a month. I had last seen him at my wedding. He started with an insider joke. He told me that when I was in Kashmir I was a proper Kashmiri, and when I was outside Kashmir, I was the complete opposite. I asked him if he was calling me a hypocrite. But he labelled it as diplomacy, an important life skill.

'What are you people doing, fucking up the whole dynamics of Kashmir?'

'Yup. It has been quiet for a long time and didn't feel like Kashmir. Now, it feels good. Non-violence here felt so awkward,' I replied.

'Indu would be afraid, won't she? She is seeing all this for the first time up close,' he asked.

'She wants me to take a long leave and go to Jammu or Delhi with her.'

'Bro, that's great. My boss says he will shift the company headquarters to Delhi or Noida in November. Come, we will stay together then,' he said.

'Damn, that is awesome. Now this is what I call motivation. I'll check with the school tomorrow. But you confirm first. When are you planning to move?' I asked.

'Will tell you by the weekend. Why do you want to apply for leave? Pandits have already come to Jammu. If nobody asks them, nobody is going to ask you. You are also in the PM Package,' he said. 'Or try for some Covid-duty. Some online work like you did during August and September. Then you will get your salary and can stay wherever you want,' Bhanu suggested.

He called me again on Friday and told me he was supposed to join the Noida office in the first week of November, probably after the Diwali holiday. He was given a hike in salary to compensate. For the prospect of a brighter future, stability in his job, and most importantly, to have a life full of freedom where he could live without his father's constant vigil, he was happy to shift out. He would be taking a rented flat in Noida, and he told me we could live together. Indu could join whenever she could.

Bhanu and I often talked about the *Kill Dill* movie, about renting an apartment, cooking, chilling and enjoying life to the fullest, clubbing on weekends, doing up our own spaces and all. This was our chance at it. I reiterated the plan with Bhanu on Friday evening, and he also got excited. We had lived together for a long time, and those were the best days of our adult life. And ever since the 2019 lockdown and the subsequent Covid lockdown, we hadn't lived together much. We kept meeting occasionally and would have stayed together for a day or two. He had come to my wedding for a day, and that was the last I saw him.

I met Bhanu during a trip to Vaishno Devi in 2013, where another good friend of mine, Jatin, had brought his friend Abhimanyu. Bhanu was Abhimanyu's plus one. We gelled immediately, and during the whole trip kept talking to each other. We exchanged numbers and Facebook IDs. But after the trip ended, we did not meet for another two years. It was during the winter vacations of 2015–16 that I met him again when he was working as an assistant professor, teaching programming to the MCA students at Meerut Institute of Engineering and Technology. During that time, he was seriously considering appearing for the civil services exams and wanted to prepare for it. I, too, for a year, thought about the same but never wholeheartedly worked toward it.

Most evenings, I would go to meet him at Bahu Plaza, a central place in Jammu City where you could find coffee houses and restaurants. It was also a major banking and private companies' office space, always bustling with people. In the Nescafe Coffee shop, we discussed preparing together for the civil services on a serious note. He decided to appear for the 2016 June exam just to measure it up and then maybe quit his day job after that to prepare seriously. I also agreed to it. During that vacation, we frequently met at Nescafe and became closer than ever. After he attempted the exam, he quit his job and came to Kashmir to stay with me for the next five months, so we could prepare together. And the next two years we stayed together in Kashmir, and under the pretext of preparing for the civil exams, we did all things against it. We founded the Unfound together, organised events, and went on treks and trips and unplanned travels. We did not clear the civils, as expected, but we did enjoy our time together. We found our true goals—a number of times—and then we lost them again and again, somewhere down the line.

When the prospect of living together, one more time, came in Noida, all those memories of fun, adventure and madness came back. Good memories, in desperate times, were a refuge and in times of prosperity, ornaments.

The first thing I wanted to do was to tell Indu about it. But then, it would raise her hope, and I was not sure if things would work out according to plan. I had a firm superstition that whenever I told someone, anyone, about my plans, they were bound to fail. If I told Indu and gave her hope only to take it away later, it would make her more tense and angry than she already was. I decided to talk to my father first and then, check with the school authorities about the leave or the Covid duty.

The rest of the days, except Saturday evening, passed in boredom. Other than the Poonch encounter update, nothing else happened. I binge-watched *Lucifer* season four. Indu's anxieties about the situation dulled a little. She did not get restless or irritated like she used to for the first two or three days after Supinder's killing. Our nonchalance had rubbed onto Indu as well. She became calmer during the week despite all this news. One reason, which I thought, was that I was home all the time and she felt reassured by it. She had gone back to her studies. I promised her that we would move out once I figured out a few things. She only wanted to know when.

Saturday evening was, in particular, very boring. We had become used to going out to Dal Lake almost every Saturday and coming back home late, around 11.30 p.m. or 12.00 p.m. The last Saturday, everything was too chaotic to go out. But now even after a week, we were stuck at home.

'I miss the momos and the cheesecake,' Indu told me, as we watched another episode of *Big Bang Theory* in our bedroom.

'Me too. I hope everything will be fine from next week. Then, I'll take you out on Tuesday or Wednesday,' I pulled her closer.

'You know, I told you once, that I feel sad and depressed looking at the mountains behind the Dal Lake. But I did not know why they invoked such a feeling.'

'Uh!'

'I realise now. Kashmir is such a nice and beautiful place. But there is eternal unrest, uncertainty and an underlying sadness and depression here. So much life lost, so much violence, and so much hatred, that people become prisoners in their own homes. Those big snow-covered peaks, they, somehow, are prisoners too, an eyewitness to all that is happening in Kashmir, and still quietly standing,' she said.

'That's some highly philosophical conversation,' I said. When she came for the first time to Kashmir, during our drive from Sonamarg to Srinagar, we ended up talking about some life philosophies and spirituality. After an hour of that conversation, I had a heaviness in my head, like a benign migraine. I told her, 'It's enough for a day. Let's play some music now.'

'Kashmir is a retirement place, not for young people who want to live freely,' she added. I wanted to tell her about the conversation with Bhanu, about the plan to move out to make her mood a little better. But I did not. I told her, 'Monday, I will check with the school and then, tell you, alright.'

'The maximum I can do today is take you to the library if you want. It will change our moods a little. The whole week we have been sitting inside. I might have forgotten to walk as well,' I told her.

'Okay. I'll change first, and then we will go,' she said without any arguments. I guess she, too, was tired of sitting at home.

12

Lives and Livelihood

Srinagar, Kashmir
16 October 2021, Saturday

While Indu went to change, I called a few friends and told them to meet up at the library. Only Raman and Sudeep agreed to come. Komal Library was a second home to all of us, especially me. It was our community library and was situated inside the complex of Gurdwara Shaheed Bunga, less than a mile from my home.

Veerji was the volunteer caretaker and librarian for the last thirty years or so. Because he was the senior in the library, everyone called him Veerji—elder brother—and the name got stuck, so much so that even his own family now called him Veerji. Every evening he opened the doors to the library between 5 to 5.30 p.m., come what may. As a child, when I was in Kashmir, I used to go to that library every evening. I learned how to play chess and carom there, I learned to read and write the Punjabi language there, and I made a lot of friends and memories. Veerji was a fun person. He knew how to deal with kids. The library was not like the usual silent place. In fact, this library was a fun-filled, discussion and debate-inciting place, with a lot of ruckus and chaos. Anything but quiet. Veerji was the first person I sought out when I came back to Kashmir in 2010. And he is the person I would still seek whenever I wanted any information about anything related to the Sikh community.

When we reached the library, Sudeep, Raman and Veerji were already animatedly talking about something. They greeted us, asked how we were, and continued with their conversation, inviting us to join.

'There are a lot of people at Supinder's home every day,' Sudeep, who lived next to her house, said. 'Everyone has a different story.'

Sudeep worked in a private company as a medical representative. Brutally honest and straightforward, he got into fights for his inflexible ideology.

'People don't have much to do these days. Free tea and gossip both are available in abundance there,' Raman replied.

'These masters,' Veerji pointed at me, 'They don't have anything to do, one class a day and then sleep the whole time. We, Central Government employees, have to go. No excuses. If it was up to them, they would keep us in the offices for the night as well.'

Veerji worked as a Central Government employee. Other than Sundays and a few other national holidays, I hadn't ever seen him taking the day off. He and his colleague were the only employees in his office, so he could not take leave unless the head office provided a substitute for him to keep the office running. He always teased me by saying, 'You masters (teachers) are born on the day of Eid, the most comfortable and easiest job.'

In Kashmir, the first thing that got affected due to any strike, encounter, or hartals was the school. Plus, there were more than two months of vacations, all the state and national holidays, leniency in attendance, and over fifteen casual leave days. All these clubbed together brings the working days to less than two hundred days in a year. And the working hours were also less compared to any other job. There was a general dislike towards the whole teaching community in Kashmir, where people keep accusing us of being lazy and sluggard. But only we knew how much work pressure we had.

'Other than the last Friday, I have also been going regularly,' Raman replied. The bank was an equally strict place when it came to attendance.

'Can we talk in English? She can also understand then,' I proposed. Everyone nodded. 'And yes, I didn't go this week. But I guess from Monday, I too will have to go.'

'You are a privileged class of people, who have permanent government jobs that pay good and will pay even if you don't go for a month, especially you,' Sudeep pointed at me, 'But for those who were doing their businesses, or people like me who work in private companies, for the days we don't go, our already pittance of a salary will be deducted. If I don't go for a week, I won't ever have to go again. They will throw me out. People like us don't have options like you do.'

'Then why don't you move out of this place and work in Jammu? With your profile you will easily find a job there, and a better paying one than it is here,' I said.

'You say it so casually. Do you even know how practically impossible it is?' Sudeep asked

'This is what our previous generations thought, and as a result, we are the ones who are suffering,' I replied.

'Why did you come back the moment you got a job? When you yourself don't stand by your ideology, how do you think anyone else would? Just talks, nothing else,' he said, sounding agitated.

'I will move out soon. I can't live here anyway. And I have been planning already, not because of these killings, but because of the general conditions here. Veerji knows, and Raman also knows. I have talked in detail with them about it,' I met Sudeep after a long time, almost after three months. Moreover, during the last few years, life had been so busy and fast for both of us that we didn't get to meet very often, and whenever we did, it was mostly a quick catching-up. I never discussed my plans with him.

Raman, by far, was my closest friend in Kashmir. We met almost every other day after his day at the bank. We were gym partners for a few months. I met him in the library when both of us were teaching a free community class to bank probationary officers and clerical aspirants. Our vibe matched, and we ended up becoming very close friends.

'We know. That is why he married an outsider. Such an educated wife. What will she do here in Kashmir?' Veerji teased me again.

'Yes, that is true also. It would be like presenting you with all the good food to eat in the world and then taping your mouth so you can't have a bite,' Raman came to my defence.

'But jokes apart, Veerji, you tell me, you have been keeping track of all of us. Do you think the youth have a future here?' I asked.

At the library, we had some de-facto responsibilities. One was to make a gazette of Sikh students who appeared for various examinations, like the class X and class XII board exams, the state- and national-level entrance examinations to various institutions like the Indian Institute of Technology (IIT), All India Institute of Medical Sciences (AIIMS), and other entrances like All India Engineering Entrance Exams (AIEEE), Public Service Commission (PSC) exams. The second task was to organise a bi-annual Khalsa week, a seven-day event, first in April, at the time of Baisakhi, and then in October or November at the time of Gurpurab

(Guru Nanak's birth anniversary), when hundreds of Sikh children would come together and participate in various religious, educational and sports events. On the concluding day, we would give prizes to the winners of those events, in addition to several other awards, given for academic and non-academic excellence, outstanding selfless service, and social work, among others. The third was to come up with new and innovative projects at the community level, like sports tournaments, counselling sessions, career orientations, seminars and more.

It was at the library, while organising the above activities, that I came to know how poorly our community performed, both educationally and economically. How, year after year, the results were dwindling, especially in entrance examinations. Most of our students were being sent to Jammu or Punjab for higher studies on payment seats. The mediocrity had been inculcated so deeply that even after higher education, they performed poorly in PSC exams for employment avenues, and most of them ended up doing meagre jobs with minimal salaries.

The sorry state came out in the open when we compiled the gazettes. We printed large posters of the results and went on posting them in all the gurdwaras around the city to let our community know and realise how bad it was. Veerji emphasised on data collection and storage. He would say, no one would remember what you said or I said. No one would remember what we did unless we documented it, and archived it. Even if we were not there, the data would speak for itself. For us, he was and is a walking encyclopaedia, an archive, and a thesaurus.

To my question about the Sikh youth's future in Kashmir, Veerji gave a precise answer. 'No. There is no future here, at least not for the next two generations.'

'Those who know how to make money can make it anywhere. Those who know how to do business, don't have to go out to work. It is one's aptitude that decides it,' Sudeep said. 'If we are not skilled or knowledgeable enough, we won't be able to make it big even outside Kashmir. A loser is a loser everywhere he goes.'

'But a fair chance of competition, an equal opportunity, and an equitable environment are what we lack despite our skill or knowledge,' Raman added. 'What do you say, Indu?' he asked her, trying to include her in the conversation.

'Sorry. I don't know the complete context of your conversations. But yes, I agree. A fair chance of competition and equal opportunity are important requirements to succeed. A loser is a loser everywhere. But even a winner can lose if he does not get a fair chance,' she replied.

'You tell me, Sudeep. Can you open your shop during a hartal or a protest march? No. But can Muslims do that? Yes, and they do it. They work with half shutters or during the night whenever there is turmoil. Do you think we can do the same without consequences?' asked Veerji.

In these thirty years, as a minority, we realised that business opportunities for us were very scarce. We knew that we could only sell to our own community customers. Some of such businesses were thriving as well. For example, there were a few meat shops, some restaurants and eateries that serve jhatka and whose only customers were Sikhs. But catering to such a small population that was distributed over such a large geographical area was an everyday challenge to these business establishments. These establishments were so few that they could be counted on one hand.

In this age, when the start-up culture was taking over the world, we did not see any entrepreneurs in our community in Kashmir. Not even one, to quote as an example. Leave alone start-ups, we did not have shopkeepers, cafe or restaurant owners, no taxis and public transporters, no hoteliers, and not even a small-scale business owner.

In our generation, the most we could see was two contractors supplying goods and vehicles to the army, one person who opened a clinic where a prominent doctor—from the majority community—visited, and one kindergarten owner. That was the sum total of our economic prowess in Kashmir.

Veerji also said, 'Do you think we stand a chance if we report a grievance in case something goes wrong? If a fight breaks out, if you have a problem with your boss, if your official government work is stuck, we all know what happens. Like an ostrich, if we bury our heads in the ground and think the hunter has gone, we are being stupid.'

That was indeed true. Every one of us had faced it in our life at some point in time. A mistreatment, a prejudice against us, and a favouritism towards their own community. The bias took various forms, like postponing our work or reshuffling the lists to push our names down. If we presented a grievance, our complaints were often closed without a solution, and inquiries into it were conveniently lost in the files. We were asked to make compromises outside the legal systems, to finish it as we commonly say, 'Kuchh le de ke nipta lo.'

'There are courts and legal systems, and after Article 370's revocation, I guess it has become easier for us to be heard and our grievances to be sorted,' Sudeep replied.

'I guess you are missing the point, Sudeep Bhai,' I said and added. 'Why, in the first place, do we have to go to the court? Why can't we get what we deserve without fighting for it? Why do we have to file grievances? And deep down, you know why. If you can't say it out loud, let me say it for you. Because we are Sikhs, and we are not liked here at all,' I replied. I was furious with myself because of the situation, but all that came out on Sudeep.

The people at the helm of legal systems, the enforcers, and the implementors were all from the majority. They had a soft corner for their own, and that clouded their judgements. Their authority was abusive towards our genuine concerns. Things that should be done impartially and without bias were somehow not done properly. Often, we felt that it was just our perception. Then again it felt like the reality too. So we fought back, and sometimes we just submitted to it.

'That does not happen only in Kashmir or just to us. It happens everywhere. Throughout the world. Otherwise, there would be no need for the police and the courts,' Sudheep replied.

'And do you think justice is being delivered?' I asked.

'To someone, it is. Their justice is your injustice.'

'We will never know if it is true or not. But the point is, we will die living in this uncertainty.'

Uncertainty was killing our community. The uncertainty and anxiety had so easily translated into a mentally depressed population that questioned everything they did. Should I open a shop? What if they stone it during the protest? Should I put a religious sign on my vehicle? What if they break the windows during a protest? Should I go out when they call for a strike? What if they beat me up for not supporting them? Should I open a business unit? What if they burn it down at the slightest misunderstanding? Should I renovate the house or build a new one? What if they make us leave Kashmir like Pandits? The what-ifs made us a financially weak, mentally frustrated and socially awkward community. It all boiled down to the most fundamental question. Would I return home alive in the evening?

'These debates will never come to a conclusion. Those who can, should go out, and those who cannot right now, will have to move out eventually. And if we think there is another option, we are lying to ourselves,' Veerji said. 'Get up, go home eat a plate full of rice and sleep.'

He continued by saying, 'Every year, almost ninety per cent of our children who clear their senior secondary, go out to other states, especially Punjab and Haryana, to pursue higher education. Recently, a good proportion of them are going to Bangladesh for MBBS. Those who cannot afford the fee stay in Kashmir and go for a bachelor's degree in arts and humanities or sciences. Also, some families believe that sending girls far away will make them bold, confident and clever, qualities which make them less marriageable. So these girls are made to stay back in Kashmir and study whatever subject they can get admission in.'

'Those who stay back, doing a graduate degree, either end up being unemployed immediately or go for a higher degree for another two years and then end up being unemployed. Those who come back from Punjab and Bangladesh after their studies waste a few years in Kashmir and then move out to find jobs in other states. A handful only gets employed in Kashmir, and that too, mostly as medical representatives or salesmen in some companies.'

As Veerji finished talking, he picked up a magazine from one side of the table and threw it on the other side. I could see the vein on his forehead throbbing. In response I told Veerji, 'Due to this low employability in Kashmir and a meagre salary, our community is facing a silent migration. And this cannot even be called a brain drain. For that to happen, our skill and ability should have value in other places. But thanks to our narrow vision, sub-par education and rusty skillset, our skills are never developed enough.

'And what is more troubling and heartbreaking is that the next generation is going to be even worse. The present generation who become parents will not be able to provide good education or schooling, and equitable facilities to their children because of their financial instability. They are already suffering from a financial crisis. If any unexpected incident happens, a medical emergency, an unforeseen expenditure, or a tragedy, then the monthly budget goes up in flames.

'Many of the youngsters are supported by the pension of their parents. The other factor that has saved us from going bankrupt is that most of the Sikhs have their own homes, and they don't have to pay rent. If not for that, we would have been failures.'

Indu clutched my hand to calm me down as my voice was also rising rapidly. I slowly brought my volume to normal.

'A failed generation will not be able to raise a successful one,' Veerji said. There was a long silence. Nobody said anything.

Veerji was particularly concerned about the children and youth. He was hopeless and optimistic at the same time; hopeless that we do not have a future here, and optimistic that if a certain number of role models came from within the community, they would be able to pull up the rest. I wondered how he kept going year after year with such disappointment. Spending from his own pocket, he bought newspapers and magazines worth two thousand rupees every month. He felt that if someday somebody wanted them, they should be readily available. I had never seen that 'somebody' ever. It was we—me, Raman and Veerji—who read those newspapers and magazines. But still, he bought them every month. Every three or four months, we sold the old newspapers to the bakery owner just outside the gurdwara at a rate of ten rupees a kilogram. We did not sell the magazines and kept piling, an indication of how futile it was to buy them in the first place.

He had bought every book, classroom note and material required for civil servant aspirants to readily give to them when they prepare for it. For IIT and National Eligibility Cum Entrance Test (NEET) exams, Veerji had the best competitive magazines, question banks and test papers. In thirty years, no one came asking for them.

'Daddy *da paisa*, Punjab *dey* college *ta naabkaar puttar* engineer,' he said every time he got annoyed and frustrated thinking about the future of our community. It roughly translated as, 'Father's money, Punjab's colleges and any good-for-nothing son becomes an engineer.'

'Chalo, it's getting late, we should leave otherwise our families will get worried. The conditions are still not good. Every other day some encounters and gunfights are happening,' Veerji said.

'It's not even seven yet. Look at us. Usually, we would leave our home after eight to going out, and now seven feels too late to get back home,' Raman said.

'Everything will be normal again. Then we will take crispy chicken from Jawahar Nagar and eat at the Dal Lake,' Veerji said.

'Aameen,' I joked. I hope so.

'Sumameen,' Raman replied in the same tone taking it further. It was an insider joke. Ameen and sumameen were Muslim terms, and we were not supposed to use them. But whenever there was any fanatic or arduous follower of Sikhism around, we used them to piss them off. It was evident that the words had made some impact on Sudeep as he was visibly irritated by now.

We were about to leave when Raman's mother called him, 'They have killed one more civilian, some gol-gappe wala again, non-local, non-Muslim. You come home fast. Father is worried,' she said in a single breath. Was Sadaam right when he said to expect more killings, I wondered.

13

Those Who Cannot Foresee

Srinagar, Kashmir
16 October 2021

Our family always had our dinners together since childhood. That was when all of us sat together and talked. Breakfast was always in a hurry, rushing for school and then college, and moreover, everyone woke up at different times. And lunch, mostly someone would be out at that time. But during dinners, I did not remember not sitting together if everyone was home. Family decisions or updates about life, or mundane discussions about day-to-day activities would happen during our dinners. Indu also liked to sit and talk. My mother and father both spoke broken English, my father much better than my mother. Indu spoke broken Hindi, so the language barrier was not a problem. However, they did not converse fluently as well.

One morning Indu had gone to the kitchen to ask my mother in Hindi for a heating rod to heat the water for a bath. She asked, '*Mamma, rod chahiye, nachne ke liye,*' which translates to, 'Mother, I want the rod, to dance.' For a moment, my mother was confused and then she understood. She asked Indu, *nahane ke liye* (for bathing)? Then both of them laughed so loud that my father and I went to the kitchen to see what happened. When Indu spoke in Hindi, or when my mother spoke in English, it was a comedy of errors. So mostly at the dinner table, I was the translator, if the subject was very complicated.

By the time we got back home from the library in the evening, one more civilian had been killed within half an hour of the first killing.

'So one was a Hindu and the other was a Muslim. But both of them were from outside Kashmir,' Papa said. 'Their stance is clear. They don't want any outsiders in Kashmir.'

'They target these poor vendors and labourers only. If they want to scare, why don't they go after some big-shot officer?' Maa asked. 'Why is it always the poor who suffers everything?'

'They are easy targets, soft targets as the IGP called them, easily dispensable, and no one cares about them,' I replied.

'And you were saying that the security has increased. There are check posts everywhere. Still, they managed to kill two people that too in the middle of markets, in a crowded space,' Indu asked me as she took another bite of her chapatti.

'This is like the 90s, but worse than that. At least then, one could easily identify the militants. They had big guns, long beards and wore proper Khan Dress. But now these hybrids, nobody knows who they are, and they just carry a small pistol, which is easily concealed,' Papa replied and added, 'The conditions will worsen I guess.'

'Who knows? They can come after Sikhs as well. Another Chithisinghpora can happen,' mother added. For Sikhs, the Chithisinghpora massacre was synonymous with an unannounced large-scale killing.

'Nobody can predict anything. All this is new. These killings of poor vendors and labourers never happened in Kashmir. Sikhs were safe, but at this speed, I don't know,' Papa said. He kept mindlessly tapping his empty plate with his middle finger.

'Take one more chapatti,' I told him. He eats two for dinner, but in all this talking, he had forgotten to take the second one. I put one on his plate.

'Papa, if it is so uncertain, then why do Sikhs still live here under so much stress?' Indu asked my father.

'We have always been living here. Where else can we go as a community? Individually, a lot of Sikhs have moved out. Whoever has a chance, tries to move out. I guess no one from the younger generation wants to live here. No one in the right mind at least should,' he replied.

'Why did you come back to Kashmir then?' she asked.

He replied, 'I never wanted to. The first time we got out was in 1991. But at that time, it was very difficult. No means to communicate like today, and then she,' he pointed at mother, 'wanted to come back, she was pregnant with Ramneek. We had to come back. The second time we went was in 2000 or 2001 after the Mehjoor Nagar *kaand*. I did not return ever.

It was because he got his job here that we came back. Otherwise, I have no liking left towards Kashmir now.'

'And I think Bupi also does not want to settle here. He has been saying that ever since,' my father added.

'Once you finish your studies, we will see what options we have to move out of here,' I replied to Indu. My dinner was already over. But everyone was on the same page, so the conversation was not very dense.

'That will take another two years. Do you think it would be wise to stay here that long? Especially now when all these killings are happening?' she replied.

'So what should I do? Book a ticket tomorrow and go to Bangalore without any plan or money? And do what?' I asked.

'No, I mean...' she did not complete her sentence. If she had, we would have ended up arguing in front of my parents. This was the first time I ever spoke back to her in front of anyone else. And I realised it the moment I raised my voice.

'We will see. Don't worry. We will rethink our plans,' I consoled her in a soothing voice and rubbed her shin with my toes under the table. She pulled her legs back.

'You take a leave for a month. Then, anyway, your winter vacation will start. That will give you four months to decide about your plan. Then you can act accordingly,' Papa said. He was voicing Indu's thoughts.

'I will check on Monday. Let's see. But the government has told me upfront that there are no leaves for minority employees,' I replied.

'There would be more killings, I guess. No minority employee is going to the office like this, especially the PM Package ones and non-locals who are working here,' Papa said. 'You send them a leave letter on Monday. We can plan to go to Jammu then.'

I had not told anyone about my conversation with Bhanu or the plan that I made with him. I still wanted to check with the school first. But these two new killings had visibly upset Indu. I signalled her to go to the bedroom. All week I had been trying to divert the conversation about moving out, trying to make her believe that these killings were going to stop and the conditions were going to be alright. But now I was hopeless about it. Amidst such tight security and hype about killings, the TRF had again killed two more, which was a direct slap to all the promises and assurance of safety and security that the government was giving.

When I sat and thought about it, I understood even I had not felt fearful about the Kashmir conditions until now. In 2016, when Burhan Wani, the commander of Hizbul Mujahideen, was killed, Kashmir went through hellfire. For four months, everything was closed down, and hundreds of people died in protests. But even then, I never feared anything. I guess the reason was that all that violence was not pointed in my direction.

But now, with non-locals and non-Muslims being targeted, I somehow felt that I might also become a target someday. After all, I was also appointed under the same package, which was considered India's move to settle migrants back in the Valley. I was one in that dataset, and nobody would ask questions and ideologies before shooting me down.

Indu waited for me in the bedroom with her questions. 'The IGP himself is saying that it is not possible to provide security to everyone, that the police cannot protect every soft target.'

'That is statistically impossible, baby, to provide security to everyone, and with these hybrid militants, the police are clueless about who to provide security against,' I told her.

The term was now being used very frequently. Hybrid militants were civilians doing normal day jobs, could be around you for years, and one day, all of sudden could bring a gun out of their bag and kill you and disappear back into daily life. Like the sleeper cells in Akshay Kumar's movie *Holiday*.

'We should move to Bangalore ASAP. We have anyway planned to settle there,' she said, getting up from the bed again. Her drooping shoulders were now wide open, her gaze locked into mine, and her palms were folded into fists.

'We've already decided to move to Bangalore after your studies.'

'No. That's two more years. I am talking about now.'

'It's not that easy. We are having this conversation for the nth time now,' The dryness in my mouth robbed me of my speech. 'Okay, you tell me what to do. Should I leave my job tomorrow and we drive to Jammu?' I had to swallow to wet my tongue. The water bottle on the bedside was empty. 'Without any salary and money, how long do you think we would survive? I won't be able to pay my EMIs even. And you, would you leave your studies and start working from tomorrow? Do you hear how impractical you are?' I was equally angry as her.

'Do you even understand what is happening? The militants are killing civilians. Everyone is saying they will kill minorities. They will continue to kill because they want everyone to leave…you don't understand. Can you guarantee you will be safe here in Srinagar, that they won't come to your school tomorrow?'

She began to pace about the room, unmindful of how loud she was. I did not know the source of all the information she was getting. But what I knew was whatever she heard was a common sentiment. It could be true. This time the militants could keep on killing minorities and non-locals. With the Taliban freeing Afghanistan from America, new rumours were already brewing in Kashmir in both communities. The Muslims were happy about it. A lot of people posted slogans of victory and videos of Taliban militants on their social media and WhatsApp statuses. They posted prayers wishing that the Taliban invade Kashmir and free it from India. The Sikhs were sad about it because everyone around them was talking about these victories and how they wished for Kashmir to be free, how Nizam-e-Mustafa would be implemented, how Islam would win its war, how Kashmir would soon become the Islamic State of Kashmir or merge with Pakistan. Another issue was that the Sikhs of Afghanistan were being killed or forced to leave for India. A similar thing would happen in Kashmir if it ever gained its freedom. And that was before Supinder's and other minority, non-local killings. Rumours could become true.

'Calm down. Come and sit down. Let's talk about it. Don't worry,' I consoled her. 'I have something to tell you.'

'You can easily earn this much by your writing. Why do you want to stick to this job?' She remained standing although she had stopped pacing.

'Okay, dear. Sit down first and listen to me,' I held her hand and pulled her towards the bed.

'This is not the first time that militants have killed Sikhs,' she said.

'This is the first time. There have been incidences in the past, but those Sikhs worked in the army. Anyone working in the army is their enemy. And even if it is a Muslim, it did not matter to the militants,' I replied.

She picked up her phone, typed something and read aloud, 'In 2000 when Bill Clinton visited India, thirty-five Sikhs were lined up in a village called Chithisinghpora and were shot point-blank.'

'That was back then, it was...' I did not know how to complete the sentence. I saw her growing more anxious, so I chose to stay silent. 'Then again in 2001, when five Sikhs were shot dead in broad daylight, that was when you left Kashmir,' she added. I never told her about these two incidents. I never wanted to. With all the keywords from our conversations, she had read about them already.

'And at dinner today, my mother was also saying that something like Chithisinghpora can happen again. What if it actually happens and then?'

'Let me speak, listen to me,' I cut her.

'We are fools if we cannot foresee what is going to happen,' she said. I tried to find a satisfactory answer to quell her anxiety, but couldn't, so I hugged her instead.

'Bhanu called today evening, I was already planning to move out by the first week of November,' I told her.

'You did not tell me. You are making this up right now.'

'When have I ever lied to you,' I replied, hugging her tighter.

'We will move out soon,' I whispered in her ear. I wanted to escape the conversation. I took the water bottle and left the room, gesturing to her that I would bring a refill. I came back, thinking of the best way to tell her about the whole plan I had made with Bhanu. But the moment I entered, she asked me, 'Tell me about the Chithisinghpora event, the Wikipedia page and other news sources have contradictory information about it.'

'I don't know more than Google knows about it anyway. Ask my father tomorrow. He was very active during those days.'

I handed her the water bottle. I had interviewed the only survivor of the incident and other eyewitnesses. I had written a detailed story of the massacre but never submitted it anywhere. Veerji insisted that I write the story, that it would be our history someday, in our own way, free from biases and prejudices. It was somewhere saved in Google Drive, and I never visited it again after I wrote it. But I did not want to tell Indu all those things, they would depress her more. And I hoped she would forget it by the morning, which she seldom did.

'And first, listen to me about the Delhi plan,' I added.

When I told Indu about the whole thing, she was elated.

'So you will move out of Kashmir in November?' She got up from the bed. 'Wow, that's so…so good, and then I can also come on Saturdays and Sundays to the flat. Superb.'

'And you can take this chance to finish your novel. You always told me that you want a take a vacation and live in some city to finish your book,' she said.

For me, hills and landscape were an everyday scene. The slow and laid-back life of Kashmir, which the writers from some cities would crave, was what I could not work in. I wanted a bustling crowd, unbearable noise, and days that merged into the night without a boundary. Over the years, I found out that I work better in cafes, public parks, or areas where there was noise and a lot of people. I could concentrate better there. In silence, I felt sleepy.

'Slow down, it's just a plan, I have to see a lot of things before that, and I might not even get the leave. So don't raise your hopes,' I cautioned her. From sulking, she went to being animated all of a sudden.

'Let me daydream then. Don't spoil the mood,' she said.

'If I get the leave, I am going to party in Delhi, not sit and write,' I teased her.

'I am not saying that you should not enjoy. Take the first month off. Do whatever you want, partying, clubbing, travelling, whatever you feel like. But after that sit and work on your novel and finish it. It's been too long now. That will give you a sense of accomplishment as well. You started it in 2012. Since then, you keep distracting yourself with one thing or another and turn it down,' she added.

'Yes, baby. This time I will finish it. I already have a skeleton draft. I just need to add layers to it,' I told her.

I was a writer but not an author. Over the years, my stories and articles had been published in several magazines and journals. But all that was a preparation for my higher goal of being a novelist. I had started a lot of projects, but left them midway when a new thought struck me. I hadn't ever completed any. I never experienced that feeling of finishing, completing and writing 'The End' in bold letters on the last page of the book.

'By the time you finish your studies, I would also have a book deal. I promise.'

'Yes, dear. work on it and you will,' she replied. 'And not just that. You can revive your other projects or start new ones. Don't limit yourself. You have much more talent than you think. I don't know why you can't see it. You can journal these happening also, the current situation, who knows someday you can write this up as well.'

She kept bouncing from foot to foot. Her grin widened with every sentence.

'Okay, okay. Now just calm down. I'll check with the school on Monday.'

I had to pull her back to make her down.

'You do that,' she said. 'Let me check my emails. Then we will sleep. I feel so tired today. But you will tell me more about the Chithisinghpora tomorrow, promise?'

'You are still stuck with that? Okay. I will tell you,' I replied.

That night, as she slept, I began to pen down all that had happened that day on my phone. I could write about the current situation someday, Indu had said. I was not someone who journalled much. I believed that most of what I could write could be found on the internet. Freelance content writing taught me that good research skills were a primary requisite for every writer. And whenever I sat down to write a story, I could recreate the emotions in myself as well. I had cried while writing them. With these two new killings, the next day was going to be very unsettling. I just hoped there wouldn't be any more killings.

One thing was sure. Sikhs would not be going to their offices for the next few days, whatever the government says. Like me, they would be questioning themselves. Whether to continue to live in Kashmir under such stress and fear of death or to leave for Jammu. They would ask themselves, as I did if there would be more killings. They would be speculating about another Chithisinghpora-like massacre. They would question the reasons for staying here and wonder who would be the next target.

Deep inside, all of us knew the answers. We just didn't want to say it out loud.

I had made my decision. I would not be a fool who did not foresee what was coming.

14

Unearthing Chithisinghpora

Srinagar, Kashmir
March 2015

On the fifteenth anniversary of the Chithisinghpora massacre, Veerji asked me to write a story about the incident for an international Sikh magazine called *Sikh Review*. He told me he knew a few people whom we could visit and interview. On the following Sunday, we could go to the village to find out more eyewitness accounts.

The first person I met for the interview was the sole survivor of the incident, Nanak Singh. Veerji called him to the library for an interview a few days later. We called two other people from the village, both younger than me. They were mere kids when the massacre happened. But both of them used to come to the library often. So, Veerji called them too.

Nanak Singh was in his late fifties and worked in the animal husbandry department. His off-white kurta-pyjama seamlessly merged with his white and grey flowing beard. He stood up to greet me when I entered, and I could see that he limped a little in his right leg. He did not seem to be at an age to limp. Immediately after me, Gurdeep and Harry entered, both of whom knew Nanak Singh personally. Nanak Singh had become the most important and talked about person in their village during their childhood. He lived in Chithisinghpora with his family. He was visiting some of his extended family in Srinagar when Veerji called him to ask about this meeting. It was by chance that he was in Srinagar. Otherwise, someday, we would've had to go to the village to meet him.

I introduced myself to him, though Veerji had already given him an overview of what I was doing and why I wanted to hear the story from him. I told him I wanted to write a story, and he asked me what new addition I would be putting to the ones already out there. He was the only survivor of the incident. In the last fifteen years, he had told his story to hundreds of people, journalists, political parties, police and army, courts, scholars and so many people like me. His calm demeanour was a result of repeating the same thing over and over again. Fifteen years down the line, the story for him had lost most of the emotions. To him, it was a mere repetition.

'There are several newspaper articles and documentaries online. Whenever someone posts one, they send me the links to them. Have you read any of those articles, or seen those interviews?' he asked me, to which I replied, 'I have, but I don't want to ask you the same questions. I am not going to record your videos or do a formal interview. I am a Kashmiri Sikh, too, and my family has suffered the same things. You might have heard about the colonel who got abducted in Budgam in 1991. That was my uncle. I want you to tell me what you want the world to know. Everyone knows people were killed. No one knows why they were killed. No one knows what happened after that. No one knows about all the years you people have spent in hardships after the incident, the agony, anger and fear. I want to know about that.'

'I will tell you what I can. You write what you make out of it,' he said. 'And I can tell you only what happened immediately after the incident. Then I was moved to the hospital and came back to the village only after a month. The account that I have is what I have heard from others. So you can ask about that to others.'

I had already seen a documentary in which a lady talked about how she lost her husband in the incident. Through the documentary, I came to know that all thirty-five Sikhs were not killed at one site but in two different places. Gurdeep had given me a description of his village and showed some recent videos he had taken in the village. So I had a pretty good idea about it. I visited the village once in 2013, on the yearly commemoration of those martyrs.

Chithisinghpora was located in south Kashmir's Anantnag district. Some five kilometres from the district city centre, you had to take a diversion towards a block of villages, among which one was Chithisinghpora. The road that led to the block was a beauty to behold, the hairpin curves climbed up the hill and led to a valley surrounded by the lesser Himalayas. Once we were up, at another five kilometres, a left turn led to a narrow green tunnel, where trees bent perfectly to cast a green roof over the road. On both sides of this narrow road, as far as you could see, were the farms and orchards of the Sikhs of the village. The tunnel led you to the village's main square from the northern side, which hosted the gurdwara.

The whole village consisted of nine localities or mohallas, six of which were in one cluster and belonged purely to Sikhs. The other three were Muslim localities and were towards the outer boundary of the Sikh cluster. Around 450 Sikh families lived in these six localities, named Showkeen mohalla, Tibi mohalla, Bhai mohalla, Akali mohalla, Changa mohalla and Jawan mohalla. There were three gurdwaras in the area, a small gurdwara for twenty families that lived in Showkeen mohalla, another small gurdwara for thirty or so families in Jawan mohalla, and a big one that was common to the four remaining mohallas and catered to the majority of the population.

From this main gurdwara, for one kilometre in every direction, there were houses. Towards the eastern end, on top of a hill, there was a large ground called Deri Sahib, where the villagers used to host big festivals. The three Muslim mohallas surrounded the Sikh mohallas on the south and west. A big village called Satrimaidan, comprising mainly of Pathans, speaking Pashto, was on the northeastern side of Chithisinghpora. The nearest Sikh village was called Ranbir Singhpora, popularly known as Hadiyanbagh (Apricot Orchard).

It was said that during the attack on Chithisinghpora, the attackers came from the Satrimaidan side and went back towards it.

I looked at Nanak Singh and said, 'I will try to write to my best effort, and for other details, I will talk to his father,' and pointed towards Gurdeep.

'Yes. He was the one who saved my life, he and two more people walked all the way to Hadiyanbagh to call the police on that fearful dark night, without worrying about their lives. If not for them, I would have also died of blood loss,' Nanak Singh replied.

Veerji left us in the library and went out, so as not to interfere with anything. Harry and Gurdeep remained inside with me. I had to ask them a few questions as well. I put my phone voice recorder on and told him to narrate his ordeal without any further delay.

'Tell me from the beginning.'

He started by narrating the horrifying incident:

> We never expected such a thing would happen to Sikhs. There were some episodes that had happened before, like the Wandhama massacre in 1998, when Pandits were killed. But for us Sikhs, it was never expected. We never had such a fear.
>
> It was around 7.30 in the evening on 20 March, the day of Holi. I was walking towards my home. We had just finished our evening prayers at the gurdwara and were coming back. My brother, Darbari, and cousin Sartaj were also walking with me. We had just crossed the road to Showkeen mohalla when we saw around seven to eight people walking up the road. They came from the side where our Deri Sahib is. It's where we celebrate Baisakhi. It was already dark. March, you know. But we could see that they were wearing army uniforms, that Chitra, leopard stripe uniform, and they had guns and flashlights with them. One of them, called Raju sir, told us that they had to talk to us about something and asked us to come to the gurdwara gate again. Some of the others scattered and brought out a dozen more people from the adjoining houses.
>
> They brought out my son, Gurmeet, who was seventeen years old, and two of my cousins, Kulbir Singh, eighteen, and Ujjal Singh, twenty-four, from our house. From our family, six were present. Similarly, Faqir Singh's family, his two sons and a grandson were brought out, and so on. A total of nineteen people were lined up near the outer wall of the gurdwara. If you go to our village now, you will see that we have preserved that wall and marked all the bullet marks on it. They stood facing us. Now there was a wall there, but at that time, it was a simple wired fence. So, one of them, who acted as their Commanding Officer (CO) told us that they had some news that some militants had come and hid in the village and that they had to carry out an identity check of the villagers. They talked to each other using the names Bansi, Pawan, Bahadur, etc. We told them that we didn't know anything about it, and that

we had not seen anyone suspicious in the village, and that there was no militant in the village.

There was this sardar, Charan Singh, among us, who had taken double retirement from the army. He had worked as a sepoy with 21 FID regiment or some such, don't recall, and he retired after twenty-two years. I told him that there was something wrong, that I feel uneasy. While I was speaking to him, the one that was their CO told us, 'Don't worry. We will just check your identity cards, and then you can go.' I started silently doing the Chaupai Sahib paath. Of late, I don't remember where I left it incomplete. He then asked us if it was Holi today, and had any of us drunk any alcohol or anything for the celebration. Ours was a pure Sikh village. Nobody touched any drugs or alcohol. So we told him, 'No, sir. We don't drink such things.' Then he asked two of his people step forward and check our cards. Those of us who had the cards showed it to them. The moment they reached the last person, the CO pulled up his gun and fired a single shot in the air.

That was the signal. The rest of them opened fire on us, round after round of bullets were fired. All of us fell down. Miraculously, I did not get any bullets though my clothes were torn. They had missed my body somehow. When I fell, I was conscious but kept silent. When they stopped firing, one of them said, 'Take your lights and see if any bastard is alive. Fire one more bullet into each one.' So one of them came and started shooting one bullet at a time. I could feel him come closer to me. I put my tongue under my teeth and grit them as hard as I could. I was lying on my right side, the arm of my son was on my body and my clothes were wet with blood. He shot a bullet in my hip from the left side. It entered and went to the right breaking the bones of my right hip and pelvis. I have an artificial replacement there. I stayed there, in deep pain, chanting Waheguru Waheguru. If I had said one word or made any sound, they would have fired at me again. In a minute, I put my hand where the bullet had entered and kept pressing the wound. My senses were all focused on what they were going to do next. But I heard their footsteps beginning to fade in the distance and their flashlights dim. They said, 'Jai Bharat, Jai Mata', in a distance.

I tried to get up but couldn't. My lower body felt numb. I heard the voice of another survivor, Sartaj. He called out at me. He called me Birji—elder brother—so I called him back and told him, 'Let us move across and hide behind the gate.' What if they came back again? I slithered across the road and went through the gate, and hid behind the wall of an adjoining house. I did not know how much damage was done to Sartaj. But he stood up and walked across, and came to sit next to me.

He had some six bullets in his torso. I don't know how he managed to stand. Within a few minutes, I heard Rajinder Singh and two others behind the wall. But we kept silent. Actually, we could not speak. I tried to shout but couldn't. A lady came after them. Fakir Singh's wife. She told him that she could hear the sounds from the other side of the village. So Rajinder ran towards the source of those sounds. The villagers were too frightened to come out. It took them some time to assemble. Meanwhile, I was asking for water from the people who had started to come. I told them, 'Everyone had died. Save us.' They carried me to my home while Sartaj, whose body was punctured with the bullets, walked.

He crashed there, in that room (he pointed to the room in front of us). It took an hour for the police to come. Rajinder and two more bravehearts went into the dark to call the police. But by the time police came, Sartaj had lost too much blood. He died on the way, just outside the home. They returned his body and took me to Anantnag Hospital. My wife saw that our son was killed by the bullets. Other members of the family too were dead. But she climbed into the police Gypsy and came with me to the hospital. She did not even care about what would happen to the dead bodies or who would cremate them. She just wanted to be with me, to save me. The district hospital referred me to the main hospital in Srinagar. But they did not even look at me properly, just dressed the wound. I told them that the bullet had not left the body, and there was no opening anywhere, but they did not pay any heed. In the morning, Dr Daljit Singh, who has passed away, came to visit me. I told him that they were not even trying to save me. So he referred me to 92 Army Base Hospital in Badami Bagh

Cantonment (famously known as BB Cantt), where they operated on me and took out the bullet. It had already destroyed my hip. I stayed there for twenty-five days. Then I was shifted to Amritsar for the replacement surgery.

It was alright for the last twenty years. Now it is giving me trouble. But I guess it is age. It is a France-imported hip. They did my surgery free of cost in Amritsar. At Dr Hardaas' Clinic. They just charged some forty-five thousand for the replacement frame.

While he was busy with his narration, I just nodded my head and mostly kept mum, so that he would did not get distracted with any questions. Once he was done, I had a few questions of my own. And some of them were the ones that not just me, but everyone in Kashmir had, the primary one being, 'Who were the attackers?'

'You say that they were wearing army uniforms, but you don't call them army men. Why?' I asked him. He continued,

Something was off. Some indications made us doubt that they were not from the army. It is not just me, the women and elderly men who met them on the way, and those people in Showkeen mohalla who saw them, also say the same. It was not like the army. It felt like they were forcing it. They were trying to act and look like army people. But they were not like militants also. Their language was different from Kashmiri or Pakistani militants that we had seen over the years, and they were not able to talk like that. Their accent and dialect were very different. We are and will always be in doubt about the identity of the perpetrators.

Bill Clinton was visiting India during those days. The next day, on 21 March, he was to sign a deal with Atal Bihari Vajpayee, for a good relationship between India and America. Whatever happens in Kashmir always points to Pakistan. So we don't know if it was done by government agencies to blame Pakistan so that India could tell Clinton how bad it was. But then again, if it was with that intention why would they try to do it in army uniforms? And if they were militants, why would they do it? They had never harmed Sikhs like that before. There is something big behind it that we will never know. No official inquiry was conducted.

Nanak Singh was telling as if to reassure himself about the incident. India and Pakistan had started to blame each other for the massacre. I remember Clinton saying that talks between India and Pakistan would resume only when the violence ended. He further added, 'There must be some way to renew the dialogue.'

The Indian PM, Atal Bihari Vajpayee, had told media houses that it was an act of 'ethnic cleansing that was underway in Kashmir' and that this 'primitive act of barbarism' was done to drive the non-Muslims out of Kashmir. India had always accused Pakistan of sending armed troops to Kashmir, and Pakistan had always denied it but admitted to morally supporting the Kashmir freedom struggle.

The timing of this incident was pre-planned, by whomsoever, because the whole international media had its eyes on Bill Clinton's visit to India. An American president was visiting India after twenty-two years. This was the best way to bring the focus to the Kashmir issue. Lashkar-e-Taiba and Hizbul Mujahideen (HM), the two militant groups, were accused of the incident by a senior Indian official, Brajesh Mishra.

HM commander Syed Salahuddin came out with his press release the next day, saying, 'The mujahideen have nothing against the Sikh community, which sympathises with our struggle. We assure them that there never was and there will never be any danger to Sikhs from Kashmiri freedom fighters.'

Pakistan also condemned the attack and accused India of exploiting the incident for political gains. But they had been doing the same for the last decade, though.

We thanked Nanak Singh for his time, as it was already getting a little dark. Veerji was outside waiting and offered Nanak Singh a lift to his home. When he left, I asked both Gurdeep and Harry, 'Where were you people then?' Gurdeep replied thus: 'I was very young, in upper kindergarten, so I don't have much idea of what was happening. But the moment this firing started, my father instructed all of us to lie flat on the ground. We did not know where and how the firing was happening. He thought they were firing at the houses, or through the windows. So lying flat on the floor was the logical thing to do. We lay down, but my father did not. He kept standing, hands folded and prayed to Waheguru by chanting the ardaas. By the time he finished his *ardaas*, the firing had also stopped.

'Immediately after that he went outside, shouted the Sikh war-cry *Bole So Nihal (whoever speaks His name, will get blessed)* at the top of his voice and left the house. Us kids, my brother, sister and I, were told to stay inside, while my mother and grandparents went to the other room, the one adjacent to the road. The next few days, we remember, there were thousands and thousands of people coming to the village, biscuits were distributed to us, and schools were closed for a month or more. We had no clue what was happening at that point in time.'

'I was in Srinagar. We used to live here only, not in the village,' Harry replied.

'I would like to speak to your father as well. Nanak Singh said it was he who saved him and was very active. I will speak to him on the phone,' I told Gurdeep. He forwarded me his father's number on WhatsApp and told me to call him whenever I wanted. That night after I went home, I called Gurdeep's father, Rajinder Singh. What he told me was something unexpected.

> It was exactly twenty minutes to eight. I was inside the gurdwara sahib. Bhai Sahib was also with me, and one more person was there. We were closing everything, and the rest of the Sangat had already left for their homes. Most days, after a visit to the gurdwara, I would go to Nanak Singh's home for some time, we would do some *gup-shup*, and then I would return for dinner at my home. That day, I did not go to his home but went to Jagdish Singh's home. He was my friend, and he also died on that day. His brother's daughter had given birth to a boy that morning, I went along with Jagdish to his home to congratulate them. They told me to stay for tea. But I smelled that they had prepared chicken or mutton to celebrate, and I being a pure vegetarian, said no to the tea as well, and went back to my home after congratulating the girl. Jagdish came out, talking to me, and walked till the gurdwara. From there, I walked towards my home while he stayed there, for someone called out to him from the other end of the street. By the time I reached home and went inside, I heard a single fire, and within a few seconds, I heard continuous bursts of fire. In my thirty years in Kashmir, I have seen so much but never heard such intense firing. There

used to be a lot of militants in this area, and a lot of encounters would happen in the surrounding jungle, but never such intense gunfight. I came out again, and my brother also accompanied me. I said *Bole So Nihal* at my house and then once again when I reached the gurdwara.

A large number of Sikhs were lying outside the gurdwara. The gunmen had already fled. There was a sea of blood there. One person, Deedar Singh, was lying next to the gate. He was breathing when I reached, but he gave up his breath when I called out his name. A lady, the wife of Fakir Singh, came running down from the other end. She told me she had heard similar firing from the other side and pointed towards Showkeen mohalla. I went inside the gurdwara and brought out sheets to cover the dead people. Everyone had at least a dozen bullets in their body, and they were destroyed beyond what one can imagine. They had fallen down, and their bodies had become one with the soil and dust. Their eyes and mouths and nostrils were filled with blood and mud. It was a gory scene. After covering them, my brother and I rushed towards the other side to see what had happened there.

Showkeen mohalla is down the road, towards Satrimaidan and Deri Sahib. The gunmen had entered from that side and exited through the same side. When I reached there, the villagers had already come out, and seventeen people were killed there. All of them had died on the spot. Everyone was worried about the perpetrators coming back again and killing more people. I ran back to my mohalla, and by the time I reached there, I came to know that Nanak Singh and his cousin Sartaj Singh were alive but seriously injured. Nanak Singh's daughter told me that she had lost her brother and uncle. 'Please save my father,' she said.

Two more people and I from the village ran during that night to Ranbirsinghpora (also called Hadiyanbagh), to call the police and the hospital to get the injured people some help. It is around three and a half kilometres from our village. Only one house had a telephone, or landline, in those days. I had the number of the police chowki of Mattan. I called the constable and told him that around forty people had been killed in our village. He came in a police Gypsy in another twenty minutes. But then, they could only save Nanak Singh, the other one died on the way due to blood loss.

I asked him, 'Weren't you afraid? How could you go to make that call after seeing so many dead bodies? Where did you get the courage to go into that dark night within minutes of that intense firing? There was a possibility of the gunmen hiding somewhere or killing more people.'

To which he replied, 'You are a Sikh as well. You know we are born under swords and guns. We are not afraid. People who got killed were confused when the perpetrators called them. They were thinking about whether they were from the army or the militants. Then, all of it happened so fast, that we did not get a chance to fight back. Otherwise, we would have killed at least a few of them. Sikhs won't die without a fight. I chanted Waheguru Waheguru while I walked to Hadiyanbagh. We had sticks and staffs with us. We were not afraid. Sikhs are never afraid. Yes, we were sad, and we were angry, but not afraid.'

He told me that for the next ten days, the village became like a mela, and thousands of people from all over Kashmir came. The army, police, CRPF, and Rashtriya Rifles (RR) made it like a fortress. Farooq Abdullah, L.K. Advani, Prakash Singh Badal, Dr Manmohan Singh, and a lot of other politicians visited them. All the bodies were cremated in a big pyre near the ground. Badal was present there. The Sikh Student Federation and its member regularly came for the next ten days. The government announced one lakh rupees and one job for every victim's family under SRO-43. Punjab Government announced Rs 2,50,000 lakh while Shiromani Gurdwara Parbandhak Committee (SGPC) Amritsar announced Rs 75,000 per head as a relief to the families of the deceased. Several different organisations came forward with similar packages in the next few months. But within a year, everything came back to being normal, and nobody bothered about the families anymore. Every year, on 20 March, an Akhand path is kept, and a small commemoration function is organised. After two decades, no one except the villagers come for that function. And that is the end of it.

'You people never thought of leaving the village or migrating to Jammu or elsewhere?' I asked him.

'Ours is a well-settled and flourishing village with rich landlords and zamindars. Why would we leave it and go live somewhere else?' he replied and added, 'And within the next few days, the government assured us of protection. A lot of army men were stationed in the village for our protection. And we are not Pandits to run away like scared cats.'

Rajinder Singh was a Gursikh, a pious, practising Sikh who lived a life of devotion and service to his community. At a young age, he joined Mahant Bachitar Singhji, a religious leader of Jammu and Kashmir, and with him, travelled to almost all the places in Jammu and Kashmir. He supervised the construction of gurdwaras and oversaw *gurmat parchar* (religious teaching) works in different gurdwaras. His belief in Sikhism was very strong, and his responses to my questions reflected that. The episodes of bravery, the stories of courage and valour, were too deeply ingrained in him.

Over the next few days, I interviewed a few more people, not the survivors, nor the people affected by the incident, but those who were far removed from it. I knew how we, the Sikhs, felt. But I had to know what the majority thought about it. I talked extensively about the incident with my Muslim colleagues and friends, and a few random people.

When I talked to one of my previous colleagues about the Chithisinghpora massacre and shared the stories from survivors with him, I asked him what he thought was the future of Sikhs in Kashmir. I wanted to know his thoughts on the struggles faced by Sikhs or other minorities in Kashmir. He replied, in a very matter-of-fact way, 'One day you, Sikhs, will have to leave Kashmir when it accedes to Pakistan because that is what this movement is all about. Kashmiris won't rest until that dream is realised.'

'Do you think it is possible for Kashmir to get azaadi?' I asked him.

He said, 'When the Indian Freedom Movement was happening, there were people who said that it would not be possible to overthrow the mighty British Empire, but it happened. How can we say that the same cannot happen in Kashmir? Like every freedom movement, there are radicals, moderates and extremists here. There are all types of people who want to participate in the movement, in their own ways. You cannot stop such incidents ever. The ones who are educated would fight with pen and non-violence. Some would not fight at all. Some would side with the occupier regime, and some would pick up the guns. There are Gandhis and Bhagat Singhs and Boses and Nehrus in every freedom movement. The Kashmir movement is no different.

'And history has taught us, wherever there are freedom movements, the civilians, and non-participative people suffer the most. There are no civil liberties, no rights, and no freedom for the citizens under the colonisers. How different do you think Kashmir is from those examples? And you Sikhs are better than us. We have to face more struggles than you. We live in a more distraught present and an uncertain future. How many times have you seen a Sikh being harassed by the police or the army? They don't even check your vehicles because they believe only Muslims can be terrorists. How many times have you seen Sikhs being pulled out of their house in the middle of the night, or made to stand up in a CASO (Cordon and Search Operation)? How many episodes of killing? We can count on our fingers. Chithisinghpora, Mehjoor Nagar, Push Kriri. Are there any more? No, and how many people were killed? Hundred? Two hundred? If you start counting our dead bodies, you will not even ask the question.'

I could see how my conversation had touched a raw wound in him, and how agitated he had become.

I did not want to answer his questions. I could not compare the suffering of one human with another and tell whose was greater. I could not compare the killing of a Sikh with the killing of a Muslim and justify one killing and be angry over the other. I was conflicted. One part of me looked at it as human loss, the other saw these killings as right and wrong. When a Muslim was killed, he becomes a martyr for the Kashmiris. Thousands of people shower flowers at their funeral because he gave up his life for their cause, the cause of Kashmir's freedom. But when a Sikh was killed, he was killed as collateral, in the crossfire, as cannon fodder, or as an example setting. He did not want azaadi, the cause was not his to die for. So what could we call his killing? A sacrifice or payment for living in Kashmir.

I wrote the story, but I never submitted it to any magazine for publication.

15

Paranoia, Alms and Pistols

Srinagar, Kashmir
17 October 2021, Sunday

The previous day's killing had brought the count to nine for the month. Seven of them belonged to minority communities or were non-locals. By morning the news was all over the TV and social media. I had no reason to get up early, but it was Indu's brother's call that woke us up. On a Sunday, 9.30 a.m. was too early for me. Indu's brother lived in Mumbai and worked as an assistant professor in a private college. He had read the news. 'Two non-locals shot dead in Kashmir'. And, another news, that two LeT militants were killed in encounters in Pulwama. Indu was a non-local and non-Muslim, who married a non-Muslim Kashmiri migrant employed under the resettlement policy, and had come to settle permanently in Kashmir. There was more than one criterion to be killed. For both of us.

While she talked to her brother, I turned on my laptop to find the story I had written about Chithisinghpora. I had not opened it for several years. I had to see if it was still there or if it had gotten deleted. The moment she disconnected her call from her brother, she received another call from one of her friends living in Bangalore. I guessed she had also called for the same reason. Civilian killings, minorities, Sikhs, Hindus, Muslims, terrorists, army and Kashmir, were the only words I could understand in her conversation. Though I have learned to understand some Malayalam words when she speaks with someone, it was too fast for me.

When she was finished with the call, before she could say anything, I said, 'I know. The same thing. How are the conditions? Are you safe? And then, finally, why are you still in Kashmir?'

'Why do they have to tell me this early in the morning, I had forgotten about it, they could have waited till midday at least,' she said and pulled the quilt again up to her neck.

'It's still 9.45. We can sleep for another half an hour. What do you say?' I told her.

'We are already so late. Ideally, a daughter-in-law should wake up first and serve the tea and all,' she smiled at me.

'You focus on your studies. Remember all this lenience is because you are still a student,' I teased her. 'Anyway, I don't feel like sleeping anymore. I was checking the Chithisinghpora story I wrote. I'll show you if I find it,' I added.

'You have written a story about it? How come you never told me?' She got up and leaned against the bedrest.

'It's not published, just on the computer. That too I am not sure. I wrote it in 2015.'

'I am going to check on parents. You do your work and show me if you find it or tell me what you wrote. You will remember that, right?' she asked. I tend to forget. One constant complaint Indu had about me was that I talked about new people every time she brought up a topic, and she felt like she did not know everyone in my life. And I told her that even though I didn't remember those people, her triggers, woke up those memories.

My mother was in the kitchen preparing breakfast. It was Sunday. So the breakfast would be something special, like chole-bhature, aloo-paratha, dosa, or likewise. I could smell the aromas in the air when Indu opened the door.

'Get ready. I am making aloo-parathas for breakfast, and I have soaked rajma for lunch. Tell Papa and Bupi to come in ten minutes,' Maa said to Indu and I could hear that as the door was still open.

When she first came to Kashmir, Indu was amazed by our obsession with food. She asked me why all our lives revolved around food. She said, 'You get up for breakfast. Then, within an hour or two, you have your afternoon tea. Then, again within two hours, you have your lunch. Another two hours pass by, and you drink the evening tea with snacks. Before dinner, you would have something or the other. Your mother spends eighty per cent of her day in the kitchen, cooking and washing utensils. By the time one meal is over, and she has cleaned and washed everything, you people ask for the next.'

'It's her ikigai,' I told her, 'She likes to cook and feed. She derives some pleasure when she sees people eating and loving her cooking. Even if we tell her not to, even if it is for just one person, she cooks food with full interest and love.'

My mother was an excellent cook. She could cook anything, Indian, continental, Oriental, Chinese, or whatever you feel like. Everyone in our extended families acknowledged her skills. Many had encouraged her to start a cooking channel on YouTube.

Regarding Indu's query, she was right. Our lives revolved around food. People lived on food, we lived for food. It was ingrained in us with our social and cultural upbringing. In our language, livelihood was called '*ted palna*', which translated as 'feeding your belly'. When someone was unemployed or did not earn, our first question would be, 'What would you feed your kids?' or 'If you didn't do anything, what will you eat?' When someone did something dishonest, they say, '*Paapi payt ka sawal*' (he did it to feed his sinful stomach).' Food became the pivot of our life. We lived so we could eat. We worked so that we could eat and feed others. We marry not for partnership but for a permanent unpaid cook. We raise kids and feed them so they could feed us when we could not earn the food or cook it ourselves. When someone was born, or there was any function, like weddings, birthdays, or death anniversaries, we visited them for the food. We said, '*chai kot uthi peesa*' when we visit someone's home unannounced, which meant, 'will have tea there.'

Indu herself was a good cook but not someone who would be spending all her time in the kitchen. She loved to cook a biryani or fish curry, but only occasionally. If cooking was an everyday job, she would be a mess. And I never expected that from her. I never wanted my mother to be like that. I told her more than enough times to switch to lighter meals, like cornflakes or oats, which were easy to cook and take only a minute or two to prepare.

'What else will I do? That is the only thing I know,' she tells us whenever we tell her to spend less time in the kitchen. 'I will get bored otherwise,' she says. It is her hobby, job and passion.

And all the women I knew in Kashmir spend at least half of their day in the kitchen, Sikh women especially. Our breakfasts were full-fledged meals, unlike the Muslim households where they had a cup of namkeen tea with a lavaas—a thin but big round bread made from maida (flour).

The Sikh breakfast usually comprises curry, tea, chapattis and sometimes fried eggs too. We truly had our breakfast like a king, lunch like a minister, and dinner like a beggar.

'Special breakfast today,' Indu announced as she came back to the room.

'Yes, I heard. I don't feel like getting out of bed,' I told her as I handed her the laptop. 'Here, I found the story, want to read it?' I asked.

'Yes. Let me. You freshen up in the meantime.' She took the laptop and sat at the study table to read the story.

When I came back from the washroom after some time, her face was a mixture of sadness and anger. She had closed the laptop and was sitting in the chair in deep thought like a statue.

'Why didn't you send it to some magazine for publication?' she asked me.

'I sent it to a few. Nobody replied.'

'Your writing style is more documentary than fiction. It felt like reading the account of what happened, the emotions were missing. I guess you need to work on that before you send it out to some magazine again.'

'I haven't planned it. But I will see. That was a long time back. My writing has improved ever since. What do you think?' I asked.

'You are still a documentary type of writer. When you tell me something, you just report. In our conversation, I talk ninety per cent of the time. You keep repeating, yes, nothing, good, I don't know, all the time,' she said. At one point of time in our relationship, during Covid, when we were away from each other for a year, she had banned the use of 'yes', 'all good', 'I don't know', and 'you tell me'.

She told me that my power of observation was too superficial and that my memory of events and incidents was cluttered, as I never spoke about anything with passion, I just reported what happened. I spoke very less.

'If I ask your father the same thing, he will give much more information, context, opinions and all, not just the minutes of the event,' she said.

'Then ask him during breakfast,' I suddenly felt a little angry at her. Feedback was a good thing. I did work on her feedback, but by the time I got it, it spurred some spontaneous emotions.

And she did ask my father at the breakfast table, 'How was it to live in Kashmir after the Chithisinghpora massacre?'

He had a confused look. He did not expect such a question all of a sudden. He took a long pause before replying. We thought he was not even going to reply. Then he said, 'For the first ten days after the massacre, we were in Chithisinghpora. I was the secretary of the All-India Sikh Student Federation (J&K Wing) at that time, and along with all the members of our organisation we stayed in Chithisinghpora with the families during those times. There was anger and rage all around. Almost 15,000 Sikhs had come out in protest against the killing. Every big name in politics and bureaucracy visited the place. But that was for the first ten days. After that, things went back to normal. What do they call it? I guess the oblivion's curse or something like that.'

'And I wanted to ask you why you waited for the Mehjoor Nagar incident to migrate to Jammu, when Chithisinghpora was so much more brutal?' Indu asked my father.

He said, 'During those ten days, a lot of things happened. I guess the HM commander said that it was not the terrorists who did it and also made it clear that nobody was to lay a hand on the Sikhs. Then the government also promised us security and protection. In every Sikh village throughout Kashmir, police posts were made, a minimum of two police personnel were kept there twenty-four seven, and the army and CRPF patrolled during the day and the evening. And then, it was a first-of-its-kind incident whose motive was not clear. And we, as Sikhs, had an inbuilt pride. They had showcased it over the years. They had been saying it out loud, too. Sikhs wouldn't run. We were not like Pandits who got scared of such things. Now admitting that they were scared and running away was not even an option.

'After that incident, nothing else was directed toward the Sikhs. But a wave of brotherhood and solidarity took over Kashmir. Muslims came out in big numbers supporting us, telling us we were their brothers and Kashmir belonged to us as much as it belonged to them. That gave us hope and renewed our belief in Kashmiriyat. And it was true, Kashmir belonged to us, not as much as it belonged to them, but in fact, more than it belonged to them.'

Both Indu and I had finished our first paratha, but my father had not eaten even half of it.

'Finish this first, it's getting cold. We can talk about this after breakfast as well,' I said.

'And then when Mehjoor Nagar happened, the memories of Chithisinghpora and the uncertainty would have come to you people. That was why you decided to go?' Indu inquired further, ignoring my suggestions.

He took a few bites before continuing. He said, 'More than the memory of Chithisinghpora, it was the fact that the whole incident was a result of misplaced anger. Mehjoor Nagar happened as a reaction to a suspicion of some SOG soldiers killing a civilian auto driver. Incidentally, those soldiers were Sikhs. It was more like 1984, where the bodyguards of Indira Gandhi were Sikhs, and the revenge was taken on the whole community. That was fearful, and if it had happened once, it could happen again whenever the majority felt like it. Some of us had decided that we would move out. We told everyone, the whole Sikh community, that there was no future for Sikhs in Kashmir. If we were going to live here, we had to live like a minority, on the whims and wishes of the majority.

'Education, employment, business, children's upbringing, nothing at that time, and at this time, has been easy for us. We had lived in mental tension. We wanted our children to live in a peaceful place. But only a handful of people migrated at that time. Every year, slowly, one by one, the Sikhs were moving out. If they had moved as a community, we could have asked for the migrant status and gotten some benefits from the government like the Pandits. But if they listen to rationality, will they be Sikhs?'

I said, 'I guess now too we are doing the same thing. I have seen a lot of my friends migrate out. Some go for studies; some for jobs. Some are moving abroad, to Canada and Australia, for better opportunities and a better future. None of them want to come back to Kashmir.'

'What's there in Kashmir to come back for, this hell?' Papa replied.

'Bupi has told me you had already migrated from Kashmir in 1991 but had to come back for some reasons. So when you moved out in 2001, was it easier for you?' Indu asked again. My father replied, 'It's never easy to leave your home, your roots. We associate with Kashmir and have always been like that. My forefather lived here. This soil is soaked with their blood and sweat, all my life I have lived here, my childhood memories, the days of my youth and early adulthood, every memory has Kashmir in it. But what to do? Sometimes, it was not meant to be, I guess. If not for

Bupi's job, I would have never come back. Ask him, I have told him many times to quit and come to Jammu. He can earn more than this in Jammu, even if he takes tuition in the evening.'

'Yes. Saying it is easy, but doing is a different thing. All these years, I have told myself I will leave one day. But then every other year, I am still here. Let's see. I have a chance to move out now. I hope we never come back,' I replied.

'When you go to Australia, find some opportunity there, settle there and take us out of this misery as well,' Papa told Indu.

'Yes, I will. One of my friends is there. She is also a clinical psychologist from NIMHANS. She has settled there with her husband, and they are doing well,' she replied. 'But we still have to figure out what Bupi will do.'

'Tesla Truck, or waiter at a Coffee house,' I replied. 'Don't worry about me. I will find something, and figure it out before you finish your studies. I will make freelance writing my main work, and keep writing literary works as well. If worse comes to worst, I can still manage a decent earning from my content writing alone.'

'I feel you will be good in some editorial role for some magazine or journal. But then, I do not know how the literary environment is in Australia.'

'The writing world is more concentrated in the US and the UK. I will check what all magazines or book agencies have offices in Australia, and try to find something.'

'You still have more than a year to figure out those things. For now, work on your writer profile so that the transition is easy,' she replied.

After breakfast, all of us went outside to sit on the lawn to get some sun before I could get back to writing and Indu could go back to her research. It was around eleven thirty when someone knocked on our main gate, which was never bolted. A middle-aged man entered, wearing a phiran, an ankle-length woollen overcoat, with its sleeves hanging freely while his arms were tucked inside. When he came, I stood up to see who he was. Indu and my mother were facing away from him, while my father and I were facing him. He greeted us with an *As-salamu alaykum*, the Muslim greeting, and then started to pull out something from his phiran. For a moment, my father and I could hear the thud of our hearts. I thought he would pull out a gun and shoot me and the others. First, I froze at the thought of it. Then I picked up the stool I was sitting on and rushed towards him holding it aloft. What he took were out a few sheets of paper that looked like something pertaining to a hospital. We realised he had come for financial assistance for his wife's ongoing medical treatment. But he was unaware of what emotions he had brought forth in us. I stopped dead in my tracks when I saw the papers in his hand but I could not hear what he said at all. When he saw me with the stool, he had a confused look. My father had also stood up. He told him to go ask for money somewhere else. I stood there until he went out. And then I laughed hysterically.

My face was flushed red, my heart was racing at breakneck speed, and my knuckles were white because I had held the stool so tight. Indu and my mother had also stood up, seeing me run with the stool, and were completely puzzled at what had transpired.

'What happened?' my mother asked, still confused.

'I don't know. I thought he had a pistol,' I replied.

'And what were you going to do with the stool?' Papa asked while he sat down again.

'No idea. I am going inside. I have to sit and write something,' I told them and walked away.

After a few minutes, Indu also came inside. I was still thinking, overthinking, about all the possible scenarios. I was two or three leaps away from him when he pulled out the papers. If it was a gun, he could have shot me before I could smash the stool on his head. And if he had not brought out the papers, I would have hurt him without him knowing what he was being beaten for. What if he or someone else had directly started shooting the moment he came inside? We would all be dead.

My mind was on overdrive when Indu asked, 'So, feeling fine?'

'Yes, baby,' I smiled, though I could still feel my heart pounding. I was lying spreadeagled across the bed.

'Baby, can you move a little? I have an online meeting at twelve. You will have to go out of the room in another fifteen minutes,' she said.

'Ok. I will. For now, let me rest for a while.'

'This is what happens when we live in a place so uncertain. We start looking at normal situations with paranoia. It is not your fault, dear. Relax,' she told me. I felt dejected. I was expecting a more heated argument about leaving Srinagar as soon as possible. But she handled it better than I did.

While she sat inside for the meeting, I sat re-reading the story, thinking about how the human mind worked. At first sight of fear, we would either freeze, run away or react with the most primitive action, violence. I was perplexed at the thought of my reaction.

What Rajinder Singh told me during the interview years back, that Sikhs were not afraid, and that the people of Chithisinghpora died because of confusion flashed before my eyes. It stood half true and half false in my encounter with the beggar. It was fear that I felt, the pure fear of being shot, the fear of my family being killed after he shoots me, the fear that what if he just killed the four of us sitting on the lawn and left Ramneek there, orphaned and unattended to for the rest of his life. Then there was a reaction. In those moments, I did not even register that I was a Sikh, or that we were not supposed to be afraid, or we were a brave community. My mind just went back to the primal instinct of killing the predator before being killed. With that instinct, I leapt towards him with the stool. The paranoia kicked in only after the beggar left.

When people dressed in army outfits came to their village, this primal instinct did not rear its head in the villagers' minds. They died because of that misunderstanding. If they had a hint that they were going to be killed, out of instinct, they would have attacked the gunmen, despite knowing that they would be killed. They would have taken out a few of them along when they died.

But the fact that I reacted with violence, instead of freezing or hiding or running away in the face of fear, was what I believed to be a trait of a Sikh. Something that had sparked on a genetic level. Even studies had proved that in humans, the flight or fight response to the environment was a genetic characteristic. Throughout history, Sikhs reacted to fear and violence with overwhelming opposition. They had fought impossible battles, held the bravest last stands, and upheld their principles in the face of death. Death never scared them; they celebrated it.

So what Rajinder Singh said was true. But again, society and the environment played a vital role in this. The times had changed, and our upbringing resulted in much weaker personalities. The moment we regained consciousness and logical thinking, the moment our belief weakened, we became tamed, domestic beings again. Long ago, there were ferocious battle-hardened Sikhs, who lived nomadic lives, going from forest to forest, fighting Mughals and the British. The twenty-first century had turned them into comfort-seeking, nine-to-five job holders who looked for a means of escape at the first hint of danger.

In three decades of militancy, that was the first time we bolted our main gate from the inside in broad daylight. Precaution or fear, whatever it was, had compelled me to stay indoors for more than a week. Now we realised that we could not even be safe or have a sense of safety inside our homes.

None of us talked about what we had witnessed, but all of us had the same feeling. I could see my mother keeping herself busy in the kitchen but keeping an eye on the main gate. Father sat on the lawn, scrolling through his Facebook account, in between calling different people and asking for updates, listening to the same thing over and over from different people. When he came inside, it was already time for lunch. Indu's meeting had also ended just a few minutes before, and she, too, came to the living room. Mother asked us if we would have lunch and if she should make the Kashmir chutney with walnuts, green chillies, mint and onion. Ramneek was busy with the Manga series *One Punch Man's* commentary on some YouTube channel. Ever since we bought the Smart TV and subscription to YouTube, Netflix, Amazon Prime and Disney Hotstar, he watched all his anime on it.

Other than the morning incident, the day was boring like all other days since the last week. I had zero energy to do anything, so I went to sleep for a few hours while Indu worked on some data for her studies. I was told to get up for the evening tea at around six thirty.

Within an hour of the tea, we had another disappointing news. Two more non-local migrant workers, both Hindus, were killed, and another one was seriously injured. The killing took place in the Laran Gangipora Wanpoh area of Kulgam. The victims were all from the same family and belonged to Bihar. The incident happened close to the residence of a former Member of the Legislative Assembly (MLA). What was more distressing was that the victims were sitting inside their rooms when someone entered and started to shoot at them indiscriminately. The two who died on the spot were Raja Reshi Dev and Joginder Reshi Dev, while the one injured was Chunchun Reshi Dev. I came to know about the news when I was scrolling and came across a tweet in *Asian News International*

(ANI) news. I went to QNS, a news channel on Facebook immediately to find out more. In the morning, the Lieutenant General of J&K, Manoj Sinha, had said they would avenge the death of every civilian. He had told in his monthly radio talk, *Awaam ki Awaaz*, 'I pay my heartfelt tributes to the martyr civilians and condolences to the bereaved families. We'll hunt down terrorists and their sympathisers and avenge every drop of innocent civilian blood.'

And now, these killings were a direct reply to his speech.

Within an hour of the killing, all the district police headquarters were instructed to bring all the non-local migrant workers to the nearest police stations for safety, and where there were no police stations, they were to be taken to the army or paramilitary camps. The IGP had told the police that 'this matter is most urgent.' When it was out in the open, a sense of anxiety and fear spread to everyone. Local and non-locals alike. Muslims and non-Muslims alike. One of my friends, who was a cafe owner and most of whose staff were non-local, was worried for them. He wanted to drive all the way to his cafe and bring them home to keep them safe. Everybody thought that the internet would be snapped and a media blackout might happen.

But it was not so. I was glued to Twitter, and within a few hours, all the major politicians tweeted something or the other. The former CM Mehbooba Mufti condemned the attack and wrote, 'There are no words strong enough to condemn the repeated barbaric attacks on innocent civilians. My heart goes out to their families because they leave the comforts of their homes to earn a dignified livelihood. Terribly sad,' while Omar Abdullah wrote, 'Another day, another dose of bad news from the Valley. Two civilians, both non-local, were shot and killed in a terror attack in Kulgam district of south Kashmir. I reservedly condemn this attack and pray for the souls of the Raja & Jogindar Reshi Dev.'

Everybody referred to the victims as civilians, non-locals, or migrant workers, but no one called them what we actually felt they were—minorities, non-Muslims. This thought of classifying the dead by their religion and not as just another human life was the result of the recent religious dipole created by the media.

With these two, the total count of the dead was eleven. There were three attacks in the last 24 hours, and it felt like the violence was never-ending. The news echoed my belief that no one was safe, even inside their homes. Indu was scrolling through her phone when her brother messaged her the link to some news website that had reported the current killing.

I was sure that someone from her family or friends would call and repeat the same question, 'What are we still doing in Kashmir?'

Rationally speaking, it would have been hard for them to understand what we were still doing in Kashmir. People were being killed, non-locals and non-Muslims were on the hit list, and Indu was both of them. Her parents, on the other hand, did not interfere regarding this. They believed whatever she did had a reason and had complete faith and trust in her decisions, one of the decisions being, marrying me. They were equally concerned about our safety and well-being. But they did not show any urgency or anger toward our indecisiveness. But when her father called after dinner, I was sure that their threshold of patience had crossed. When she cut the call, I was already waiting for her with interest. Her tone had shifted from excited to angry to irritated to distressed to low, over the call. When she finished, she was a mix of it all.

'What?'

'Same. Why are you still sitting there? What are you waiting there for?'

'What did you say?'

'What could I say? Do we even have an answer for it? I told him we would leave in November, but he said that was still too far away.

'What are we supposed to do all this time here?' she asked.

'I have to look into a few things, baby. I'll call the school principal tomorrow and see what she says. The problem is, if I go on leave, I won't get my salary, and that would be very difficult. Without money, I won't be able to survive in Noida,' I said.

'Anyway, you check that tomorrow. I feel drained. Let's sleep now,' she said.

I guess she wanted to turn off the overwhelming thoughts running through her mind. It was the same for me as well.

16

Men Are From Mars, Women Are From Venus, Sikhs Are From Punjab

Srinagar, Kashmir
18 October 2021, Monday

That night I had a disturbed sleep. My mind was stuck on the encounter with the beggar. I had some very vivid dreams where I was the hero.

In my dream, I was at school. An armed man came to the office where I was sitting at my desk and he pulled out a gun from his bag. The moment I saw the gun, I threw my bag at him to disarm him, and in the meantime, I jumped up, got hold of a globe lying there and smashed his head. In another scenario, an armed biker stopped next to my car and pulled out his gun from his jacket. I opened the door and kicked it in such a way that the door banged against his bike, making him misfire a shot in the air before he fell on the other side. I grabbed my big kirpan, which was always under my driving seat, and stabbed him repeatedly.

When I woke up, I was smiling at the stupidity of my dreams. There were other fleeting dreams. But the harder I tried to remember them, the more I forgot them. Evading dreams, I guess. I did not tell any of those to Indu. For me, they were mere dreams. But for her, they would be a reminder of what happened yesterday. It would also mean putting in her head possibilities of what could happen. Both of which I did not want.

I was supposed to call the headmistress and inquire about the leave, but before I could do that, she called me herself. She told me that it had been more than ten days since I went to school, and she did not know what to do with my attendance. She gave me two options, either apply for a leave or rejoin. If I did neither, I would be marked absconding from my duties, which could result in my suspension or my salary being withheld. I had already given it a lot of thought.

It was still the middle of October. The winter vacations would start in the first or second week of December. Once the winter vacations were announced, I could easily stay in Noida up to the end of February. All I had to do was to somehow manage the one and a half months, beginning from November until the start of winter vacations. I already had a plan for that.

I was given a temporary, data uploading duty for Covid vaccine status on the government's website in August and September, which I did for some time and then went back to school for a few days. For that duty, I had to go to a nearby government-run vaccination centre at a Primary Healthcare Centre (PHC). If I could get that duty again and convince the doctor that I could do the data uploading from home, I would not have to apply for leave or worry about attendance. I had already worked with him and established a good rapport. With that in mind, I thought of visiting him and then the school with the proposal of assigning me that duty again.

Over the phone, I had requested the headmistress to give me two days of casual leave for the time being so that I could think and decide what to do further.

'I am going to school,' I announced in the dining hall when everyone was having afternoon tea. 'I'll just go for an hour and come back. I need to see what I can do about the leave.'

'Can't you do that on the phone?' Indu asked.

'I have to give a handwritten application, signed by me if I have to take the leave, and then I have to apply for a station leaving permission as well, to move out of the state.' I did not disclose the other idea of getting the Covid duty, for I was not certain if it would work out.

'Did you tell the headmistress that you are coming?' Papa asked me. He heard me talking to the headmistress, and now I was planning to go to school.

'No, I haven't. I will call and tell.'

'No. Don't call. If you want to go, then go unannounced. They won't know that you are coming,' he replied. 'Who knows who is working with the militants? What if she tells any other staff member, and then it reaches the TRF or any others? They can do anything.'

When Supinder was killed, she was identified and killed, and the gunmen had the necessary information before the attack. Every attack was planned, and not just a random killing. They knew who lived where and who worked as what. My father's statement echoed the belief that the information was provided by the insiders. I never thought of it as a leak or providing insider information. But rather as common knowledge that flowed and reached the gunmen. When you worked at some place, a lot of people knew your whereabouts, and the news travelled, the information was available for anyone to use however they deemed fit. I agreed to my father's suggestion of going unannounced, not because I thought anyone would inform the militants. I had complete faith in my colleagues. But because I knew if they knew I was coming, the information would flow among the staff and then to the people they could call or meet.

I had already told them that I wanted two days of casual leave, and if I went unannounced now, it would be a complete surprise to everyone. Nobody would suspect I would be coming.

'Should I come with you,' my father asked.

'No, I will go alone. I will return in an hour or two before lunchtime.'

I thought it would be better to go alone. If I was killed, there would be someone to take care of the family.

'You come fast. What will you do there for two hours? Write and take the application with you from home. You don't have to sit there and write it,' Maa said.

I wondered how one incident had changed the way I was thinking and acting. Was it my paranoia or my fear of acting out? I did not know. Going to school felt like going to a battlefield. My parents and wife were asking me questions and telling me the dos and don'ts.

My school was located just outside the municipal limits of Srinagar city, in a locality called Kralpora. It was a small locality of three to four smaller mohallas with a total population of over 4000. As a result, our school was upgraded from a middle school to a high school in 2019. Since 2010, I was working in the same school. So most people in the locality knew me. The students who passed out from our school were still in touch with me, and I had a very good relationship with them.

When I reached school, everyone was surprised. They asked me how I was feeling and what my parents and my wife were feeling about the situation. I had been absent for over ten days. When I saw the arrival attendance register, I had casual leave against my name.

'Are you planning to join duties again?' one teacher asked.

'I don't know yet. It is still unsafe for us, and moreover, the whole community has decided that nobody will attend duties for now. The PM Package employees are not going to join for another month I guess,' I replied.

'Yes, but there is no official order about giving leaves or dealing with their absence. So we don't know what to do with the arrival attendance register,' another teacher said.

'Let's see how things develop. Nobody will ask the Pandits anything. But you have to take care of your own job. They have *jacks* and *jugaads*. You don't,' a senior master said.

'I will ask for a leave of absence for forty-five days until the winter vacations start. I can go to Jammu after the leave is sanctioned,' I replied.

'Earlier they were targeting Pandits. Now it is not safe for Sikhs as well,' said another teacher. 'Your wife is a Hindu. She would be traumatised right now,' she added. Everyone in school knew that I married a Kerala Hindu. And not just in school, all the teachers who I had worked with earlier also knew about it. It was gossip for a while that a Sikh boy had married a Hindu girl from another state.

'As a tourist, everything is rosy and cheerful for them. But now that she is married to a Kashmiri, she would be thinking, "What did I get myself into?"' another one said.

'Next, it is the Sikhs' turn. They will have to leave Kashmir,' she added. 'Sikhs should have left when the Pandits left in the 1990s. What did they get here? In Jammu, they could have lived a happy life among their people.

'We don't have our people there. All our people are here. Why would we go to Jammu?' I said. I wanted to shout back at her, but I chose to keep quiet at her utter ignorance.

'No, no. I meant Hindus are much closer to you,' she replied.

I did not feel like answering her. If she was thinking along those lines, there was no point in explaining to her. Most Kashmiri Muslims didn't know anything about the Sikh religion other than we wear a turban and never cut our hair.

I was amazed, when I came back to Kashmir as an adult after a decade, at how misinformed and ignorant the Muslims were about us. Those who had a chance to work with Sikhs or were friends with Sikhs only knew about our culture and religion. But that they would have learned by repeatedly saying something wrong in front of a Sikh and then being schooled by the same person.

I remember when I went to a Muslim friend's house, his parents offered me food. They had made some gushtaba, a mutton dish, and when I told them that I don't eat non-vegetarian, they told me to have the curry only. My friend had to explain to them that it was because of the difference between jhatka and halaal, which they could not understand. They did not understand the logic of slaughtering the goat in a different style and then only being allowed to eat it. It was an interesting concept for them.

A lot of Muslims did not know about 'such' things. Then they would say that Pandits didn't differentiate between jhatka and halaal and that they buy from their shops. Most of them thought of us as derivatives of Pandits and Hindus, who believe in some other God and not, Shiva, Krishna, or Vishnu. One Muslim colleague usually cut the call by saying, Jai Mata di, thinking that he was making me comfortable. Some would say namaskar or namaste to us.

For us, jhatka was not just a style of slaughtering. There was a philosophy behind it. It was during the period of the sixth Guru in the 1500s that the Mughals ruled north India. They had a strict policy of selling meat. Nobody was allowed to cut livestock at home, and everyone was forced to buy it from shops owned by the Mughals. Mughals being Muslims, always cut the livestock by first reciting the name of Allah, reading the Kalima, and sacrificing the livestock in the name of Allah, cutting in from the underside of the neck in a very slow manner, the halaal way. Everybody else had to buy it from them. As a rebellion against the authority of the Mughals and on the principle that one should take responsibility for his actions and not kill in the name of God, the sixth Guru declared another way of killing the livestock and boycotted the Mughal style and shops. Killing to eat and calling it a sacrifice for God was against the Sikh philosophy, in which one had to stand up and take responsibility for every act and deed.

As a teacher, I came to know how none of these things were ever told to the Muslims and how they were never sensitised towards minorities in the state.

'You give an application for leave and sit home for now. Let us see how things pan out. Then you can come back to school,' a senior master said.

I told the headmistress that I was willing to go for Covid duty and that it would be good for the school if the other teacher who was deputed for Covid duty could join back the school and teach, while I could go to the dispensary. She agreed and told me to ask the dispensary in charge for further advice.

After school, I went to the dispensary, which was nearby, and met the in-charge doctor. Doctor sahab, as I used to call him, was a very bold and straightforward person. He was brave enough to say things to your face and fight for what he thought was right. He greeted me with a hug.

'You got scared and went away. What kind of a Sikh are you?' he asked me referring to my absence from school. 'When someone had to die, they would die even in their bed. The time and place of the death are already written. You don't have to worry about that. You come and join again.'

I told him I was planning to rejoin and would attend office intermittently till the end of the month. Then, I planned to do the work from home. He just had to send me the photo of the register, and then I would upload the data from it.

'Bupinderji, when someone comes to kill you, I will be standing in front of you. He has to kill me first,' he told me. 'Kashmir is not someone's father's property. It belongs to you as much as it belongs to us,' he added.

'Nothing like that, sir. It is not that I am afraid of dying. When death has to come, it will come. But you know, my parents are worried. They are getting anxious, and my wife too. She is seeing such things for the first time in her life. So whenever I come out of home, they are on their feet all the while.'

'You don't worry as long as I am here. I will send you photos of the register, but you have to finish the work before 2 p.m. Your job is to update the data. That work should not suffer. To me it does not matter where you are working from and how you do it,' he replied. 'Those people who are doing all these killings, they don't know anything about Kashmiriyat or Islam. They are brainwashed scums. They succeeded in ousting the Pandits, but they won't be able to do that with Sikhs.'

Throughout his career, the doctor had worked with a lot of Sikhs and pretty much knew a lot of things about our culture, ethics and stories.

During my previous working period with him, he told me how he had a very dear Sikh friend who was like a brother to him and how he respected his honesty and integrity. That friend had taught him everything about Sikhism through words and through actions.

With his assurance that I just needed to do the assigned work without worrying about attending the office physically, I was relieved of a major worry. This way, I wouldn't have to apply for leave and would receive my salary also. The work was online and I had to upload it from the portal. It would be a lot easier for me to do it from home, where I could use the laptop, instead of doing it on the phone at the dispensary. It was good news for me.

I went back to convey the information to the headmistress and told her that I would be working from the dispensary from now on, and a duty slip would be sent to school at the end of every month, on the basis of which my salary could be drawn. Doctor sahab had already called the higher-ups and told them to sign a formal order to depute me to his office as a data entry operator for the Covid vaccine.

'Once the order comes only then can I mark you being present on duty. Otherwise I will mark it as a casual leave,' the headmistress told me. That was the protocol, and breaking it would mean jeopardising her own job. I told her that I would try to get the order as soon as possible.

'You would have some relatives in Punjab also. You can stay with them for some time,' a teacher asked me. She was a new recruit and had joined the school recently, and we had not had much interaction.

'Why would I have relatives in Punjab?' I asked her.

'All sardars are from Punjab only, no? That's why I asked,' she replied.

'No. We are from Kashmir, not Punjab. If that is the case, are all Muslims from Saudi Arabia? Do you have relatives there?' I asked her. I wanted to directly tell her, 'Are you stupid or what?' But I controlled myself.

'Arre, no, no. I did not mean it like that, but was talking about your ancestors or grandparents. Somebody would have been originally from Punjab,' she replied.

I did not want to give her a lesson in history, but like always, I was amazed. What astonished me was that she was a young teacher, my age or maybe younger than me, and in this day and age, when information was available at a flick of a finger, she was assuming such a thing.

'Oh, okay. No worries. It's alright,' I told her, controlling myself again.

It was already 2 p.m. and my mother had called me twice in the last one and a half hours with some excuse or other. First, she called and told me to bring some curd while coming back, and then she called again to tell me to bring one kilo of onions, which I clearly remembered were still in stock at home. I bid goodbye to the staff before some other new conversation could pull me in and take more time.

When I reached home, I told my family about what happened so far. I would not need to apply for a leave anymore and I would be able to go to Noida and work from home. I would get the salary on time. With that, most of my immediate hurdles in the way of leaving Kashmir were solved.

What the new teacher said somehow made me angry. It was not the first time, but in the context of all the things happening in Kashmir. This simple question had vexed me.

I remembered that one of my friends, Kulbir Singh Badal, who had done his PhD on the Sikh History of Kashmir during the reign of Maharaja Ranjit Singh, told me how such questions had steered his life. He was repeatedly asked this and several such questions at his college where he studied history. 'Where did Sikhs come from, and how did they settle in Kashmir? Do all Sikhs want to go to Punjab and live there? Why is the Sikh Rule in Kashmir called Behbooj Raj (a state of lawlessness)? Do the Sikhs of Kashmir have any different religious rituals than the Sikhs of Punjab? Are they related in any way?' And a plethora of similar questions.

Instinctively I called him to check where he was and what he was doing. He told me that he had come to Kashmir just three days before Supinder's killing. I told him to come to the library sometime so we could catch up. The library was named after his grandfather, Sardar Kartar Singh Komal, and was called Komal Library. His grandfather was an eminent personality in Kashmir, a teacher and a leader who had worked for the welfare of the community for a long time.

I knew about most of the eminent Sikh personalities of Kashmir and had recently come to know about the two major incidents, the Mehjoor Nagar, and the Chithisinghpora massacre, in some detail. For a novel I was writing, I had extensively interviewed the survivors of the 1947 Sikh massacres in Kashmir. I had a good knowledge of the history of the Sikhs in the last hundred years. But of the time before that, I scarcely knew anything. To know more about the period, I messaged Kulbir to send me a copy of his thesis, so I could have some idea of the earlier periods. He would be meeting me in some days, and if I read his thesis before that, I could ask him questions which I did not even know I had to ask.

INSTRUMENT OF ACCESSION OF ....JAMMU AND KASHMIR STATE

WHEREAS the Indian Independence Act, 1947, provides that as from the fifteenth day of August, 1947, there shall be set up an independent Dominion known as INDIA, and that the Government of India Act, 1935, shall, with such omissions, additions, adaptations and modification as the Governor-General may by order specify be applicable to the Dominion of India;

AND WHEREAS the Government of India Act, 1935, as so adapted by the Governor-General provides that an Indian State may accede to the Dominion of India by an Instrument of Accession executed by the Ruler thereof;

NOW THEREFORE

I *Shriman Indar Mahandas Rajrajeshwar Maharajadhiraj Shri Hari Singhji* Ruler of .....JAMMU AND KASHMIR STATE.......... *Jammu Kashmir* in the exercise of my sovereignty in and over my said State Do hereby execute *Naresh Tibbet* this my Instrument of Accession and *Tibbet adi Desh adhipati*

1. I hereby declare that I accede to the Dominion of India with the intent that the Governor-General of India, the Dominion Legislature, the Federal Court and any other Dominion authority established for the purposes of the Dominion shall, by virtue of this my Instrument of Accession, but subject always to the terms thereof, and for the purposes only of the Dominion, exercise in relation to the State of JAMMU AND KASHMIR (hereinafter referred to as "this State") such functions as may be vested in them by or under the Government of India Act, 1935, as in force in the Dominion of India on the 15th day of August 1947 (which Act as so in force is hereinafter referred to as "the Act").

2. I hereby assume the obligation of ensuring that due effect is given to the provisions of the Act within this State so far as they are applicable therein by virtue of this my Instrument of Accession.

3. I accept the matters specified in the Schedule hereto as the matters with respect to which the Dominion Legislature may make laws for this State.

4. I hereby declare that I accede to the Dominion of India on the assurance that if an agreement is made between the Governor-General and the Ruler of this State whereby any functions in relation to the administration in this State of any law of the Dominion Legislature shall be exercised by the Ruler of this State, then any such agreement shall be deemed to form part of this Instrument and shall be construed and have effect accordingly.

5. The terms of this my Instrument of Accession shall not be varied by any amendment of the Act or of the Indian Independence Act, 1947 unless such amendment is accepted by me by an Instrument supplementary to this Instrument.

6. Nothing in this Instrument shall empower the Dominion Legislature to make any law for this State authorising the compulsory acquisition of land for any purpose, but I hereby undertake that should the Dominion for the purposes of a Dominion law which applies in this State deem it necessary to acquire any land, I will at their request acquire the land at their expense or if the land belongs to me transfer it to them on such terms as may be agreed, or, in default of agreement, determined by an arbitrator to be appointed by the Chief Justice of India.

7. Nothing in this Instrument shall be deemed to commit me in any way to acceptance of any future constitution of India or to fetter my discretion to enter into arrangements with the Government of India under any such future constitution.

8. Nothing in this Instrument affects the continuance of my sovereignty in and over this State, or, save as provided by or under this Instrument, the exercise of any powers, authority and rights now enjoyed by me as Ruler of this State or the validity of any law at present in force in this State.

9. I hereby declare that I execute this Instrument on behalf of this State and that any reference in this Instrument to me or to the Ruler of the State is to be construed as including a reference to my heirs and successors.

Given under my hand this......2.6.10..........day of ~~August,~~ Nineteen hundred and forty seven. OCTOBER

Harisingh

Maharaja Dhiraj of Jammu and Kashmir State
Rng

I do hereby accept this Instrument of Accession.
Dated this...*twenty seventh*...day of ~~August~~ *October*, Nineteen hundred and forty seven.

Mountbatten of Burma
(Governor-General of India)

Instrument of Accession.

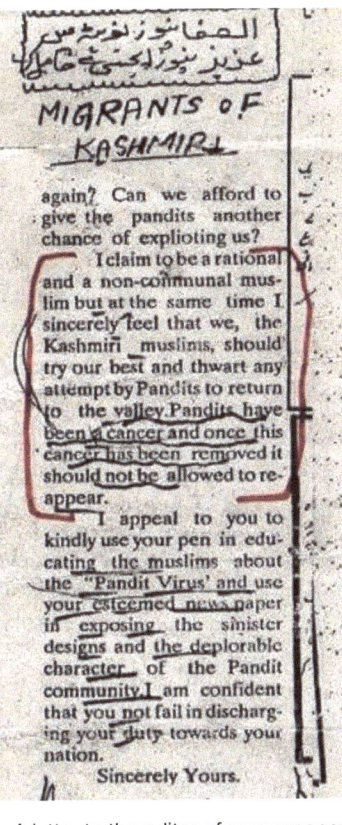

A letter to the editor of a newspaper expressing animosity towards a certain section of society.

A warning against Kashmiri Pandits in the Kashmiri newspaper *Alsafa*.

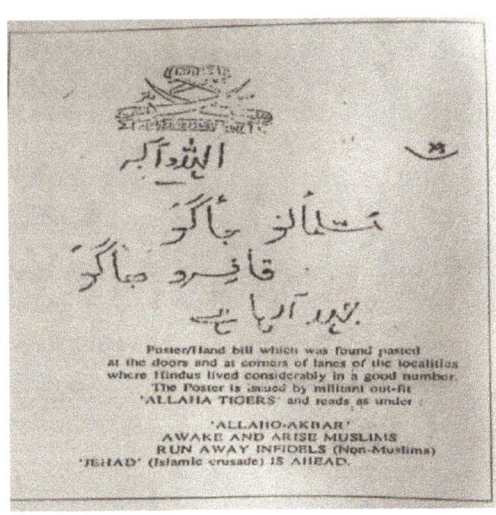

Poster that reads: '*Musalmano Jago, Kafiro Bhago, Jihad aa raha hai.*'

The present condition of the author's village house.

Thousands attending the funeral congregation of the Mehjoor Nagar victims.

Victims of Push Kriri: Julie (12), Rosy (18) and Simmi (16).

Poster at the village entrance with photos of those killed in the Chithisinghpora massacre.

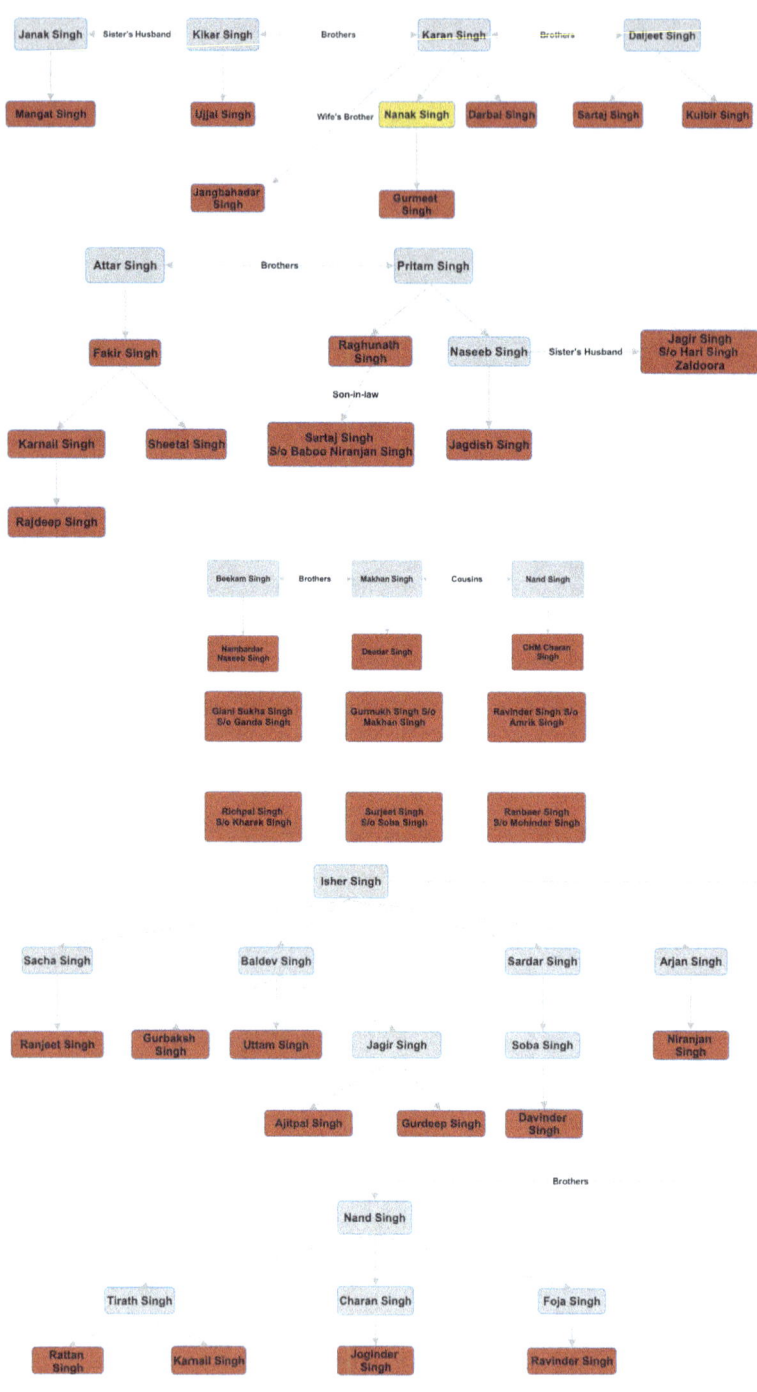

Flowchart showing the intensity of loss to the families involved. Out of the 36 people who were killed, six were individuals, three were from one family, seven from one, eight from one, and eleven from one family each.
Red=Dead, Yellow=Injured, Grey=Not involved.

A contingent of Kabalis entering Kashmir allegedly with the help of Pakistan.

Victims of the Kabali raids being relocated to Delhi.

Rescue, relief and rehabilitation efforts by Sikhs during the Kashmir floods of 2014.

17

The Sikhs of Kashmir, Circa 1490 to Present

Kulbir's thesis was titled 'State, Society and Economy in Subha-i-Kashmir under Sarkar-i-Khalsa'. It was extensive research that depicted the life of people, their rights and duties, the administrations and governance, the society and economy in the province of Kashmir under the reign of Maharaja Ranjit Singh, also known as Sikh Empire Rule from 1819 to 1846.

According to his research and the works he quoted, he established the fact that Kashmir was inhabited by Sikhs since the 1490s when Guru Nanak, the founder of the Sikh Panth, visited Kashmir for the first time. It is estimated that many people who were primarily Brahmins (Hindu) converted to the Sikh Panth and followed the teachings of the Guru.

Guru Nanak Sahib visited Kashmir Valley during his second Udasi travel between 1487 and 1490 via the Ailapather–Khilanmarg route on horseback. He visited places like Pahalgam, Mattan, Awantipura and Beerwah. He held conversations with the local people, and after listening to his sermons, a large population adopted the Sikh faith. The Kashmiri Brahmins of south Kashmir were the first to adopt it. At all of these places, the Sikh Community of Kashmir has built gurdwaras to celebrate the visit of the Guru.

During the Guruship of the fifth Guru, Guru Arjan Dev ji, Sikh missionaries were sent to Kashmir to preach the tenets of the Sikh faith, and as a result, a large followership emerged in Kashmir.

Subsequently, Guru Hargobind ji, the sixth Guru, visited Kashmir in 1620, while Guru Har Rai ji, the seventh Guru, visited Kashmir in 1660 to meet their followers and had conversations with them. The places where the Gurus stayed and held their conversations and preached their sermons were sites of gurdwaras in present-day Kashmir.

Even the tenth Guru, Guru Gobind Singh, sent a Sikh missionary to preach the Sikh faith to the people of Kashmir. The physical manifestations of the ten Gurus were condensed into the Guru Granth Sahib, the final and eternal Guru of the Sikhs in the eighteenth century. During that time, Afghan rule was established in Kashmir, and a prominent Sikh personality, Sant Rocha Singh, took charge of all missionary activities in Kashmir. And after him, when the Afghan Rule was overthrown and Sikh Rule was established in northern India from the then Punjab to Multan, Sant Mela Singh was made in charge of the missionary activities by Maharaja Ranjit Singh.

It was during the rule of Maharaja Ranjit Singh that a huge number of Sikhs from other areas relocated to Kashmir. By this time, the Sikh presence in Kashmir had become strong. Several places were given Sikh names. Hundreds of gurdwaras were constructed, and the Sikh ethics and school of thought began to gain importance in Kashmir during the Sikh rule.

According to a Kashmir historian, Abdul Rashid Khandey, the author of *The Sikh Rule in Kashmir*, after the conquest of Kashmir by Maharaja Ranjit Singh, the government under his monarchy did not attempt to change the existing demography nor attempted any forceful conversions like the previous rulers. But during the governorship of Hari Singh Nalwa, many Kashmiri Pandit families who were earlier forcefully converted to Islam adopted the Sikh faith as their brothers (Hindus) did not accept them back to their faith (Hinduism).

Another historian Mohi-ud-Din Fauq, in his book, *Tawarikh-i-Aqwam-i-Poonch*, claimed that during the period of Sarkar-i-Khalsa, the propagation of Sikh faith was done by the Nihangs and Bhai Mela Singh. Meanwhile, Sikh preachers were able to establish the centre of Sikhism in different parts of the Valley, such as in Muzaffarabad and Sialkot (Baramulla). During the period of Sarkar-i-Khalsa, areas like Maisuma, Habba Kadal and Basant Bagh in Srinagar city were densely populated by the Sikhs. Other parts of the Valley such as Trahal Pargana, Krihun, Hamal, Baramulla and areas of Muzaffarabad were also inhabited by the Sikhs and a large-scale migration of Sikhs took place from Punjab to Kashmir at the same time. By this time, gurdwaras and other religious institutions of the Sikh faith, such as dharamshalas and gurmat vidyalayas, were established at Poonch, Hazara, Muzaffarabad, Sialkot (Baramulla) and other places in the Valley.

The question that made me angry would not be answered by this, for I was told again and again that the ignorants asked questions not to get answers but to get emotional reactions, while the wise when they asked questions, was to seek knowledge. Moreover, I could not go on answering everyone who threw such stupid arguments and statements telling me that all Sikhs came from Punjab, or asking me if I had relatives in Punjab. As our oral narrative, I knew all this. But the fact that it was documented properly and had been retold by different historians and yet had been unheard by the local majority population was sad, especially when the ones who asked me such things were highly educated people.

The misconception stemmed from the misappropriation of the word Kashmiriyat and Kashmiri. The word which should signify culture started to signify religion after the Pandits were exiled from Kashmir. Anyone living in Kashmir and following the culture could be called Kashmiri. We have Kashmiri Muslims, Kashmir Pandits, Kashmiri Sikhs and Kashmiri Christians. The common thread of culture should have held us together, but the replacement of the cultural interpretation of the word Kashmiri with the religious affiliation of Islam diluted the meaning of it. Similarly, the word Punjabi and its association with the Sikh Panth was another misappropriation and resulted in identifying every Sikh, anywhere in the world, as Punjabi.

As Kashmiri Sikhs, we did not even speak the language Punjabi but were fluent in Pahadi, Urdu and Kashmiri, the major languages spoken in Kashmir. At home and within our community, we usually spoke Pahadi or Hindoo, a dialect that was a mixture of Pahadi, Punjabi and Urdu. When speaking to others, we used either Urdu or Kashmiri, depending upon the other person's conversational fluency in the language.

In terms of food habits, other than a few differences, all the Kashmiris had a common culture. The use of mutton and chicken was prominent, and the famous Kashmiri Wazwan which included around thirty different dishes were a part of our household cooking as well. The only difference was that we as Sikhs ate the jhatka, and Muslims ate the halaal cut. The use of spices and condiments, the style of preparation, and the use of peculiar vessels were all common. As Kashmiris, we used a lot of chilly and oil in our dishes, and it was the same for everyone, be it Muslims, Hindus, or Sikhs.

Our clothing was influenced by the weather and was as Kashmiri as can be. The turban was mandatory by religion. Other than that, we were free to choose what we wore, with a sense and sensibility to know what was appropriate for what place. Sikhs in Kashmir did not have any particular type of clothing in the summer, and they seldom wore the kurta-pyjama, the major dress of Punjabi Sikhs. In winter, you would find Sikhs wearing the phiran, woollen overcoats, and carrying a kangri, a small mud firepot underneath to keep the cold away, which was very specific to Kashmir. The winter asked for layers over layers of clothes to keep the body warm.

Kashmiri houses were built in a different way, and most outsiders from the rest of India found it very amusing to see such constructions. First thing, being a winter place, houses had sliding tin roofs, so the snow and rain did not accumulate on top. Most houses had three floors, in which the uppermost was always a single large hall used as an attic. The sliding tin roof was supported by an intricate mesh of wooden logs, which made the attic area very low towards the sliding ends of the roof, while the centre had a lot of head space. This hall was called Kaini and was used to store all the off-season belongings like beddings, and sometimes excess food stock.

Most rooms had a minimalistic look, as Kashmiris preferred to sit and sleep on the floor which was thickly carpeted and foam-padded to keep it warm. This made the room look empty because there were no bedstands and chairs, or tables in the room. In the richer households, the walls were panelled with woodwork which gave them a posh designer look and, at the same time, kept the room warm. One room on the ground floor had a hamaam, an improvisation of the Turkish hamaam, in which big limestone blocks which were hollow underneath, lined the floor. In extreme winters, firewood was lit inside the hollow space to make the whole floor warm. Houses of common people rarely had hamaam and the winter cold was fought using a bukhari, a metal firepot in which wood or coal, or kerosene was burnt to radiate the heat to the whole room. Small kangris with coal were carried by individuals, usually under the phirans.

Another cultural commonality in Kashmir was the lack of privacy in the households, though some modern families were more considerate nowadays. In winter, when the cold was intense, only one or two rooms in the whole house were used for daily activities. Everyone sat in the same room, and often, everyone slept in the same room. Imagine the whole family in one room. By family, it meant, not just a nuclear unit. It meant the kids, the parents, the grandparents, any guest who came, and any extended member of the family in case of a joint family. If there were more members, then a second room was used. But that would mean a second bukhari and double the cost of firewood.

Another peculiarity was that the bedrooms were open to everyone and usually used to entertain guests. The closer the guests, the more accessible the bedroom was to them. Only the very distant relatives or strangers would be seated in the living room. In most houses, the drawing room or the living room was also sans any furniture and instead has a plush carpet on the floors and big cushions placed against the walls. The living room was called baithak, or *Bethaak*, meaning sitting space. Most bedrooms did not have an attached bathroom. There was a common bathroom for the whole house, which in earlier constructions was in a separate structure. Modern houses had attached bathrooms, as in winter, it became very hard to go to the toilet building which was adjacent to the main house.

Kitchens in Kashmir were also built a little differently, as they are divided into two areas, the cooking-cum-washing area and the sitting-cum-eating area. The sitting-cum-eating area was not a dining room, as it had no dining table. People sat cross-legged on the floor forming a circle around a polythene or cloth sheet where all the food was placed. In Muslim households, the food was served in a trambi, a big plate on which four people share the food, while in non-Muslim households, people ate on separate plates.

In the Sikh faith, cleanliness was a strictly followed kitchen ethic. Anything defiled or consumed by others was considered unclean and could be consumed only by whoever ate it in the first place. While cooking and serving the food, the chef should not eat or use any vessel or spatula which was used by someone else and thus had been rendered unclean by them. By the same logic, eating from someone else's plate or food that had been half-consumed by anyone was thought to be sacrilegious. So eating in a trambi was not seen in Sikh households.

All these things were the opposite of how my wife had lived her life. In south India, privacy was a big deal. Even parents would not come into the bedrooms of their children and vice versa. Guests were hosted in the living rooms and would never enter any bedroom. Bedrooms were strictly private spaces. The houses were loaded with furniture, like beds, sofas, chairs and dining tables.

As we had lived in Jammu for a considerable amount of time, we had a fair respect towards privacy and knew how important it was, but at the same time, the roots and culture of Kashmir made those boundaries blur a little sometimes.

Most living spaces in Kashmir were common to every member of the household. This was true for everyone from all religious and social communities in Kashmir.

On the community level, the Sikhs had gurdwaras, where they assembled on an everyday basis. Every Sikh village and all the areas where the population of Sikhs was concentrated had a gurdwara where Sikhs living in the vicinity would assemble every morning and evening for community prayers. The morning prayers began with the sunrise and would last for an hour, after which tea was served in the dining hall of the gurdwara. Similarly, in the evening, the prayers started with the sunset and would last for an hour or so. The hymns from the holy book were sung in the classical ragas accompanied by the use of musical instruments like harmonica and tabla.

Gurdwaras were the central place for every life event of a Sikh. The birthdays, naming of children, baptism, marriages and death commemorations, in every happiness and sadness, the Sikhs went to a gurdwara to celebrate or to commemorate. For such functions and commemorations, a three-day event was held in gurdwaras wherein the Guru Granth Sahib was read from end to end. The whole family and their guests would be invited to the gurdwara for the function. The start of such a programme, usually around seven or eight in the morning, was with a reading of Shabd Kirtan, and then a holy sermon from the Guru, followed by an ardaas. The programme ended exactly after seventy-two hours of constant reading of the Gurbani from the Guru Granth Sahib and was followed by an elaborate function where a sumptuous langar was served after the recitation of the musical rendition of hymns. This whole programme of three days was called the Holding of Akhand Paath, or simply Akhand Paath.

In addition to such local area gurdwaras, there were a lot of gurdwaras that hold special status because of being historically important for the whole community. These places which were visited by the Gurus themselves or other prominent missionaries during their preaching were later used to construct big gurdwaras. The examples of such important gurdwaras are Gurdwara Pehli Patshahi at Awantipora, Gurdwara Pehli Patshahi at Beeru, Gurdwara Pehli Patshahi at Mattan, Gurdwara Chatti Patshahi at Shadi Marg, Shopian, Gurdwara Chatti Patshahi at Kathi Darwaza, Srinagar, Gurdwara Chatti Patshahi at Baramulla and Gurdwara Chatti Patshahi at Uri. Pehli Patshahi meant the first guru, Guru Nanak Dev ji, while Chatti Patshahi meant the sixth guru, Guru Hargobind ji. Other than these, there are some other famous gurdwaras like Gurdwara Shaheed Bunga at Srinagar, Gurdwara Kalampura, Gurdwara Tapiyana Sahib and Gurdwara Paranpeela at Baramulla.

Festivals like the birth and death anniversaries of the Gurus, the celebration of Vaisakhi, the birth anniversary of Khalsa Panth, the commemoration of the July 1984 attack on Harmandir Sahib, the martyrdom commemoration of Sikhs who fought the oppressiveness and persecution, etc., were all held in these gurdwaras by holding the Akhand Paath (Kashmir's major festivals).

Ever since I came to Kashmir, I had visited all these gurdwaras at least once. The Komal Library was housed in the compound of Gurdwara Shaheed Bunga and was just a kilometre from my house. My parents would walk to the gurdwara every morning in the summer and spend an hour or two there praying. My mother was the most religious person in our house, and sometimes, she asked me to take her to the other gurdwara, Gurdwara Chatti Patshahi at Kathidarwaza, Srinagar, which was some forty kilometres away from our house. As a child, she used to go to that gurdwara with her father and had a special affinity towards it. She felt some kind of calm there. She used to tell me stories of how she would sit behind her father on his bicycle and go to the gurdwara. She had happy childhood memories associated with the trip to the gurdwara, so whenever she asked me to take her there, which was very rare, I could not say no.

She was the one in our home who followed the proper Kashmiri customs. Her social makeup showed a Kashmiriyat to the core. My father and I found it hollow in the present context as we felt that the rituals and customs had lost their meaning in the modern world, especially when they were being done only as a formality and not from the heart.

In Kashmir, the true spirit of Atithi Devo Bhava was seen, especially among the Muslims who did not even know that such a phrase existed. The people of Kashmir were known for their hospitality, not only to their guests and acquaintances, but to strangers as well. When a guest came to one's home, the customary tea would consist of at least half a dozen snacks. In Muslim houses, chicken or mutton kabab was the most common, while in Sikh houses, the snacks would be mainly biscuits, salted mixtures and boiled eggs. As a guest, one could not return home without eating something. If the guest stayed for a meal, non-vegetarian food was mandatory. People who did not eat non-veg food were those who were specifically told not to eat by their doctors. Hence if you said no to non-veg food, the first question would be, 'Oh! Are you sick?' Another mandatory custom was to never go empty-handed to someone's house. You always bought something for the hosts, most likely fruits.

While these things were a part of hospitality, I felt burdened by this materialistic exchange. It became a burden, especially if one was poor. The host was required to feed the guests with expensive preparations, and at the same time, the guests were obliged to buy something for the hosts. One had to buy all the fancy crockery, cutlery and other fine dining articles to host a guest. In times of happiness, the custom was bearable, but when there was somebody sick at home and people came to inquire about their health, the already burdened family had to treat every visitor with utmost hospitality.

My father and I hated the forced serving of food, but my mother thought it was a necessary hospitality, a sign of being a good host. You forced the guest to eat more, even if they said no. One would ask at least three or four times before giving up. The same mentality was prevalent among the guests as well. If you didn't ask them three or four times, they would not eat. It became a match of push and pull over every meal. We tried to do away with this at our home by keeping the bowls and casseroles filled with all the dishes in front of the guests, but the custom was so deep-rooted that they would not take anything of their own accord without being forced.

One custom or so-called cultural formality that I stood up against, and was kind of successful in breaking was the wedding functions. A typical Kashmir Sikh wedding would last for a week. It had a dozen mandatory rituals and customs which had to be followed in a proper sequence and with full rigour. The first function which began two weeks before the official start of the wedding, and which was only customary now, was the rice-cleaning evening, where women from close family circles and neighbouring areas would come together to clean the rice bought for the marriage function. Rice was the staple of Kashmir, and an average person ate a kilogram of rice every day. Tea and some snacks would be given to all the women who came for the function. It was a small gathering of not more than thirty to forty women.

The next was the first official function, the Akand Paath, to take the Guru's blessing before the marriage. This was a three-day function, mostly held in the local gurdwara, and most people were only invited on the final day of the Akhand Paath. A vegetarian meal was served to all the guests who came for the event. This was also a small event with not more than fifty people.

Then after a few days, all pomp and show started with *geetan* or ladies' sangeet, a musical night for the ladies, where the whole family and extended family and another seventy to eighty acquaintances came together to sing traditional songs, folk narratives about weddings, and dance to them. This was an important function, and a full course non-vegetarian meal was served during dinner.

The next day's function was called *Chappa* and *Kangan*. It began in the morning when the bride and groom in their respective houses were massaged with a concoction of sandalwood oil, saffron, turmeric and some flour. At the same time, the sisters and other young women of the house would dig some soil and put walnuts and other seeds, symbolising the start of a new life. They would bring some soil back and add some colour to it, and then the sisters and cousins would smear a little of that soil on a chart, announcing the names of the two partners and the start of the official wedding ceremony.

In the evening, around six elderly men and women from the family would come and pour curd over the bride and the groom. After the bathing ceremony, the people from either side of the wedding party, that is from the bride's as well as the groom's side, would visit each other with bags full of new sets of clothes and four out of five Kakaars; *Kada* (iron bracelet), *Kanga* (wooden comb), *Khachera* (boxers) and *Kirpan* (small sword). The fifth was the *Kesh* (hair) already in every Sikh, the reason for uncut beards and hair. Both the bride and the groom had to wear all four items. These assortments of smaller ceremonies took place after that and finally, the day ended with a full course non-vegetarian meal. That night everyone danced and sang until they were too tired to continue.

The next evening was the grand function of *Mehendi Raat*, where all the invitees sat together and drew mehendi on their palms. The bride and groom were required to apply it on their hands, arms and feet as well. This was an important function, and over two hundred people attended. Meals, snacks, cold drinks, etc., were served throughout the night.

On the following morning, the main wedding ritual, which was the central agreement, and the only religiously mandated event, happened. A *baraat* from the groom's side consisting of around 100 to 150 people would go to the bride's house early in the morning and would be treated for breakfast. After that, a few people from both parties would go to the gurdwara for the *Anand Karaj* (marriage) along with the bride and the groom. The couple would take the four pheras or rounds around the Guru Granth Sahib, while the Bhai Sahib—priest—recited the four commandments for the couple.

This was the actual wedding ceremony, after which a lunch buffet, which was also a grand feast organised by the bride's side, was served for all the people who were invited by the bride's side, as well as all the baraatis who accompanied the groom's side. The groom and bride then would go for a tedious photo shoot, after which both of them, now a married couple, would go to the groom's house. But the ceremonies did not end there. In the evening, all the relatives of the groom came for another ceremony called the *mooh-dikhai*, which meant seeing the face of the new bride.

The next day was a grand feast given by the groom's side to all the relatives, and the close relatives of the bride were invited for a meet and greet. Earlier, the bride's relatives would not join this feast but would come on a separate day after three or four days of the wedding for a meetup. A small function called *Andar Badhna*, meaning going inside the groom's house would be organised for this.

All these functions and event span over a week, and on an average, ten to fifteen lakh rupees was spent on all these events by each side respectively. In addition to that, a lot of gold and apparel were exchanged between families depending on each person's financial status. Even in a humble household, during these functions, the meals served consisted of at least two varieties of mutton, two varieties of chicken, around seven vegetarian dishes, an array of chutneys, rice and chapatti in the main course, and around five to ten snack stalls for small eats like aloo-tiki, dahi bhalla, gulab jamun, coffee, ice-cream, gol-gappas, etc.

The invitees and guests also help the family in any way possible to lighten their financial burden. Gifts in the form of money had to be given to the hosts, the first being Thali, which was the amount given on the day of the mehendi, the second being Nindra, or the amount given on the day of the feast, the third being Sastrikal, given to the groom on the morning when he went to the bride's house for the wedding, and then finally, money given as mooh-dikhai, to the bride when she came to the groom's house. The first two were common to both the bride's and groom's sides, and the latter two were specifically given to the groom and bride, respectively.

On average, a guest spent around two to three thousand if he attended a wedding. Even if one did not go to the wedding, he was obligated to send all these monetary gifts to the host's family, in lieu of weddings the host had attended or would attend in the future. So it became an eternal give-and-take ritual.

In my wedding, I broke all the rules and rituals and just organised a small function on the first day of mehendi, that too without any ritualistic events of putting the mehendi on my hands and feet, and then the Anand Karaj and the feast next day. There were only seventy guests for the feast. All other ceremonies were left out, and there was no exchange of gold or clothes between the families.

The culture of expensive marriages had put a lot of people under a severe burden, both Sikhs as well as Muslims. The show-off for the sake of society compelled the people to take hefty loans for marriage functions. The Sikh community, which was already under financial stress, drained money in this nonsensical way. Young people who earned not more than twenty thousand a month had to repay such loans for many years unless the parents took responsibility. The previous generation were landowners and had accumulated some wealth, but it was eroding fast. Without the assistance of parents, our generation was not capable of taking responsibility for their own wedding expenses. Now, our people, who were zamindars and jagirdaars, had sold their properties in the villages and came to towns and cities and built small houses. They had no more properties to sell and enjoy the lifestyles they used to have.

All the ceremonies had become financially draining; even funerals and deaths were expensive these days. In our community, the custom of grieving went on for ten days, in which for the first seven days, every evening, people would go to the bereaved family and sit together for the evening prayers. The host family had to serve everyone tea and some snacks. On the last three days, an Akhand Paath was held, at the end of which hundreds of people who had come for condolences were served food. Though vegetarian, the expense still went up to a lakh. Among Muslims, the grieving custom is only for four days and was mostly inexpensive, unlike our community.

The Sikhs had absorbed the Kashmiriyat, or we could say the Kashmiriyat of Sikhs was their cultural root while religion was their spiritual root. Kashmiri Sikhs had always been Kashmiri Sikhs. They were not outside settlers who could go back to their place, their homes, or their homelands. Kashmir belonged to them as much as it belongs to the Kashmiri Muslims and Kashmiri Pandits. They were, like Pandits and Muslims, natives of Kashmir.

18

The ISI Blueprint

Srinagar, Kashmir
19 October 2021, Tuesday
Morning

The plan was set. The first thing Indu wanted to do in the morning was to look for tickets. Before sleeping, I called Bhanu again, and he had decided on a date, 4 November, to leave from Jammu to Delhi. We would be taking my car and driving to Delhi. That meant I had to reach Jammu before the fourth to drop my parents there. But Indu had to join her institute any time after 26 October. Our Jammu house was a small one-room accommodation given to us by the government for Kashmiri migrants. So we could not stay there as there was no room. She had never visited that house. Also, Indu wanted to celebrate my birthday together, which was on 30 October. So after deliberating every possibility, we decided to book her ticket on 2 November from Srinagar, and I would drive to Jammu on the third of November with my parents and Ramneek.

We discussed it with my parents, and they were fine with it, but with one big suggestion. Before going away, we had to visit my relatives, especially my maternal aunts and uncles. And as a newlywed couple, we hadn't had our dinners at their houses. We would have to manage all that before leaving.

That meant we were to have dinner or lunch at five places and none of them could be clubbed in a single day. Indu, on the other hand, had already wasted a lot of time, and her mid-term deadline was on 1 November. Managing and planning all this gave us a new level of anxiety. I arrived at a middle ground. We would accept invitations from only three people, and that too on the dates we would decide.

'There will be a big fuss. Who will you say no to? And to whom will you say yes?' Mama asked me.

'I guess I will say no to Kaki masi and Manjit uncle. We can visit them the next time we come to Kashmir. It is not a big deal. Both of them will understand. I will talk to them personally,' I replied to her.

It was very hard to say no to my mother because she never forced anything on us. She would ask only once, and if I said no, she would oblige but with a visibly sad face. All my life, I never argued with her, ever. Mostly I agreed with whatever she said, and whenever I didn't agree, she wouldn't push again.

Pavaam only, Indu often said about my mother. Over the years, I never understood the proper meaning of this Malayalam word. It could mean different things depending on her tone and the situation she used it. But I always knew what she intended to say. It could mean naive, innocent, gullible, a person who knew nothing about the ways of the world, sweet, or lovable. It was not a feeling of pity but of empathy and love that came when someone was too good.

'They haven't even asked or invited us yet, and you people are planning the decline as well,' Indu was bemused at our confidence.

'The moment we tell them we are leaving, that is the first thing they will do. Because you had a strict schedule, I have been declining their invites for the last month,' I told her. 'Three days, that too only three hours for one feast. That is the maximum I will ask of you,' I added, sensing her discomfort.

'I have already met everyone. We can just go and meet them. Why do we have to have meals at their places?' she asked.

'It's a tradition. Doesn't it happen in Kerala?' I asked her. 'Remember when I visited in February, I had meals at most of your relatives' 'houses?'

She did not reply immediately.

'Ok, I will make time. But then, I want to cook biryani on your birthday. So don't agree to visit anyone on the thirtieth,' she said after a long pause.

Inviting a newly wedded couple for feasts was a tradition in Kashmir, organised mostly to introduce a new member to close relatives. There would be big feasts, and the hosts would go all out with their hospitality, cooking and entertaining. It was no different in Kerala as well. When I visited her house in Kerala, I was invited by most of her relatives. Their cuisines were a lot different than ours; their textures and aromas were something that I had not experienced much. I got to taste a variety of food other than the famous idli-dosa-sambhar. I relished dishes like appam, idiyappam, puttu, kozhukkattai, ada and others. Indu's parents prepared different kinds of fish; ayala, kilimeen and karimeen. The most noticeable difference was the use of coconut in every preparation, sometimes as oil, sometimes as milk and sometimes grated.

Until the afternoon of that day, we kept on planning the dates and my birthday. Indu's anxiety kept swelling when we started talking about how much work was left for her to finish before the deadline. We decided to keep our planning and daydreaming aside and work.

'I will not be able to give you any time for the rest of our stay here. So you also find something to do,' she told me as we entered the bedroom.

'I have to go on Covid duty from tomorrow,' I pulled her into a hug.

'For three or four hours, you will go. I mean to say find something to do when you are home as well. Why don't you revise the story and send it to some magazine, or write something about the current killings, or Kashmiri Sikhs? Anything along those lines,' she said as she pushed me away and took her laptop out of the bag.

'Ok. I'll brainstorm on it, and see what I can come up with,' I told her and took out my laptop.

'I can stay in the room, right? You don't have any meetings?' I asked. When she had a meeting or saw any patients, she wanted complete privacy. She never shared details of her interactions with patients with me.

What she suggested put my mind on overdrive. I could see how many things I could write about and how many topics about Kashmir had never come to light. I could foresee all the stories I could write, about Mehjoor Nagar, about Chithisinghpora, about 1947, or the battles, the survivor stories, the eyewitness accounts, the current killings, the last thirty years, and so on.

The first thing I wanted to do on that day was to revise and finalise the Chithisinghpora story, as it was already complete. Once I got into writing mode, I could carry the energy to new stories. It took me three hours to do that, and then I gave the new draft to Indu to read when she got a break from her study.

'This is far better than what you gave me earlier. Well done,' she told me after reading it. She also said, 'Now send it to some magazines.'

'No, I am not sending this. There is no relevance to it right now. But it's October. If I write about 1947, that would be better, because, unlike the rest of India, Kashmir killings and incidents happened at the end of October and the first week of November. So as a commemoration of that, if I submit a story to some magazine, it would be more relevant,' I said.

'You have already written a story about that in *The Week*,' she replied.

'No. That was 1947, but not Kashmir. It was a different story from Pakistan, a place called Thao Khalsa,' I told her.

'And the Ravneet wala novel you are writing is also based on 1947. Why don't you pick that up and work on it?' she added.

'No. That's a different project, and that's too big to finish. It will take me another six months to finish that. I am talking about Kashmir's 1947. How do I explain it to you?' I replied to her.

She did not understand what I meant because she could not intuit ninety per cent of the thoughts. She called my major work, a multi-generational historical fiction, partly covering 1947, the Ravneet wala novel after its protagonist.

'Then you do it. Write what you want, and then show me instead of talking about it,' she replied in an equally irritable tone.

In 2015, a group of people from Punjab, led by a historian, Dr Sukhpreet Singh Udoke, came to Kashmir to make a documentary on 1947 and how it affected the Sikhs. Veerji was their contact person in Kashmir, and as a result, I was roped into the project. They conducted a lot of interviews with the people and made a documentary about it. I listened to most of those interviews at Veerji's house when they came back with the video recording. Veerji told me to pen down the essential details so that if we ever wanted to write something about it, we would have the notes. Again in 2018, we went to those villages for a different reason, realising the questions we asked them during our previous interview did not bring out a complete picture. Earlier, we were concentrating on the incident alone, not the trauma and the mental agony after it.

I had those notes on my Google Docs. And the completed documentary was also on my laptop. Instead of talking to Indu more about it, I thought of writing a skeleton draft of what I could. I was never a writer who planned ahead of writing. So I went with the flow. By the time evening tea was served, I had a rough draft with places marked in bold where I had to add more information when I revised this draft.

I was too engrossed in writing that I hadn't checked the messages on my phone. During tea, I replied to them. One message from Veerji was a link to a news article. The same news article was forwarded to Indu by some of her friends from Bangalore, and co-incidentally she had also not looked at her phone during the day. She had a three-hour-long Zoom meeting, and all of us were waiting for that to end so we could have the evening tea together.

The popular news channel Zee News published an article titled, 'Pakistan's ISI's conspiracy against Jammu and Kashmir exposed. Blueprint reveals a major plot', with the subheading, 'The development comes at a time when eleven civilians have been killed by terrorists in Jammu and Kashmir in October.'

In the article, the news claimed that an alleged directive of the ISI—Pakistan's intelligence service—had emerged, which listed twenty-two points to be followed. They were enumerated as follows:

1. Target every non-local official, whether in the Valley or at their native place.
2. Target non-locals who came to the Valley to stay for long.
3. Target Kashmiri Pandits who migrated from Kashmir in the early 1990s and were now planning to shift back.
4. Every non-local employee, whoever it might be, irrespective of the department he or she was employed with.
5. Target every house of J&K police personnel whoever was involved in the anti-Kashmir struggle.
6. Petrol bombs, stones, etc., to be thrown at informers' locations locally.
7. Wherever any non-local was located, he was to be warned to leave the Valley at the earliest.
8. Local government employees should show their resentment against occupier regime orders and circulars which tried to curb their freedom and went against their work.

9. Sports events organised by the occupier regime and their stooges to be banned/boycotted.
10. Whoever was involved in government/occupational forces events to be dealt with harshly.
11. Kashmiri Pandits who migrated from Kashmir and were now showing their faces again in the Valley not to be welcomed.
12. Target those heads of educational institutions who were hand in glove with the occupier.
13. Boycott all those media outlets whose names emerged as collaborators.
14. Maintain distance with the occupier stooges and their forces, especially J&K police, whoever was directly or indirectly involved in the anti-Kashmir cause.
15. Identify every collaborator and traitor.
16. Freedom fighters to prioritise their targets according to the Kashmir cause.
17. Locals should shun their dependence on non-locals.
18. Keep distance from elements that were against the Kashmir cause.
19. Try to understand the negative impact of non-locals residing in J&K.
20. Non-locals were to be targeted irrespective of their nature of work. In the directives, it was written that 'this act might look vague, but in the long run it will prove beneficial and effective for the Kashmir cause.'
21. Since outsiders came to J&K for harassing, brutalising and controlling J&K affairs, it was mandatory to expand operations outside J&K, and it would be intensified.
22. Target government properties, developmental projects, bridges, schools, colleges and sports infrastructure.

Indu and her concerns about the list and our future in Kashmir were serious. By the time we finished reading it, the tea was cold. One look at Indu told me that she had evaluated all the scenarios with different permutations and combinations of Kashmir's future and ours.

'This is complete bullshit,' I put my phone down and took the cup.

'This is not bullshit. This is very disturbing and serious,' Indu told me.

'I don't know. But I can't believe this news. Not everything is done by ISI,' I replied.

'How does it matter? Who and why do they do it, that's not even the point. You read points two, five and twenty, and you read points eight, eleven, twelve and twenty-two. That makes both you and me their targets,' she said as she held her cup without drinking the tea.

'We should leave earlier,' she added, her gaze fixed on the teacup.

'We have booked your ticket already. It is only two weeks away. We will be leaving soon,' I replied.

'And how do you know nothing will happen in these two weeks? They killed those two civilians at their homes on Sunday. How do you know they won't come here?' she put the cup down without even taking a sip. She got up from the chair and left for the bedroom.

'Hey, sit, don't go,' I called out.

'I am not feeling good. I need to go to the washroom,' she replied. I knew that feeling. The stomach is the first organ that revolts when we hear something like that.

While she was not there, I kept asking myself, what if this list was actually true? What if they actually start killing everyone, according to the list at their homes? Would it be like 1947, when people were sitting inside their homes and had no clue what was happening?

They had already killed two people in their houses the day before, and with this new list claiming to intensify such killings, it could be true as well. The whole day I had been reading the notes and watching the documentaries of the 1947 victims. Was it a sign for me? Should I act on it?

I had just finished writing the story of a survivor who was a kid in 1947, sitting in his attic eating apricots when his village was attacked. Could the same happen in 2021, I thought to myself.

19

Survivor Stories

Baramulla, Kashmir
October–November 1947

As narrated by the survivors

I was ten or eleven years old when it happened. The winter had already kicked in as it was the end of October, and I remember most of the villagers were still busy with the apple produce. The harvest was almost over, but storing the apples in wooden caskets was tiring work. One had to first arrange a layer of apples, then spread a thin layer of hay over it before putting another layer of apples. A casket would hold three or four layers of apples, and you had to be careful that there was no bad apple in the casket. One bad apple could spoil the bunch. Most men from the village would go to their orchards by sunrise, taking their lunch along, and returned once the sun set.

One day, I was eating the apples and apricots, stealthily, in the attic and looking out through the small window. It was evening, the sky was orange in the horizon, and the men had already started coming back from the apple orchards. During the harsh winter, people preferred to stay indoors. The snow would usually be knee-deep, and going out to buy anything was not possible. Kashmiris adapted to this weather by rationing a large number of food grains, lentils and dried vegetables. At home, we had already installed the *Bukhari*, and the attic was full of firewood for the winters. There were dried eggplants and gourds, a lot of red chillies, and a box of apricot. Every house would have such a store, either as a roof-top attic or a backyard, where they would keep everything.

As a protection against this biting cold, heavy quilts and blankets were brought out and used. The same blankets were useless in the summers. All those heavy quilts and blankets and winter items would also be kept in the attic in the summers. In summer, I would never visit the attic because a lot of bees would make their hives under the roof.

Our schools were already closed due to the Partition. The past few months were very troublesome. India had gained its independence, and a new country called Pakistan was formed. Muslims from all over India were crossing over to that newly formed country, which they said was exclusively for Muslims. All the non-Muslims who lived in that country were coming to India.

Two months after Partition, Jammu and Kashmir was still a politically single unit under the rule of one king, Maharaja Hari Singh. Demographically, there were two different areas. Kashmir, a Muslim-majority area and Jammu, a Hindu-majority area. And when they were asked to decide whether they wanted to accede to India or Pakistan, the people stayed in limbo. Kashmir was a state with a large Muslim population and a Hindu ruler. The limbo was broken when Muslim revolutionaries from western Kashmir, tribals from Pakistan and Afghanistan called Kabalis, entered the state through Dir district to capture and annex Kashmir with Pakistan forcibly by invasion.

Notwithstanding the invasion, mass massacre and annexation attempts, Maharaja Hari Singh signed the instrument of accession with India on 26 October 1947. The 'Kabali' raid was devastating, destroying and shocking. Thousands of people were killed, mostly Sikhs and Hindus.

When I was eating those apricots, I heard a loud clamour. Hundreds of people poured into the village from all sides. They were big, over six feet, and carried axes, swords, spears, staffs and guns. A lot of them were shouting some profanities or others, their slogans were, *Sardar ka sar, Hindu ka zar, aur Musalman ka ghar*' which meant a Sikh's head, a Hindu woman and a Muslim's property. Their mission was to kill or convert as many non-Muslims as they could so as to shift the demography of Kashmir to a Muslim-only place and help the Kashmiris to accede to Pakistan. This happened on 27 October 1947. At that time, we did not know that the ruler of Kashmir had already signed an annexation with India. The Kabalis were trying to liberate Kashmir, and a lot of Kashmiri revolutionaries were supporting them and guiding them to our villages. Later I came to know that they were marching towards the Airdome, the Kashmir Airport, in Srinagar. If the invaders captured it, the Indian army would not be able to come to Kashmir and defend it. On the way to the airport, the invaders were annihilating every non-Muslim village.

Ours was a small and beautiful village consisting of not more than fifty households, all Sikhs. The single-story mud-and-wood houses with sloping tin roofs lined the path to the village centre. The centre of the village had a large playground and a gurdwara. The village spread out from the centre like a web and ended with the jungles on two sides, and step-farming lands on the third. The fourth side formed the entrance to the village. There were only two two-storied buildings in the whole village. One was the house of the sarpanch, and the other was the gurdwara. Green with trees and golden with rice fields on its periphery, the village had the lesser Himalayas in the background and was strikingly picturesque, the kind that people now photographed, framed and hung on living room walls. The villagers practised step-farming during the rice season and also grew apples and walnuts.

The Kabali entry into the village was not by stealth. It was a brazen one. The tribal people were savages. They loved to slaughter. The smell and taste of blood fuelled them. They killed not because they were told but because they enjoyed it, they loved it.

The Kabalis ran into the village and unleashed all their rage on the villagers. Shouting slogans and roaring like wild animals, they put a sword in anyone that they saw. Kids were playing, and women were cooking while men were doing different work. Before they realised what was happening, they were already dead. The handful of people tried to run or hide. Those running were chased, killed, and then dragged back to the village. Those hiding were hunted which proved to be an exciting exercise for the Kabalis. They played hide-and-seek, calling them out, telling them what was waiting for them and how they would chop off their hands and feet before killing them.

There were a lot of slogans and noise, cries, and people shouting. "*Naso, Kabali aye* (Run! The Kabalis have come)". I was scared. I was frozen, seeing everything from the window without moving.

They put spears through the people and left them hanging there. With their brutal force, they cut people in half, and there were headless bodies everywhere. When a big man with an enormous sword brought it down on the head of a person, he was cut from his head to his torso in one blow. When he withdrew his sword, all his insides splattered out. I vomited on myself.

By the time they reached my house, the hue and cry in the village had already reached us. My father was out somewhere while my mother was on the ground floor, cooking dinner. My younger brother, who was just a two-year-old toddler, was mostly in bed or crawling beside my mother. I saw a big man drag my mother out of our house. He was holding her by her hair. Another one tossed my brother onto the ground in our courtyard. I wanted to run downstairs. I wanted to cry. I wanted to close my eyes so I couldn't see what was going to happen. But I could do none of that. I was wet with my vomit and sweat, and my body did not move at all. They kicked my brother repeatedly, and then someone just put him out of his misery by putting a spear through his heart. The one holding my mother's hair with one hand had a big sword in the other. He pushed her towards another guy who tore the front of her shirt, impaled her on the ground, and rode her while the former ran into the opposite house. When he was done with her, he stabbed her with a sword multiple times till the ground was red with her blood.

After a tireless bloodbath, and a ground full of bodies, the village looked like a graveyard. The large central ground between my house and the house into which that guy ran was filled with multiple bodies. I knew them all as it was a small village, and everyone knew everybody. More Kabalis were arriving, each dragging bodies and throwing them like they were bringing sacks of rice to a warehouse.

Several women and children were captured alive and brought to the central ground. They gave them a choice, to convert to Islam or die. They cut their hair and told them to recite the *kalima,* the initiation verse, and threatened them with death. My body was stiff. Even breathing had become difficult. Those women and children were not ready to convert. And they did not ask twice. The moment they said no, a sword travelled across their body. One after another, they killed them, sometimes torturing them before they were killed.

A guy came holding a woman who had an infant in her arms. I knew her, too. I used to call her chachi, as my father was friends with her husband. They first snatched her infant from her. They placed a knife on the child and told her to convert or they would kill the baby. She fell, crying hysterically, begging them to spare the baby. The monsters liked the view. Slapping the kid had a direct effect on the women. It worked like magic on her. She gave up and yelled repeatedly, 'I will convert to Islam. Please don't harm my child.' A lot of the attackers spoke the same language as us, Pahaadi, the language of the hill people. When they heard her, they told the big man something, which was inaudible to me. They gave the baby back to her. She embraced her with all her love. She was asked to recite the verse as proof of converting to Islam, and then she could accompany them. One of them claimed her as his own and said that no one else should lay a hand on her. She said something to them. The one who had claimed her slapped her so hard that she fell to the ground. And everyone around started laughing. There were no more villagers left. I could not see my father in the pile of bodies. I did not see his head in the heap either. He had gone to the orchard. I kept praying that he would come and save me.

Many Kabalis started marching out of the village, but a handful stood there around chachi and her infant. Then, the person who slapped her picked her up by her hair. She was holding the child and crying loudly. After that, something unusual happened. The remaining Kabalis dragged all the bodies to my house. It took them a while as there were more than a hundred people. They kicked the heads like they were footballs, spluttering blood in the air. And then they set fire to the house. I guessed my chachi had asked for a proper religious cremation for the dead and that she would convert to their religion and marry one of them after that. They had been destroying the villages since they entered Kashmir, but they had not able to convert even one Sikh so far. Some of the women would jump into the wells, some into the Jhelum, or kill themselves. They always choose death instead of converting. My chachi here was something they could make an example of, tell others that this woman was the one who loved her life more than her religion, which the Sikhs were so proud of. Chachi kept crying the whole time, hugging her child, and kissing the child like a madwoman all over his face. She asked the man something again, who let go of her hair. She walked a few steps forward and bowed in front of my house like we used to bow in front of our holy book, our Guru. Then she stood up and walked to the man who had set fire to the houses. All eyes were on her. She said something again. There was a loud cheer all around. The flames had started to grow bigger and bigger. I could now feel the heat. I tried to move, to jump, but my body was paralysed with all that I had seen. I feel the heat more and more. Though the fire had not reached the attic yet, the smoke was now cluttering my view of the outside.

 I closed my eye and gave up. I knew I was going to be burned in a few minutes. My mother and younger brother were dead, and I did not know if my father was alive or not. I thought it was better to burn and die along with them. I had no other option. It was then, when my eyes were closed, that I heard a loud cry, which I recognised as the war cry of the Sikhs—*Bole So Nihal Sat Sri Akal*. I had heard it hundreds of times in my life; I myself had shouted it several times. It was my chachi.

 I opened my eyes and looked around. Chachi shouted again, '*Bole So Nihal Sat Sri Akal*' with a smile on her face. She ran, not to flee, not to get away from the Kabalis, but towards the burning houses and jumped into the flames along with her child. Their faces became pale and their laughter disappeared. They yelled profanities at her though she was away from their sight, embracing the fire. The Kabalis lost her. The last thing they heard before she jumped into the fire was screaming, *Bole So Nihal*. I heard that and, in my heart, I answered with, *Sat Sri Akal*.

Somehow that gave me courage. I ran towards the rear window and jumped out. After a moment of dizziness, I found myself in pain both from a burned arm and from the uneven landing. At least, I was alive. I ran to the only place that came to my mind, my aunt's home in the next village. I ran and ran, not knowing for how many hours. My feet were bleeding, but I kept on running. When I reached the village, it was already burning. The ground was red with blood. There were bodies everywhere, a few of the men were still alive but bleeding. I sat near one until he, too, died. I slept next to his body, the blood from him and others had drenched my clothes as well.

I was woken up by some people when it was already night. They took me to their home and dressed me. I don't know how many days I stayed with them. When I was able to walk again, they took me back to my village where some survivors had come back.

I came to know later that it had been almost six days, the Indian army had come to Kashmir, and the Kabalis had gone back after the battle with the army. We, then, stayed in the camp in Srinagar for many months. I could not find my father. He was also killed. I lived with one of my uncles, who had survived the ordeal somehow. He had also lost his family.

What haunted me over the years was not all the goriness that I encountered but my chachi's smile. She jumped into the fire with a smile. That smile I would never forget. It was godly. I felt guilty for too long for running away from there.

Like me, hundreds and thousands lost everything, their family, their loved ones, their homes and their hopes. It was with Waheguru's blessing that we survived and have come so far again from that massacre.

Whenever I thought about it, I asked myself the question. What was my fault, my Karma for witnessing all that? Why was I kept alive? And more than that, I asked myself about that woman, my chachi. Why did she do it? How could she do that with a smile? And what did her smile mean?

Was it pride in that moment of death, feeling satisfied that she did not give up her religion and faith? Was it the satisfaction that she had fooled the Kabalis into doing her bidding, the last rites of her villagers? Or did she lose her sanity and smile like a mad person? Whatever it was, the truth died with her.

We met this person accidentally one day in the library when Veerji, Sudeep and I were talking about how our community was still lagging. He was around eighty-four-years-old now, but his memory was sharp. He had come to visit the gurdwara and had come into the library. He was looking through a picture book while we were talking, and he interrupted us all of a sudden, saying, 'You have the privilege of sitting and talking about how our community is lagging because your parents and their parents have done a lot to empower you. They have come from nothing, zero, and still managed to come this far. With 250 rupees and a log of wood we restarted our life.'

When we asked him what he meant by it, he narrated to us his story. After he finished his story, he asked us a question, but we were in shock so we could not reply.

He asked us again, 'You are saying the Sikhs are a hundred years behind other communities. You should be thankful that they are at least this far-educated and prosperous. What other community would come back from that kind of trauma in seventy years and prosper so much despite all that? The majority blamed us for decades for fighting against the Kabalis and providing the Indian army with a safe passage during 1947. The contempt and anger we faced all those years! We were still recovering from it when the era of militancy started. You people, tell me how will such a community not be hundred years behind?'

A scathing agony took over our consciousness. My cheekbones ached from trying to control my tears, and my eyes were blinking trying to keep the tears away. Veerji had a line of tears that formed droplets sticking to his beard. Sudeep was quiet. Nobody could reply to him. It took us some time to speak again.

It was as if he could read us. He knew we were not in a state to reply. So he stood up and said, *Waheguru ji ka Khalsa, Waheguru ji ki Fateh* and left with a smile. We could just fold our hands in reply, nobody uttered a word. When he left, I went to the washroom and cried to calm myself, to release the pain. I washed my face and came back to the library. We were all so dumbstruck by his story that we did not even ask his name and his whereabouts.

We did not know about this incident at all. Later, we traced the story and came to know that the lady's elder son, the one the man referred to as chachi, had also survived the massacre. For us, this story was thought-provoking.

The story gave us an impetus to find more stories like that. We made a plan to visit the villages where there were survivors and interview them. After several visits, I had enough material to write about it. I gathered a lot of knowledge from the visits, and during that season of intense activity, I made a lot of notes. Some people we met had a very ghastly story to tell about their survival.

***

One such person we met, was the sole survivor from his whole contingent that tried to escape the Kabalis who were chasing them. They were a group of sixty to seventy people including more than two dozen women and around fifteen to twenty children. He was nine years old at that time. A resident of some village in Muzaffarabad, which the Kabalis had annihilated. These few survivors were running for their lives through the mountains and were being chased by the Kabalis. Harsh winters and hunger were chasing them as well. After two days of running through the thick forest, they reached a meadow and could see a village in front of them. Their hopes were snuffed when they saw the houses in that village already burnt down in the fire. They knew the Kabalis had already reached it, and the villagers had met the same fate as theirs.

The people in the group unanimously decided to take the last step. In the meadow, there were many huts, remnants of the Gujjar-Bakarwals, the nomadic community of shepherds who would stay in such meadows in summer and go to the valley in winter. Those nomadic hutments had three large compartments to accommodate the shepherds and their cattle. All the fleeing villagers assembled in front of one hut and instructed the women and children to go inside and rest while the men went to the surrounding forest to bring branches and twigs. They covered the hut with a lot of wood. All the men also went inside. Then, they set it on fire with all of them inside.

The person who told us about this escaped the burning hut through a small window and ran away from there. He remembered running and crying until it was evening and then falling unconscious. He woke up at a Muslim's house in a nearby village. Later, he was given off to a Sikh family who adopted him as their son.

In another such case, somewhere in Baramulla's Uri, on the bridge over Jhelum, a thousand Sikhs were surrounded from both sides. When they knew that death was imminent, the men went to fight and buy some time for the women and children to jump into the mighty Jhelum. The women did not want to be captured. For them, capture meant a worse fate than death. Faced with the choice of being captured or dead, they happily and willingly chose death. There were no survivors from the group. The story was told by the Muslims of the nearby village to the journalists and newspapers and later became an oral tradition.

In a place called Chura, located some fifty kilometres on the highway connecting Srinagar to Baramulla, an orchard full of fruitless trees were made into a spectacle with the heads of Sikh men tied to the branches. Their bodies were under the tree. The grass had turned red.

The Kashmiri Muslims who saw it said, 'It was like *Kiyamat*, like something out of *jahaannum*. We could not eat or sleep for days after seeing the massacre. If you dig the orchard anywhere, you will still find human bones there.'

More than two thousand people were killed in this small village. A small memorial stands there today.

Throughout the district of Baramulla, wells were full of dead bodies of women and children who had committed suicide to evade capture by the Kabalis. They attacked not only Kashmir but also the bordering areas of the Jammu province, like Mirpur, Rajouri and Poonch.

In Mirpur, in one of the villages on the border, over 19,000 Hindus and Sikhs were killed. The village had a population of over 25,000, and due to Partition, another 15,000 refugees from other villages had come to Mirpur. When the Kabalis attacked Mirpur, they were faced with tough resistance on their first invasion. But the next day, again, they came with all their might and invaded the village, and burnt it down. They killed the people mercilessly and raped and humiliated the women. Scared of losing their integrity, hundreds of young women committed suicide by jumping into the wells. Some begged their fathers to behead them or kill them before they were raped by the Kabalis. Many fathers killed their daughters on that day. The Kabalis took about 5000 girls from both communities as captives, who were later raped and tortured. They were then sold in the flesh markets of Pakistan, Afghanistan and Arab countries.

Similarly, in Rajouri and Poonch, two areas with a population of over 5000 and 10,000, saw an influx of refugees from Pakistan. Their population swelled to 40,000 and 50,000 respectively. When the Kabalis invaded the town, over 30,000 Sikhs and Hindus were killed in both areas.

In Kashmir, the worst affected area was the Baramulla district where an estimated 25,000 Sikhs were killed. The number of Hindus was uncertain as the district did not have much population from the Hindu community. But observers placed it over 2000. There were thousands of suicides, where women and children killed themselves. In some villages, the women folk requested to be beheaded by their own family members rather than being captured. The elders came together and beheaded dozens of women to protect them from being raped, tortured or humiliated at the hands of the Kabalis.

One mind-numbing story that we came across was from a village called Satarna, where a survivor told us how women were so frightened that they fought among themselves to get beheaded first. When one woman fell down, the other would instantly line up behind her and bend forward to bring their neck to the executioner's blade. Most of these were young, unmarried girls. Those who had children chose to jump into the wells along with their children.

In our Budgam district, which was farther on the trail the Kabalis had taken, the loss of life was less as compared to Baramulla, where people had been caught unaware and were slaughtered mercilessly. By the time the news of the Kabali raids had reached the district, the small villages had already been evacuated and people from those villages had reached Attina and Ichahama where the Sikh population was very high. The Sikhs prepared for an offensive to fight the Kabalis instead of retreating or evacuating to Srinagar. They had the privilege of time, knowing beforehand about the invasion, which the people of Baramulla did not.

My father had told me that during the Kabali raid, our village house was burned to the ground, and my grandfather built a new house at a new location years later. At the place of the old house now stood a small plantation of pears and walnuts. There was no loss of life in our village as everybody had vacated their houses well in advance and moved to other villages. Some had gone to the adjoining village of Ichahama, where the deciding battle between the Kabalis and Sikhs took place. That was the game-changing battle that decided the fate of Kashmir. If not for that, Kashmir would have been a part of Pakistan.

These battles not only changed the fate of Kashmir but also changed the fate of Sikhs, for better or for worse.

20

Battle of Ichahama and Attina

Budgam, Kashmir
November 1947

The Kabalis kept moving towards Srinagar Airport. They were keen on capturing the airport as it was central to their plan of occupying Kashmir. Kashmir was connected to the rest of India through two roads and the airport. The Mughal Road, which was built by the Mughals, encountered high snowfall from October till May and was usually closed for traffic then. It is considered one of the most dangerous roads in India, narrow and lined by steep mountains on one side, while the other gives way to deep cliffs and gorges. The route was traditionally used by the Mughals for trade, and was in a very bad shape before Partition, so much so that it could not be used to transport the army from Jammu to Kashmir. The other highway, built by the English, was much safer but due to weather hazards in winter, it remained closed for short stretches frequently. It took a few days to reach Kashmir from Jammu by highway. So it was important for the Kabalis to capture the airport as it was the most feasible route for the Indian army to come to Kashmir for the counterattack.

The Kabalis moved from Baramulla and took the shortest path they could to reach the airport. It was through the lower reaches of Budgam district and it avoided the main city of Srinagar. The route, unfortunately, had two of the most populated villages of Sikhs, Ichahama and Attina, on it.

When the Kabalis were raiding Baramulla, a lot of survivors and escapees had come to the Budgam district for refuge. With them, they brought the eyewitness account of what had happened and the warning of what could happen if the Kabalis were to raid their villages.

More than two thousand people had come to Ichahama alone, including a few hundred Pandits. It was a big village with over two hundred household units, and the influx of such a large population had made the village population swell to around 4000 people. The village was divided into two different areas, called the upper mohalla and the lower mohalla, based on the elevation gradient. It was an open village on three sides while on the southern side, it merged with a Muslim village named Astanpora.

The refugees were given space in the houses and the halls of the gurdwara, while the whole village brought food stock to the gurdwara, where they cooked food in bulk for everyone. Every gurdwara had large-sized utensils because, on the days of festivals, food was usually cooked for thousands of people. The refugees and the locals came together to feed everyone. The people who had come to the village urged the villagers to leave and go to Srinagar, the capital city. But the village elders were keen on staying and planned to put up an offensive. The Sikhs in Baramulla were surprised by the attack, otherwise, they would have also fought. It was genetically ingrained in the community not to run away from a fight. Now when the people of Ichahama came to know that they would be attacked next, they set up several bunkers on all sides of the village. A lot of the villagers had simple gunpowder-filling guns, which they used for hunting. Sikhs who used to be in the army during the Maharaja had old rifles with them.

I wanted to visit both the villages, Ichahama and Attina, in the hope of finding some survivors and talking to them. When I told Veerji about my plan during our casual session in the library, he came up with a few names of people living in those villages. We called them to know if any survivors were still in good health and if their memory was intact. It was important for me that they remember what transpired during the Kabali raid. We decided to visit one Sunday and talk not just to the survivors but to the villagers in general.

During those interviews, I came to know some astonishing facts. One Karan Singh, who was the president of the local gurdwara of the village Ichahama when I interviewed him, was a child at the time of the attack. He told me he 'remembered the story clearly as if it happened just yesterday.'

It was the first of November, early morning, around six or seven. We had just had our breakfast at home while several adults from the family had gone to the gurdwara for breakfast. My father and uncle had gone to our orchard to cut the blackberry trees for firewood for the langar that had been arranged in the gurdwara. There were thousands of people in the village who had come from different places. Our family was busy tending to their needs, and so was every other family in the village. The food was cooked there for everybody. The whole ground was full of people. They slept there in the cold weather. In our house, some ten people had come to sleep the previous night.

We were told that the village would be attacked soon, so the adults had set up three barracks on the three sides of the village. We were expecting an attack from the north side, the side on which Baramulla was located. There was one elder named Sardar Ujagar Singh. He, with help from some others, had made a canon out of a propeller shaft of an old Chevrolet car. Most of the adults were helping to set up barracks and filling the gunpowder in the topidaar (muzzle loading) and buckshot guns.

By morning, the first shot was heard from the expected direction. The barracks were well prepared for it, and they fired a shot back in the direction. Nothing happened for the next one hour or so. They heard shots, but none of those shots came to their village. It was clear that they were firing at some other targets. Everyone had gone back inside their homes and were lying flat on the ground.

According to what I have read in the news reports from that year, and later heard retellings by different historians, the number of attackers who raided the village was around a thousand. Three different contingents of invaders had assembled to launch an offensive on the village. The first one was under Captain Sherkhan's command, which took the shortest route and reached first. There were around four to five hundred men under his command. The second contingent of similar strength was led by Major Khursheed Anwar, who had just captured the Pattan area of the Baramulla district, a strategically important place to counter the Indian army, which had started to join the fight. The third was a special column led by Latif Afghani, with one hundred highly trained National Guards who were the heroes of ethnic cleansing during Partition. The three columns had camped on the northern and northwestern sides of the village, but their first target was a nearby village called Dalwash.

The first shot that Karan Singh told me about was fired by Latif Afghani but not towards their village. It was towards Dalwash. The village did not have much population, and only a handful of people had guns. There was an intense gunfight, after which several people escaped and came running to Ichahama. Dalwash was later looted and burned, which gave the escapees time to reach Ichahama and warn the people about the impending threat.

It was mid-morning, between ten and eleven, that the gunfight erupted on the northern side of the village, where a fortified and well-trenched barrack was set up by the Sikhs. Other eyewitnesses and survivors validated the story told by Karan Singh.

> When the firing from the same direction started again, it lasted for an hour before going silent again. The barrack closest to the side fired back in between. They stopped it so they could surround the village from all sides. Within an hour or so, the village was surrounded from all three sides and we could hear the attackers firing from all the sides. The other barracks also returned the fire. Several people got injured in the firing. There were a lot of bodies lying on the grounds.
>
> Ujagar Singh fired a shot from his canon, which stopped the attackers for some time. His canon was made from a shaft, and when fired it became red hot, and he could not fire from it until it cooled down fully. Otherwise, it would burst and kill him and others around it. In between, some of the Kabalis entered the village but were immediately killed either by swords or guns. Casualties began to pile up on both sides. Their rifles were also confiscated and then used against them. The battle lasted for three hours. Then everything went silent when the raiders retreated. A lot of our Sikhs perished in the battle, but there was a huge loss on their sides as well.

Kawal Kashmiri, a local Sikh writer and a witness to the battle himself, said in his article about the Ichahama battle that the first thrust was ferocious but was unsuccessful. The second in command, Captain Sherkhan, fell on the spot, while Major Khursheed Anwar received a buckshot to his right thigh. They retreated to a safe distance. The injured were taken to Pattan and then subsequently to the field hospital set up by the Pakistani army at Chukothi to aid the raiders. Khursheed Anwar was later sent to England for his treatment but succumbed to gangrene. When he was removed from the battle, it was rumoured that he had gone to fetch reinforcements. The Masood tribals in his contingent were enraged and, in an attempt to avenge their fallen comrades, initiated a second offensive. This was fiercer and deeper. To confront them, two brave hearts took the command, one Sardar Bhagat Singh, and the other, Sardar Mohan Singh Nirman, and motivated and inspired the people to fight back. The injured, women and old, everyone came forward with a regenerated spirit to fight the Kabalis head-on. This second offensive lasted for another two hours. The sun had already begun to set, and along with that, the hopes of the people.

Another survivor, a Pandit family from Larikpora village, who had also taken shelter in the village, said the following:

> After the second thrust, there were heavy injuries. The raiders went back, but there were dozens of dead bodies lying on the ground. The ammunition was depleting at a faster pace. A lot of people among Sikhs had died and many were injured. Everybody feared the next attack. Deep inside, we knew we would not be able to survive another attack. During the pause we got after the second attack, people decided to march towards Srinagar.
>
> We exited the village and had walked for hardly five minutes when the Kabalis came out of their ambush and started firing at us. They came out from field demarcations and clay covers and began firing indiscriminately at the people. Hundreds of people died in the firing. Many others got crushed in the stampede. Those who were at the front and in the middle suffered the worst, very few of them survived. The survivors who were in the rear moved back to Ichahama.
>
> One of our relatives, Shobhawati, was pregnant and had a three-year-old daughter in her arms. She was shot in her hand,

and someone bandaged her hand with their turban, but she was unable to carry the child with her. She dropped her three-year-old somewhere near the bush.

When everyone assembled near the gurdwara, a decision was made that the survivors among the refugees would assemble in two three-storied dharmshalas near the gurdwara and would commit self-immolation instead of falling into the hand of raiders. The women and children were weeping and wailing, feeling helpless. The granthi asked refugees to wait for ten minutes before making any hasty decision. Suddenly the firing stopped.

Meanwhile, a raider entered the dharmshala compound. He was a very tall man, with magazines around his neck. He positioned himself to open fire on the survivors but before he could do it, the volunteers fired at him. As the raider did not relent, the lady volunteers dragged him in and hit him with swords.

The granthi then asked us to reconsider the decision to self-immolate. He said that we have survived despite all odds. So we should not give up our lives, but make a last stand. The other people who were fighting on different fronts also suffered great losses. It was, then, that we heard a very loud shot. That was the canon shot. After that, the firing stopped completely. It was already evening. The raiders had retreated after suffering three consecutive losses.

Some of the Sikhs went to check the status and came back with the news that they had started to camp and wouldn't be fighting without more reinforcements, which he had heard was coming by the fall of night. Another Sikh came with the news that a party of well-trained and armed men would be coming from the fourth side, where there was no fortification or barrack. It was where the village merged with the Muslim village of Astanpora. The locals aided them and gave the Kabalis a way to attack the village from their village.

Karan Singh also corroborated this information and added the following:

When we heard that the Kabalis will be coming from Astanpora, Sardar Darshan Singh took it upon himself and made a plan. He asked all of us to bring any amount of kerosene oil that we had. He was a very good horse rider and owned a horse. It was already dark, and the October sun sets early. But for us, the day passed in a blink of an eye. Sardar Darshan Singh mounted his horse and took the flambeau and set pace towards Astanpora village. The village houses were made of grass and wood. He took bottles of kerosene oil along with him. Within twenty minutes we could see huge flames erupting from that side. He burnt the raiders along with those houses.

The invaders had a great lust for loot, arson and abduction. The losses were infuriating for them. The only thing they achieved so far was the deaths of their comrades. The payback for being mercenaries was the loot, which was their only remuneration. Money, ornaments, precious metal and young women. Anything else they destroyed mercilessly, massacred. This was the second time they were facing the battle, the first at Muzaffarabad, where they were delayed for four days, and now in Ichahama, which delayed them by another day. The burning of the houses by Sardar Darshan Singh stopped the fight for the night.

Latif Afghani, on his return, when counting his loss, noted that one-third of the National Guards he commanded were killed in the battle. Overall, the horrific day robbed them of their fellow men. Messages regarding the day's failure were wired to the concerned quarters. The advance guard that was camped at Wuterhail was called back, and reinforcement was called for from Baramulla and Pattan.

The next morning, just after sunrise, the invaders launched another offensive. This time they were loaded with machine guns and heavy mortar. They bombarded the village for half an hour but did not get any response. They sent in a small exploratory party to see what was happening in the village, but to their surprise, they found the village deserted. There were bodies of the dead and the wounded were lying all over the village, including their own fellow raiders. Ujagar Singh, who manufactured the canon, lay next to his creation. Due to continuous use, the canon had exploded and killed him in the process. He had fired at least a dozen shots from it during the whole day.

The preceding night after the invaders retired to their respective camps, the villagers and the refugees, some three thousand in number, wounded and injured had escaped from the village towards the Narbal camp of the Indian army which had already started coming to Kashmir from 27 October. There were less than 700 troopers who were flown to Srinagar. Most of them were then sent to different areas to fight the Kabalis. One major party had stopped the Kabalis coming from Pattan, while a troop of fifty was posted at the airport to defend it in case the army failed to contain the Pattan thrust. This party had made its camp in Narbal.

The Ichahama raid was completely fought by the Sikhs without any assistance from the army. They delayed the march of Kabalis towards the airport by more than thirty-five hours. The airport was less than fifteen kilometres away, a mere three to four hours' distance. The National Conference volunteers came forward to help the refugees and took them to Srinagar camps. Amongst them was comrade Sant Singh Tegh, who drove one of the lorries and carried the aged, wounded, women and children to the exhibition ground in Srinagar, a new refugee camp set up by the Emergency Administration.

Similarly, the village Attina, which was smaller than Ichahama, had somewhere between six hundred to thousand refugees. Its own population was less than a hundred households. They had opened up the gurdwara for the refugees, along with their own houses. There was only one mansion in the village where around forty to fifty people took shelter. Attina was at a distance of seven kilometres from Ichahama and it took not more than two hours on foot through the shortcut to reach it. People of Attina had also braced for an offensive, but being a less populated village, it had only a few guns at its disposal. Every Sikh household, though, had a sword and some other weapons as they practised Gatka and took pride in owning swords and Khandas (heavy double-edged straight swords).

On the night of 31 October, Pir Manki Sharif, who accompanied the invading forces, did not want to see the brutality that the Kabalis would unleash upon the people, and he straightway went ahead and stayed at Wuterhail in a house of a Muslim Conference activist. A section of the invading force had come with him as advance guards. During their stay, the section came to know about the village Attina, where many Sikhs lived and lured by the prospect of good loot, they launched an attack on it on the afternoon of 1 November.

The first one to die in the village of Attina was Mata Gangi Kour. Naive and filled with motherly emotions, she went out to negotiate with the Kabalis, calling out to them, 'You're also some mother's children. I am also a mother to you. Why do you want to kill us? If you want anything, take it. Don't kill your fellow humans, your fellow brothers.' In response, she was shot in the chest.

Some of the villagers, with their few guns, started to fire back. They held the small party of Kabalis at bay till sunset while the rest fled through the other route. Women and children who took refuge in the two-story mansion next to the gurdwara, fed by the fearful stories of the survivors, set fire to the house they were in and self-immolated themselves. A survivor recalled, 'While we were running out of the village for the first time, one of them dropped his bag which contained utensils. At the sound of it, a bullet was fired and it hit the person in his left leg. All of us fell to the ground and returned to the village again. Then again, after an hour or so, we made a second attempt at escape while the Kabalis entered the village. The ammunition we had was over. Some of us were fighting them with sticks and swords. A lot of people died, but we somehow managed to escape. This Kabali contingent was also delayed and lost a lot of people before Pir asked them to return. They set the whole village on fire the next day after looting.'

The importance of these battles and the sacrifices of the Sikhs were never acknowledged. It was not hard to imagine that had those invaders, who were hell-bent on liberating Kashmir from India, not met any resistance anywhere, they would have reached the airport before the Indian army even made it to Kashmir. They would have taken it easily. The two days that they battled the people of Ichahama provided enough time for the Indian army to assemble their troops. Only on the third day, the army troopers of 4 Kumaon under Major Somnath Sharma came to fight the already miserable Kabalis.

The attack started on 22 October and the first contingent of the Indian army landed on 27 October. The Kabalis with their 6000 strong men in over three hundred lorries had to travel only one hundred and eighty kilometres to reach the airport. There was no one to halt their rampage other than the Sikhs of Kashmir. Their first encounter was with the State troopers of the Maharaja's forces, ninety per cent of whom were Muslims and who deserted and joined the Kabalis. That offensive was fought by the Sikhs living in Muzaffarabad and by Brigadier Rajinder Singh, who fought till his last breath and was killed on 27 October. The Kabalis had already breached and pushed his small force of around two hundred men from Muzaffarabad to Baramulla, from where the Kabalis started their plunder and massacre on 27 October. They divided themselves into three different parties, unbeknown to the Indian army, which concentrated all its forces to fight one party at Pattan and held it up there until 4 November.

The other two parties, almost 1500 men, marched to conquer the airport and, on their way, met with the ferocious offensive from Sikhs who stalled them till 3 November. It was only on 31 October that Major Somnath Sharma, who was given the Param Vir Chakra for his sacrifice fighting the Kabalis, landed in Kashmir airport. On the first and second of November, when the Sikhs fought against the Kabalis and delayed their forward march, all the Indian forces were concentrated on the attack at Pattan and were completely unaware of this contingent of Kabalis who were marching towards the airport. Only after 3 November, when the survivors and refugees started coming from that side, that three parties of two hundred men from the Indian army went to survey the Budgam area. Out of those three, only one party of 200 men under the command of Major Sharma camped at Budgam. The rest were sent to fight at Pattan as they did not find any information about the attack from the locals. It was a grave miscalculation on the army's part because they did not know the locals were supporting the raiders. Major Sharma's party came under attack from the Kabalis, whose number was cut to 700 from 1500 after the battle with Sikhs. The attackers were already injured, and their spirits had taken a hit. They still managed to overpower Major Sharma's party, in which Major Sharma lost his life. Meanwhile, reinforcements had come to aid the army, and finally, the Kabalis were pushed back.

Had the encounter at Ichahama and Attina not taken place, the Kabalis would have reached Srinagar airport by 31 October or 1 November. They would have captured the airport, making it impossible for further reinforcements from the Indian army to come to Kashmir. Napoleon lost Waterloo because of a five-minute delay by one of his generals.

Sikhs, instead of being heroes, paid a heavy price for defending themselves. They became the villains in the eyes of the local people who viewed them with contempt because they were said to hinder Pakistan's plan to capture Kashmir. The majority of the locals were Pakistan sympathisers. Until the middle of the 1980s, Sikhs were not treated well. There were social boycotts, taunts, glares, everything that made the Sikhs feel like culprits.

And what felt like salt in their wounds was that the contribution of Sikhs in saving Kashmir was never acknowledged. Though it did not hinder the Sikhs from developing, it did put them in a dilemma as to what their existence in Kashmir meant to the country and the state.

21

Closures Matter

Srinagar, Kashmir
19 October 2021, Tuesday
Evening

Indu was worried about the directives allegedly given by the Pakistan ISI to the Kashmiri militants. When she returned to have her tea, I was already lost in my thoughts. She took a sip of it and shrugged.

'I am not feeling good about all this. I have a bad intuition,' she said.

'Let me reheat your tea,' I took the cup from her and went to the kitchen. I did not know what to reply to her. I, too, was having a bad feeling about the whole thing. She followed me into the kitchen.

'Should I check with the airlines, to see if I can reschedule the ticket? Can we leave earlier?' she asked. She kept straightening her hair with her fingers.

'I don't know. I will talk to my parents during dinner and see what they have to say,' I replied to her.

It was a very productive day so far, and then all of a sudden, with one news article, all our focus and peace went flying out of the window. But that was how it had been all those years living in Kashmir, uncertain and erratic. Many a time, I remember the internet being cut without any warning in the middle of video lectures. Sometimes, I would be in school when we received news about unrest in some area and we would have to close the school in the middle of the class.

After our marriage, Indu had to return to her university. But I requested her to stay for a few months and work from home. She wanted a stable internet connection and power supply. In Kashmir, even in the metered areas, electricity was cut at least for four hours a day. I had to buy a UPS for the internet router so her connection did not get disrupted in the middle of her session.

But within ten days of her arrival in Kashmir, on 1 September, Syed Ali Shah Geelani, the most powerful figure in Kashmir, died. The internet and cellular network were immediately cut off for two days. It was like the blackout of August 2019 when Article 370 was revoked. Indu did not know what to do about it, how to reach her patients, and how to reschedule sessions with them or contact anyone outside Kashmir.

'What kind of a joke is this? What will I do now?' she had asked me then.

'Welcome to Kashmir,' I told her.

Many times, I had shouldered losses due to such uncertainty. I was working with a high-paying client on a project in 2019, designing educational material for K-12 kids before the lockdown. While in the middle of the project, the internet was cut off, and I became missing in action (MIA) for the client. I could not even write him an e-mail or tell anyone to inform him what had happened to me. I just hoped that he read about Kashmir and understood that I was not an untrustworthy person but a person in an untrustworthy place. He never worked with me again, even though he liked my work.

At this point of time in her studies, Indu could not afford to have such blackouts, which I was expecting would happen sooner or later. I, too, wanted her to go to Delhi as soon as possible.

'You check with the airlines and go to Delhi by the end of this week,' I told her, handing her the tea again.

'And you?' she asked.

'I will go to Jammu by the end of the month, and then come to Delhi as planned on the fourth of November.'

'No. I cannot go leaving you here. It will be too stressful. I will die of anxiety,' she replied. 'Why don't you also leave for Jammu by this week?' she asked.

'I just asked for Covid duty. I need to go there for a week or so, at least, before I ask them for favours. We will be fine here. You don't worry, baby. You reschedule your flight.'

'I will do that tomorrow. But you are not going for Covid duty tomorrow, or for a few days,' she replied.

It meant a no to rescheduling the flights without me rescheduling my drive down to Jammu. But she did not want to argue any further, so she just said that. Even I was in no mood to pick a fight.

'Ok, I will not go,' I told her, knowing that I had to go, come what may. That evening we spent scrolling our phones, unable to do anything useful because of our anxiety. The only person who did not get much affected by all this was my mother. Or she got affected in a completely different way than the rest of us. I think, being a housewife, it did not matter to her what happened outside the house unless it had a direct implication on us. When I went out, and she knew it was not safe for me, then she would be worried. When my father left his phone at home and came back late, she would be walking on thorns, waiting for him, overthinking, because Kashmir was never safe. She would be worried about how her brother's business would suffer if the situation worsens. Her anxieties were all about the well-being of others. But then it might be just what I think. The truth could be entirely different, because she never reacted to any news, beyond asking about our well-being and how it was going to affect us. Sometimes I felt sad for her, for her devotion towards her family was so much that nothing else mattered to her. She would not ask for anything that she might need or want. She had given her everything to raise her kids and serve her husband. The stereotypical perfect, selfless, compromising and accommodating Indian mother and wife. The notion of which I despised. She had given her youth to her siblings, raising them as the eldest sister, when her mother died at a very young age. The moment her siblings became independent, she got married and started her new life as a housewife. After she had me, I became the centre of her life. She never lived for herself. When Ramneek was born, I was five years old. I saw her raising him, a child with cerebral palsy (CP), with dedication. It was one of the most difficult jobs in the world to be a mother of a CP child, that too in a patriarchal society where the woman was the primary caregiver and the man the breadwinner. Whatever remaining aspirations or dreams she had, got buried in raising him. Though our household had never been a patriarchal one, with our father helping out with most of the work whenever he could, the silent privileges of being a man were always available to him. Whatever he did was considered as an effort, a help given to her, and not a duty he had towards the household. She was and is the primary caretaker and caregiver of our house.

But I was wrong on so many levels, as a man trying to understand the world and emotions of a woman. I could never grasp the entirety of it. I have immense respect and love for her, not because she is my mother, but because she is the most practical and reasonable person I have known. The way she handles life and its problems inspires me to become like her. Her quick response when everybody else panics, and her clear thinking when everyone is crying over anything that happens are qualities I try to emulate.

When I was three or four years old, I swallowed a bottle cap and it got stuck in my throat, choking me. We were at my grandparents' home, and there were a dozen people in the dining hall including my father, mamus, masis and grandfather. When they saw me choking everybody panicked but were not able to do anything about it. Before they could collect themselves, my mother just rushed, hung me upside down and slapped my back so hard that it pushed the cap out of me. And during several other incidents where life and death were dependent on a split-second decision she could somehow make the right choice. I had seen her rushing towards the burning kitchen when everybody was rushing out. She did not think about herself and went to detach the gas cylinder and take it away from the fire to avoid any blast. She is my Captain America. When I was a child she taught me a life's philosophy, which had shaped my personality in a very profound manner. She told me, 'Don't get tensed about the problem, because there are only two options for you. One, the problem cannot be solved. So, why get tensed if it was not in your control? How can being tense help it? Two, the problem can be solved. Then, why get tensed? Instead, work on it and solve it.'

That has been my guiding principle for life, but it was hard to stand by it. I was anxious for weeks now, trying to find a solution to my situation. My head was being pulled in different directions. On one hand, I wanted Indu to go to Delhi. On the other, I wanted to celebrate my birthday with her. I wanted to take her to all the relatives for dinner. But I also wanted to take her away from Kashmir as soon as possible. I was conflicted. And then the whole day writing about 1947 had already put me in a contemplative and low mood. The stories of survivors were heartbreaking.

In a way, every killing was the same, be it in 1947, Chithisinghpora or Mehjoor Nagar, or this new wave of killings. People busy with their lives, working at their jobs or sitting in their homes, who knew nothing, did not even an inkling that their lives were going to end in a few moments for no fault of theirs. Anyone who died in these incidents was killed because somehow, somewhere, the killer's rationality and logic were dead. And they would never know why it happened to them. Sacrificial lambs, chosen at random.

After Indu read my story about Chithisinghpora, and then the Wikipedia and other Google material about it, she asked me, 'So, who did it? What do you think?'

I told her what I knew, that nobody knew, that it would always be a mystery. I told her that what I thought did not matter. What anyone thought, or why or who did it did not matter. Thirty-five people were killed. The families lost their members, children had been orphaned, wives were widowed, parents lost their children, and none of the theories mattered to them.

But what she said was an eye-opener to me.

'You are wrong. It matters. That's how justice works. When someone knows whom to hold accountable, whom to direct their anger and rage towards, and whom to punish, they get a sense of closure,' she said. 'Think about losing someone and not knowing whom to blame, who to shout at, or who to punish. That's more agonising than we can imagine,' she added.

I had never thought about that. How people deal with trauma, and how having someone held accountable would pacify them. Probably, Indu knew because she studied that in psychology. But more than just the blame, there was a relief when justice was served, when the criminal was punished. The human mind worked like that, the consolation of seeing the criminal go to the gallows, of justice being served, soothed the victim or his family more than anything.

When I think of those eleven civilians killed during the month, I felt the same for them and their families. Nobody knew whom to shout at, whom to vent their anger at, whom to blame. Most of them would be blaming themselves for living in Kashmir, for not leaving while they still had the time, for ignoring all the signs and tells, and for being stupid.

What I learnt about the survivors or the eyewitnesses through my interviews and writings made me panic more. It was not just the terror of the incident alone that was painful, but the aftermath of it. The emptiness after the loved ones were gone, after the homes were destroyed and after the families were killed. The years it took to get used to that emptiness, the time it took to rebuild a life. A life full of despair, regrets and guilts. During my interviews with the survivors, I realised that everyone, including me, had concentrated on the brutalities of the Kabalis and the days of the attack. Nobody bothered about what happened after that. When I realised that later and went with new questions to the villages, I was too late. Majority of the survivors were either dead or too old to give further interviews. I found only a handful of reliable sources, the accounts of whom were too harrowing for me.

Regarding the present situation, I did not want to end up guilty of not acting on the clues and signs. I had scores of stories in front of me as warnings. And if I learned nothing from them, I would be the fool who did not foresee what was to come.

22

Aftermath of 1947

Kashmir

I was hopeful that the children and younger family members of the people who survived 1947 would know something about the aftermath of the Kabali raid. Surprisingly, they repeated only the popular narrative of people being killed and all the other brutalities they had to face. When I prodded them further, I learnt that the raid itself was too quick to process as and when it happened. They did not realise the enormity of the aftermath immediately. A survivor recounted this:

> Most of our villagers were killed, then our houses were looted and the whole village was set on fire. We kept hiding in the forests for seven days. It was very cold. We did not have anything to cover ourselves with, or anything to eat. We were too scared to move. And we were trying to be as far from each other as we could so that we could not be found from a distance. A few young men who were injured soon succumbed to it because, without food or medicine, their injuries were not able to heal. We just applied leaves and mud to control their bleeding. But it did not help. Some people kept watch on the borders of the forest. Those days were very hard. The forest was not too dense in certain places, but in others, the foliage was very thick and infested with bears and leopards. So we did not enter them. Later some of our people got to know that the Indian army had come to Kashmir and pushed the Kabalis back. Then we went back to our burned-down village.

Another survivor from the same village said the following:

> When we went back, there was nothing left. Our houses were burnt to the ground. And it was during winter. You know how

cold it is in November here. And in those days, the winters were harsher, not like winters today. Then we did not have electricity in our village. Our source of warmth were the bukharis and the firewood, which was already burnt by those devils. We had to cut down trees and make wooden and mud homes for the winter. Most of the adults who could work were either dead or injured. So women and children also joined the workforce. But most of the trees that belonged to us were also burned down by the raiders so we couldn't return. After three or four days, when all the rebuilding felt overwhelming, and a few more people succumbed to injuries, we shifted to Srinagar camps for the next seven to eight months. We came back when the winter was over and started building our homes. The government gave us two logs of wood each to build our houses. But we are thankful to the Waheguru, that we were able to survive and come back to our places within a year. Think about those thousands who had to jump in the Jhelum to save themselves from the Kabalis. Death was an easier option for them. Think about those who killed and burned themselves. Think about those who were shifted to Delhi for years, or had to live in the Srinagar camps for half a decade. Then there were those who never came back, and those who came back and found nothing, their sisters, daughters and mothers taken to Pakistan. There were people who could not take their children with them while they were fleeing. Those people got their children back from the local Muslims after seven or eight years after they came back. Nobody knows what and all had happened to their loved ones. When we look at them, our pain and angst seem too small.

From one of the survivors of the Attina battle, Basant Kour, I heard some very tormenting facts. She was only eleven when their village was attacked.

By nine o'clock in the night, we were able to run from here. But they had already started to enter the village and burn and loot the houses towards the south boundary. A lot of people died here, especially those who had come from other places to stay here.

There were hundreds and hundreds of people in our village. Oh! My poor mother had to serve water to the refugees for three days. They kept yelling and cursing her to bring more water and to be served first. But there was water scarcity. So she and a few others had to go all the way down to the stream to fetch water and then serve it to everyone. The children of the village also helped in fetching water or bringing small items from the village houses to the gurdwara. If you write something from our conversation, tell people that Paro Kaur, that's my mother's name, served water to the survivors day and night.

I asked her to tell me what happened after the attack, where and how did they go. What she said shocked me.

We fled the village at night. When we ran, we were again attacked with sticks and stones by the villagers from Dhansa, a neighbouring area. A lot of locals were eagerly and happily helping the Kabalis. They wanted Kashmir to be with Pakistan. But not all of them did that. Two small girls were left in the village after we abandoned it. They were raised by Muslims for four years and when we returned to our village, they gave the girls back to us. In another instance, a Muslim family hid a person in their bukhari for, I don't know how long, but until everything was fine. They fed him there, cleaned his urine and stool inside the room and did not allow him to come out, so he would not be found out and then killed. There are good people and bad people in every religion.

When running, we were very scared and fearful. It was like a stampede. On that dark night, we fought each other because of mistaken identities. My uncle died by his brother's sword who thought that he was an attacker and stuck a sword in his stomach. There was a lady who came from Baramulla. In Baramulla, she had jumped into the well with her two children. But the well was already full. So her husband pulled her back. Her two children, however, died in the well because of suffocation and the weight of others who jumped after them. But she died here. In our village, there was a one-year-old infant who died because her mother could not carry her anymore. She left her sitting on the ground, but people walked over the child, killing her instantly.

The outsiders died here, too. Those who had come from other villages, those poor people did not know the routes to escape and where to run. There was a newly married couple whose mehendi was still fresh, both of them died together.

It was a living hell for us. Sometimes, we thought that it would have been better if we were killed. For four years we lived away from our village, first in camps and then in some houses that the Sheikh (Sheikh Mohammad Abdullah, the first elected Prime Minister of the Princely State of Jammu and Kashmir) had opened for the refugees. There was nothing there. Every day we had to fight for survival. For water, for rice, for bed, for blankets. We were constantly in a survival battle. For months we did not eat proper rice, but only husk and hull, with water-like dals. But what could we do? We had nothing else.

From other survivors, I gathered similar stories. The Kabali raid had three outcomes, death, despair and desolation. A rough estimate places a total of 33,000 deaths in our community. Hundreds of villages were completely burned down, and the people who survived were either taken to Srinagar or Delhi and had to stay there for somewhere between three years to a decade. They were given 250 rupees and two logs of wood to return and build their lives from scratch. During the run, a lot of people died, some from their injuries, some from fatigue and hunger, and some at the hands of locals who joined the Kabalis.

During the escape from the Ichahama battle, an eyewitness narrated about one of the raiders named Ramzan Kabali, who had taken a young girl in her early teens from her fatally wounded grandparents as they lay unconscious near the site of the battle. When the locals of village Khanpur Badgam requested him to hand over the girl to them, so they could take care of her until her family returned, he said, 'During the last twenty days, ever since I have left my home on this expedition, I could only earn this kafir girl. At least, it will fetch me some money. I am not giving her away to anyone.' She and several other girls were, later, sold in Pakistan and

Afghanistan. Some of the girls who returned after many years told me how miserable their lives had been.

Another survivor, Mastanaji, talks about the time in greater detail.

> There was a person from the neighbouring village of Gundipora. Everyone called him *Am Gunda* because he was well-built and brave, but he was a goon.
>
> He came to our village and told us that some of the Sikhs had come from other villages and were waiting near the outer boundary of the village and that we should send some of our village chiefs to escort them inside the village. Some seven to eight people went with him. Only two returned. It was an ambush. The Kabalis also used to wear turbans, not like ours but from a distance they looked like sardars. But they fooled us by crying the *Sikhi Jiakara, Bole So Nihal* in a very loud voice. When our people replied with Sat Sri Akal, they opened fire at them. Those who returned warned the village that the attack had started. It was four in the evening. There was a strong fight, but our village had only a few guns. Nevertheless, we fought bravely. The fight went on for five, six hours. Charan Singh Bali, Sardar Singh, Inder Singh, Gurbaksh Singh and Jaswant Singh were the riflemen from our village. They went into some houses and returned fire in the direction, which held the Kabalis at bay for some time. But the Kabalis were also clever. They set fire to the village from afar by throwing flambeau on the houses. Everything was burning. I heard children and women crying, being burnt alive. People were badly injured, with bullet wounds in their arms and thighs, blood flowing from them. Still, we managed to escape. In the dead of the night, we were able to escape the Kabalis through those fields, on the west side. You can see them from here. Running and fleeing, we somehow reached a village called Bhatpura, a Pandit village. But when we approached it, we realised the Kabalis had already taken it over and were forcibly converting the Pandits to Islam by asking them to recite the Kalima. We had to run from there as well.
>
> It was only when we reached Budgam that the locals came to help us. Those Muslims had kept water, roasted rice and some

dry fruits for the survivors. They told us thousands of people had crossed to Srinagar before us. They helped us with all they could. They bandaged our injured, gave us food and best wishes, and told us to keep moving towards the town, that big camps had been set up by the National Conference volunteers and that they were taking care of everyone.

When we reached Narbal camp, we saw hundreds of volunteers, and among them were our two prominent leaders, Budh Singh Tyagi and Sant Singh Tegh. They were also members of the National Conference, and they took us in trucks to the camps.

When we came back after nine years, everything was gone, no homes, no fields. The raiders had even burned our trees so that when we came back we could not cut them and rebuild our houses. Some locals looted and carried away our things. I remember my father found out that all the utensils and furniture from our local gurdwara were taken by the people of Sewdara village. He had some connections in that village. So he went to them and asked them to return the things. That is how we cooked the langar for the village till we were able to build our individual houses again.

During those nine years, we stayed, first in Delhi refugee camps at Tees Hazari for one and a half years, and then at Rajbagh camps in Srinagar for the rest of the years.

In the Delhi camp, there were thousands of people, those who came from Pakistan before and during Partition. We had only one motto there, to survive. It was very difficult. We were scattered and had to live among Pakistani Sikhs and Hindus. Their languages were different from ours, though most of them were conversational in Punjabi. We were given two full meals every day, and we did not have any space to cook our own food. There was only one tap for hundreds of families. Those years were very miserable, more for us than for those who came from Pakistan. Those who came from Pakistan knew that they would be living in Delhi or would be settled by the government once everything stabilised. But for us, we had not lost our lands as Kashmir was a part of India now. We were expected to go back and resume our lives in our own places. We did not belong to Delhi. In the hope of returning to Kashmir, we refrained from setting up our business or moving ahead with life in those camps. While those who came from Pakistan opened shops, worked in railway stations, distributed newspapers and did other meagre jobs.

Some of our girls got married to those people and never returned to Kashmir. Those Sikhs who were educated set up classes outside their camps and taught the children. I went to one such school for more than a year. I worked at a few odd jobs, but we always knew that all these things were temporary for us and we were to return to Kashmir sooner or later. And so we did.

When we came back to Kashmir we did not go directly to our village or our homes, but we were put into another refugee camp for eight years. It was in 1956 that we returned to our village. There was nothing left for us. We had to start from scratch, again set up a temporary camp for months till we could build our homes.

The loss of property and life was immense, but mental distress was far greater. The people who returned were not the same as those who lived there once. Those happy families were broken. There was not a single family that had not lost someone to the gory raids.

In our modern-day science, we would have associated Post Traumatic Stress Disorder (PTSD), depression, trauma, anxiety and a myriad of other mental health issues with those survivors. But no such evaluation was carried out for them. People who were in their budding and growing years, and went through all that turmoil, would have undergone severe personality changes, which would have manifested into their adulthood years later. All those things were never talked about. Those initial years of struggle were far easier than what came after it. Contempt, blaming and discrimination.

In the last decade, ever since I came to Kashmir for my job, I asked the same question to many people, both Sikhs and Muslims and got a similar response from them.

To my question, 'What do you think would have happened if the Kabali raid had never happened, or in the first place, the Partition never happened?'

Everyone said, 'We would have been a lot happier and prosperous.'

Both communities felt that it would have been more beneficial for them when compared to present times.

'We lost thousands of people, our homes and properties. It was only our will to live and prosper like how our Guru taught us, that we have managed to leave that horrible time behind and forged ahead. Imagine, if there was no Kabali raid or Partition, we would be zamindars and landlords. We would have been the masters of Kashmir,' said a Sikh uncle when I had asked him the question.

A Muslim elder from a village in Baramulla told me, 'If the raid did not happen if there was no Pakistan. Then, where would we go? We would be homeless.'

When I told him that if there was no Partition, he would still be a Kashmiri and an Indian as well because there would be no Pakistan.

'Astaghfirullah Allah, why would there be no Pakistan? How would we be Indians?' he replied.

It was an interesting premise for me, when I asked a few more people from that village and the adjacent villages, I understood that for them the scenario where Pakistan did not exist was unimaginable. They could not even comprehend that, at one point in time, there was no Pakistan and that the whole area was Undivided India.

A younger person, who worked as a mechanic in the city, had a different view. He said, 'Then, we would not be fighting for azaadi, but we would be fighting for some other things, fundamental rights or something or the other. Because whatever happens, the Hindu government will always torture us minorities in India.'

I wanted to tell him that the Muslims in the other states never thought about azaadi, and the fighting he was talking about was not specific to minorities, but to everyone in India. Every faction was fighting for something or the other, and that was true for every country in the world. Everywhere the citizens were fighting with the government. That was how democracy works. Through fights, opinions were formed. Through opinions rebellion, and through rebellions new governments came and the cycle started all over again.

Another middle-aged person who worked as a contractor and who was building the nearby government school building said, 'Kabalis came to free us from India. But they failed and we are still living miserably. But if they had never come, we would have also lost the will to fight against India, because Pakistan always takes our side. If they did not take our side, then we would have nowhere to go.' For a lot of Kashmiris, even the idea of a peaceful existence as a part of India was non-existent. Even in my close circle, my friends and colleagues were divided on it.

I had a long conversation with Snowber about azaadi and how she perceived it. Being an ardent Gandhian she always talked about diversity and secularism. 'No Bupi Bhaiyya, azaadi or Pakistan, both are not good for us. I don't know how and why people can think that a majoritarian state is good for anyone. Pakistan by itself is in deep shit. How would it take care of Kashmir? They are politically and financially unstable. And any state which rules based on religion is not good for its citizens.

'You look at India. It is a diverse country, full of different cultures, languages and religions, even though the majority are Hindus. And the fact that the majority of the population is Hindu and still most citizens are against a majoritarian government, tells us that most people are smart enough to understand how it would be if a single religion had absolute control. If we go to Pakistan or get azaadi, it would be a big problem for women. That far, I know. The freedom and rights we have grown used to will be snatched away in a blink of an eye. There would be restrictions everywhere. And then, what about the minorities in that future? Look at Afghanistan and Pakistan and Saudi. The minorities are always in fear, and looking out for trouble.'

Another friend who lived in the innermost parts of the city called Jogi Lanker, had a completely opposing view. He said,

> We will live in poverty, starve to death, and be politically unstable, but at least we will be all that in a place where we belong. Come to my home someday and you will see. Ever since I was born, I have never seen what the neighbourhood looks like at night, because after eight, we are not allowed to go out. There are army men and CRPF at every exit and crossing, and barbed wires are at our perimeter. And if I ever come late, I have to go through two check posts to reach my own home. Every part of my body is searched. At one point in time, in every fifth house in our locality, the attic or one of the rooms was occupied by the army people. They stayed there for the night,

and then in the day they would go out on duty. They said it was for our protection. Ha ha. Protection from whom? It is better to die in Pakistan than to live in India as a second-class citizen.

And then a friend, who owned a business establishment, had another view, 'Bhai, *apne ko paisa kamana hai*, India or Pakistan or China, doesn't matter. Those who have nothing to do want to pretend they are important. They have to blame their incapacity and incapabilities on something. So, they want to do this drama, azaadi and Pakistan Zindabad.'

Sometimes I felt my asking such questions was a futile activity. I knew what they would say, but I wanted to hear it from them. And every one of them said what I was expecting them to say. It became evident to me that in all matters of Kashmir, there were only three divisions, the ones who wanted Pakistan or azaadi, the ones who felt it was better to stay with India, and the ones who did not mind whatever it was. And everyone was extreme in their stance. There was no middle ground in Kashmir.

23

To Leave or Not to Leave

Srinagar, Kashmir
20 October 2021

The day started with a scuffle when I got up early and announced that I had to go for my Covid duty. The day before, Indu had told me not to go out for the next few days. Waking up to indecisiveness made me irritated. The first thought, while I was still in bed, was confusion about the next plan. Should I go to the office or not? Should I tell Indu to reschedule her tickets or not? Should I tell my parents about how we were feeling or not?

The best I could do was to find the strength to report for duty so that all other decisions could be kept aside temporarily. Also, it would give me some space to think. When Indu saw me getting ready, she asked, 'You said you will not go for the next few days.'

'I have to go today. I need to mark the attendance before joining for duty. Otherwise, it will be considered a default, and the order will be cancelled,' I told her, not sure if she would believe it or if it made sense to her.

'Then let it be. You take a leave without pay. We will manage. I have some savings that we can use for a month or so. Then your vacation will start,' she slammed the door behind her before going back into the bedroom. could feel my heart start to race suddenly. I wanted to tell her to leave for Delhi and stop talking about the issue. It had not been two months since we got married, and we were fighting because of what was transpiring around us, letting it seep into our lives and upsetting us from the inside. In the two years of our long-distance dating, we seldom had any arguments. The stress around us had made us a fatigued and pessimistic couple, full of unprovoked anger, general irritability and constant melancholy. It affected me more than her.

On 22 August, when we got married, Kashmir was a peaceful place. Nothing major had happened for the past several months, at least not big enough to land in the national news. During the first month, because Indu was busy with her work, we kept our plans for travels on standby and decided to travel in the winter or after her review presentation. We requested our friends and relatives, whoever invited us for the customary meals as newlyweds, to postpone their invitations to November. We only went out on weekends to some new cafes or places. Our long drives and cheesecake dates around the Dal Lake were our only respite.

Indu did not have any friends in Kashmir, and due to the language barrier, she was not able to freely and easily join my friend circle. Other than Raman, she did not befriend any of my friends as well. Most places where I took her, she felt left out because sooner or later, we would start using our mother tongue or Kashmiri or Urdu.

Every time we went out I was mindful about it and kept her close so that she wouldn't feel left out or alone. We knew that our time in Kashmir was limited. She was expected to join her university sometime in November, and I was to visit her in Delhi in December. She had to apply for her visas and other paperwork to go to Australia the moment international students were allowed to join after the Covid relaxations, which would be anywhere in the first half of 2022. We daydreamed about our time in Australia when I would visit her for a month. We would sit and google places in Australia, especially lakes and beaches, to make a list for our visits. We would plan our expenses and our travels. Indu being a planner, had an organised way to go about it, and I being a pantser would go with the spur of the moment. 'We will see once we reach there,' I told her.

When I was ready to go to the office, she did not even come out of the bedroom to see me off. When I told my parents I had to go, they, too, had a similar reaction. I was feeling suffocated. I understood that this was what my father meant when he said that it was not one event or incident that triggered his decision to move away from Kashmir. The daily living conditions filled with uncertainty and mental pressure with no prospect of a better future would be killing us slowly.

At the vaccination centre, the vaccine was not available for the day's session, and the government portal to upload the vaccination status was also closed. We had nothing to do other than discuss some random topics. I was done with my joining and then talked with the in-charge about my going to Delhi again. He had already assured me that I had to do my work, and that was all that mattered to him. But still, he wanted me to talk to the higher authorities so that they were also in the know about the whole thing. When I called them, they said the same thing, that work should not suffer, and if the immediate supervisor was fine with it, they did not have any problems with it. On that note, I came back home happy and optimistic.

When I reached home, they were already in discussion, this time about the TRF militant who was caught in the morning and the increase in the number of encounters between the police and militants. I was tempted to tell everyone to go out and see for themselves how everything was back to normal and that we were just holed up inside our house, on our own accord, because of our pessimism and negativity. Indu asked me about my take on the news, which flipped me somehow.

'Why do we even have to talk about it? How does it matter what we think? Nobody gives a fuck about your opinion or mine, just live your own life and chill.'

I was fed up with what was right, what was wrong, what one thought, and what would happen kind of questions. But what made me raise my voice was the sheer pessimism we were in. We were not able to think about anything in a positive light. We were depressed most of the time and felt irritated with everything in general. Something was wrong with us. And when I went out that day, I felt like everyone else had gone back to their lives again like nothing ever happened. At home, it was completely different. I wanted them to go out and see how the world was moving on with all these killings. Even the Sikhs and Hindus started going back to their jobs and resumed their duties. My uncles were all going to their shops and business centres. Veerji and Raman were going to their offices all these days without any fear or anxiety. I felt I was being too cowardly, and so was my family.

'Why are you overreacting to a simple question?' Indu asked.

'Why do you have to keep asking such questions? What else can I do? We are leaving in a week anyway? How does it matter now whatever the hell was happening in Kashmir?' I replied. My tone was still raised.

'You don't care about others. Your relatives will still be here. Whatever is happening involves every Kashmiri.'

'Then what do you want me to do? Leave Kashmir or not? We have been talking about leaving all the time, and now when I say we will leave, you are telling me all this,' I replied.

'It's not that I want you to leave. You have always dreamt about your life outside Kashmir as well. Whenever we spoke you always said it's not a place you would spend your whole life. Even if I was not in your life, you were still planning to leave,' she said.

'And I don't have to care about any of it. I am not even a Kashmiri. I was concerned about you,' she added. Her voice kept rising with every word. I knew if I answered something mean, we would again end up in a fight. The last two weeks had been hard.

'Then do me a favour and don't act so concerned,' I picked up my phone and started going through it, acting as I was doing some tasks on it.

'Whatever,' she said and left the room.

For the next two hours, I was alone in our bedroom, thinking about why I had reacted in such a way. She was genuinely concerned and anxious about the situation. So was I. But for me talking about it over and over again did not make any sense. The helplessness of not being able to do anything about it other than just talking and discussing made me angry. It was a futile exercise.

The news channels, which were dissecting every aspect of the Kashmir issue, had suddenly gone silent on it. Nobody cared anymore until someone was killed again. The general mental, emotional and psychological well-being and troubles of the people were never discussed. When I was fed up with my musings and my waiting for Indu to come back to the room, when my patience was exhausted, and when I had self-justified my wrong behaviour, I sent a WhatsApp message to her, 'Let's go for a drive. We can have a cheesecake as well.' I waited for another ten minutes for her reply and then went out only to find her watching a movie with my parents. I gestured for her to look at her phone. She replied with the red angry emoji. I messaged her a sad emoji and asked her to come to the room.

'Let's go na, love. Anyway we will be going away from Kashmir in a few days. This would be our last date in Kashmir,' I told her. She was still angry. So she did not reply and just stood there with a cold look in her eyes.

'Baby, I was upset and irritated,' I said, trying to make a *pavaam* face. 'Forgiveness is a heavenly virtue,' I whispered.

'I don't feel like going anywhere,' she replied.

'*Paleej, paleej*. Once the anger subsides, we will feel bad that we missed an opportunity and be angry for that,' I pleaded.

'Okay. Ask your parents first. They would be worried if we go out this late,' she replied after a minute.

'Thank you. Let me check with them. Anyway, it's only six. You get ready and we will come back early,' I told her as I went out to talk to my parents. I had never taken my parents' permission before. Usually I just told them that I had to go. They had given me absolute freedom ever since I started earning. They treated me as an adult even when I was not one. So asking them was something reserved only for very serious matters.

'Is it important? You know what is happening and still want to be blind,' my father replied when I told him that Indu and I would be going out for a small drive around Dal Lake. 'Want to go, go alone. Why do you want to get someone's daughter killed?' he added.

'She has been holed up for the last two weeks, and we will be leaving in a few days. I want to take her out, if not Dal, at least to some cafe nearby,' I replied after a long pause. I controlled my anger again. I was about to lash out at his hypocrisy, but then I realised if I did that, we wouldn't be able to go out. I had already made one person mad, and that was enough for a day.

'Then go to Sanat Nagar or Jawahar Nagar, leave early and come back early.'

'Okay, I'll get going then.'

My father had always been optimistic and fearless. Even in the most hopeless times, he told me, 'Live courageously. What is the point in being scared and living a cowardly life?'

In 2019, Article 370 was abrogated, and telecommunications and internet were shut down. Following that, curfews were imposed. Even then I used to go out to my friend's house and come back as late as twelve in the night. He never told me anything but was only curious to know what the conditions outside were like. I did not expect those answers from him.

'Baby, ready?' I called out to Indu, who was in the washroom.

'Just a minute. You get ready in the meantime,' she replied in a muffled voice. Probably she was brushing.

More than the date or the cheesecake, I wanted to take her out to Dal Lake, not for the conversations or the drive, but to show her how thousands of tourists were enjoying a carefree evening. The majority of them would be Hindus from different parts of India. Dal Lake, or any tourist place, was by far the safest place in the whole of Kashmir. There had never been an episode of attacks on tourists. Even in the worst times of Kashmiri militancy, the tourists were safe. The locals would come out to help them, feed them and take them to their houses if curfew was imposed or an uncalled hartal or strike happened. Kashmiri people, without a doubt, were known for their hospitality.

The Dal Lake Road presented to her, what she needed the most, a regular day scene. Vendors were selling bhelpuris and shikara walas were negotiating with the people for boat rides, groups of young people were smoking cigarettes while tourists were clicking countless selfies and pictures. The traffic was at its peak. It was a normal day in every sense. That day we drove a little further and then a little more. We didn't talk much but listened to the songs of Piyush Mishra. She patted my shoulder in between with her small hands. And somewhere during the drive, we both cried for no reason. While coming back Indu told me in a soft voice, 'You know that I don't hate Kashmir, right?'

In the one and a half hours we were out, my mother called twice. First to ask if we would eat dinner at home and then to tell me to come back a little early. My father called once and asked to bring a packet of curd while coming back. We reached home before nine, and still, everyone felt like we were very late. Usually, we left home at 8.30 and would come back by 11 or so. The trip helped elevate our moods a little. That night we slept like a normal couple living a normal life in a normal place.

24

The Good Old Days

Srinagar, Kashmir
21 October 2021

The next morning when I got ready for office, Indu was packing my lunch. The evening visit to the Dal Lake had changed her opinion a little, and she was less anxious about me going outside. But things were so unpredictable that nobody knew when some more news would come and upset us or destroy our current moods. Every emotion felt short-lived and temporary. Anything happening anywhere could change our moods.

The day before, while Indu and I had gone out, my mother had called her brothers and sisters and told them that we would be leaving by the end of the month, and as expected, they had invited us for lunches and dinners. At breakfast, my mother asked us to give a time slot for each of them and to personally call those whose invites I was going to decline. She could not say no to them.

After consulting Indu, who was not as anxious as the day before, we decided to settle for the 24, 28 and 31 of October for our dinners. First to Bikram mamu's and then to another close relative, Harjeet uncle's house, both of whom lived nearby. We could go in the evening, have dinner and come back late at night. On the 30th, Indu wanted to stay home, cook some dishes and celebrate my birthday. It was going to be our first celebration after our marriage. On 31 October, we would have to travel to Baramulla to one of my masi's home for dinner and then stay overnight as it was far away.

By the time my mother and Indu came to see me off at the veranda, the newspaper had arrived, and I had picked it up before they could see and put it in my bag. I glimpsed at a minor headline on the front page, which read, 'Encounter breaks out in Srinagar's Chanapora area.' This was the second gunfight within a week in Chanapora.

Other news that we already knew was about Shri Amit Shah, the home minister's visit on 23 October and the much-anticipated India-Pakistan cricket match on 24 October. There was a news that said that security had been beefed up ahead of the home minister's visit, while a subheading clarified that the internet blockage in some areas and seizing of two-wheelers was not in response to it but related to terror violence. I knew my hiding the newspaper was a futile activity, for Indu would sooner or later come to know this news through her mobile, or someone would send her another WhatsApp forward to snatch away her peace and calm. I just wanted the week to pass without any more incidents that could bring unrest in our lives again. I was waiting for the winter so I could spend my vacation in Noida. With that thought of enjoying and partying in Noida, I drove to my office.

When I got the job and the financial independence that came from it, every year in winter, during the two-and-a-half-month vacation, I used to travel extensively. I bought my bike, a 150cc Hero Hunk, in the winter of 2011 with my own money, and I was very proud of the fact. I was just twenty-one and financially independent, unlike all my classmates and college friends who were still studying.

That year I drove to Jammu on the bike. Sarabjeet had come from Jammu to accompany me because the route was very risky, and it was my first ever bike drive on that route. In winter, it was considered unsafe even for four-wheelers, but the moment I told him the plan, he came overnight in a taxi, and the morning, we drove to Jammu. That was like a limit-breaker journey because, after that trip, I drove to the remotest places in Jammu and Kashmir, visiting every single place on the tourist map accessible by bike the following year.

Every Sunday or any other holiday, I explored a new place in Kashmir. But what I believed to be my biggest adventure was in December of 2012. In October 2012, I knew that in the coming winters, I would be going somewhere new, somewhere outside Jammu and Kashmir, and my first choice was Simla. My cousin, Ranvir, lived in Chandigarh at that time and was in the last year of his engineering degree. I called him up and planned the trip to Simla with him.

'Do you have so much money? Think about the petrol and food and the hotel for two people. It would be around eight to ten thousand,' Ranvir said to me.

'I have five. You can arrange another three, and we will manage. It will be thrilling,' I replied.

'If someone could give us money to travel, how cool it would be.'

'Then why would we go to Simla? We can travel the whole country if someone gives us the money,' I replied.

We started daydreaming that if we had the money, we could do all sorts of things, eat all kinds of food. After the call with Ranvir, I started to look for crowdfunding options on the web. I toyed with the idea for a few days and then concluded that we could get money for social work if our work somehow benefited the people who we would be asking for money.

I called up Ranvir and told him what I was thinking and we planned something that was beyond our initial Simla plan. An all-India bike trip, Kashmir to Kanyakumari and back, where we would sensitise people about drug abuse and give lectures in different colleges about youth and women empowerment. And for that, I wrote hundreds of emails to news agencies, colleges, sponsors and organisations. By the end of October, I had received a promise of over one lakh rupees from a Mumbai-based organisation called Young Sikh Leaders, headed by Manpreet Singh, for whose organisation we had to collect some data from every college. He also brought in another sponsor, Vismaad, an animated movie-making company based in Chandigarh. They were also willing to give us around fifty thousand and would be designing everything for us. We were to call them our primary sponsors and talk about them wherever we went, wear their logos on our t-shirts, and hang the poster whenever we spoke to the media.

Ranvir, on the other hand, asked permission from his college and convinced them to pitch another thirty thousand rupees. We had to wear their logo on the back of the t-shirt along with the logo of other minor sponsors who gave us ten thousand each. He was an army kid and, as a result, had friends all over India. He called everyone and asked if we could crash at their place for a night or so, and where there was no one, we looked for gurdwaras for free food and stay. By the first week of November, we had received the first instalment of 50,000 rupees, the design for posters, and replies from at least twelve colleges and universities where we could use the auditorium and hold a discussion with the students.

One of Ranvir's friends, who was an instructor in a college, helped us to tie up with more colleges, especially in Gujarat and Chennai. With all the developments, we were set to travel in December. We had planned a route map and a timeline of our journey. It was going to be a fifty-five-day travel, of 13,000 plus kilometres, with stops at over twenty-eight cities.

I was to travel from Kashmir to Chandigarh alone and then from there, the official kick-off journey in the presence of some dignitaries on 24 December.

Just a week before we were to start the journey, an event that shook entire India shaped our plans as well. The infamous Nirbhaya Rape incident happened on 16 December 2012. It unleashed anger in every conscious human being. A 22-year-old girl was beaten, gang-raped and tortured in a private bus in which she was travelling with her male friend. Six people beat her friend and threw him out of the bus, and then brutally raped her. The girl died within two weeks.

There were protests throughout India. Widespread media coverage and debates angered more people and made them come out in protests. Our primary focus of the trip shifted to awareness about rape and other violence against women. In every college and university we went to, we held hours of discussion and seminars about the topic to find out what the youth of India thought about it, how they perceived women and youth empowerment, and what they thought was the root cause of such violence against women.

That trip changed us, both me and Ranvir, in many ways. We had travelled the whole length of the country. We talked and discussed with tens of thousands of students. We spoke at the top institutions in the country and held debates with the most learned professors and scholars. The level of exposure we had in those two months boosted our confidence and shaped our personalities. I went into deeper intellectual readings and discussions, and that was when inside me, the aspiration of becoming a writer emerged.

The next year, in the winter of 2013, during my vacation, I went solo biking to different north Indian states, self-funded and without a mission. When I was done with biking, I had a new kind of journey which started as an experiment for the first time in August 2014, when I had to go to Himachal Pradesh to appear for an exam. I started ten days before the exam on a hitchhiking journey without any money. I decided to go as a complete backpacker and carried just a single bag of clothes, a tripod and a camera to travel around. When I successfully came back after taking the exam and having spent zero money, it gave me the confidence to repeat the journey for longer durations and to different destinations.

With that in mind, in the winter of 2014, I went for two and a half months of hitchhiking, wherein I travelled from Kashmir to Jammu, Punjab, Haryana, Himachal Pradesh, Uttar Pradesh, Uttarakhand, Delhi, Rajasthan and then back home. That hitchhiking trip was another life-changing one for me. For over seventy-five days, I was at the mercy of strangers, random people fed me, gave me lifts to different places, let me sleep in their houses, interacted with me, and let me into their lives. I spent many nights hungry, sleeping at bus stands, at railway stations, outside the shops, and on roadside benches. Many times I felt like asking a friend to transfer some money to my account, so I could take a bus and go home and end the madness. But I persisted.

Every person I met had a life story, and behind it was a life experience that I imbibed into my own. The journey brought transformation in many ways, which would be the subject of another book I intend to write someday, along the lines of Khalil Gibran's *Prophet*, a modern-day hippie telling his life stories and talking on subjects like love, life, religion, marriage and others just like how Gibran dealt with it in his book.

In the winters of 2015, 2016 and 2017, I went to visit friends in different states, living and enjoying my vacation to the fullest. In October 2018, I met Indu, my to-be wife. That winter, I went to Bangalore to meet her and stayed there for two months with some of my friends and kept meeting her on weekends. The winters of 2019 I spent in Jammu with Bhanu organising open-mic events of poetry and storytelling under the banner of Unfound Artists.

Then Covid took over, and my travels and journeys stopped. After two years of staying home on vacations, I wanted to travel during the coming winter. However, the excitement that I expected from myself was absent due to the current conditions or because I was no more a bachelor.

At one point in time, I was so famous for my travel that in my social circle and extended family everyone would be worried if I did not travel.

They would assume I was sick. 'If he is fine, he would be travelling.' That was the general opinion about me.

The whole day I kept thinking about my previous travels and journeys, and what I could do in Noida. I called up Bhanu and told him that we were going to visit at least three or four places, like Nainital, Jim Corbett, Rishikesh, Haridwar and Jaipur during the winter. I would write and I would travel. Indu would visit us on weekends or whenever she had time. The four months she stayed with me had already put her behind in her studies. I wanted her to concentrate on her studies for the next few months.

Thanks to the previous day's outing, Indu was full of energy and went back to her research work, which kept her away from reading any news or wastefully scrolling through the phone during the day. When I got back home, she was already in the room on some Zoom call.

The moment I finished my lunch, she also came to the dining hall humming a sweet tone.

'You look happy today,' I told her.

'Yes. I finished one data and coded another one today. It has been a productive day so far,' she said, taking a bite from my plate.

'Hungry?' I asked.

'No. I will eat just a little from your plate,' she replied with a wide grin.

'You know, I have realised that it is the biggest scam. You say that you will just eat a little from my plate but by the end, you eat half of it and I am left hungry,' I joked, pushing the plate to the middle of the table so that she could also have some. Whenever I ordered something, she would say, 'I am not hungry, I will eat from your plate,' and then finish most of the portion by herself.

'I read your new draft as well. You had kept it open on your laptop. It's nice,' she said with her mouth full. 'Now you have written about the two major incidents, of Chithisinghpora and 1947. Now you can write about the rest of them and then compile a collection of articles about Kashmiri Sikhs.'

'That's a good idea. I will think about that. Right now I want to finish the draft I started. It's so fresh in my head,' I replied, though the whole day I had been dreaming about my previous trips.

'And... I... don't have to go... to…mo…row,' I sang out to her, 'and most probably on Saturday or Sunday as well,' I added, not finding any rhythm to continue.

'How come?' she said, snatching the last bite from me.

'Friday, the long prayer day. So the supervisor told me that there wouldn't be many people coming for vaccination. He can send me the pictures if needed. And then, Saturday Amit Shah is coming, probably there will be curfew everywhere, and Sunday is a holiday.'

'Great. Then you can work on the articles and I can work on my data, and Sunday we have to go for dinner at mamu's,' she said.

Our plan was set for the next few days and after many days, we were having a normal conversation. No questions or anxieties about when to go and what to do. And going out had also made my mood better. The semblance of normalcy had returned.

25

Better Left Unsaid

Srinagar, Kashmir
24 October 2021

Two days passed in the blink of an eye, with Indu being busy with her research and my parents and I busy with our packing and cleaning. On Friday, I did not go to the doctor's office and spent the day writing and revising the articles.

On Saturday, when Home Minister Amit Shah arrived in Kashmir, everything came to a standstill. It was his first visit to Kashmir after the revocation of Article 370 and the lockdowns. He was on a three-day visit to Kashmir for a security review and to visit the houses of local victims of the terror attacks. Amit Shah and the army chief, Bipin Rawat, gave out a few statements that evening. First, the army chief said that there would be more curbs in Kashmir, like those that followed the revocation of Article 370, and then Amit Shah told the media that these curbs were like bitter pills for the security and welfare of the Kashmiri people. The curbs were a part of daily living in Kashmir. We were expecting a temporary internet shutdown and probably a connectivity blackout for a few hours during the day. But it did not happen. After the revocation of Article 370, the only incident of internet and phone blackout was on the day Syed Ali Shah Geelani died. There was complete normalcy in Kashmir, so much so, that it scared us.

I called Snowber early in the afternoon to check on her. She also had the same reaction. 'Oh, your network is working? I thought it might have been cut down. The almighty home minister has come. Then how come?' she had asked.

'When have you seen protests and hartals and shutdowns after 370? This is the new Kashmir now,' I said.

'By the way, there is no curfew or any other restriction as well. The traffic might just get a little affected, that's all. The rest is completely normal right now,' I said that loud enough so Indu could hear and feel relieved.

'That is good. How much Kashmiris have suffered because of all that? It was a vicious cycle. First, they pass some policies. Then people protest against it. Then the government aggressively suppresses it, and then people protest more,' she said and added, 'Nightmare! In the end, it was the Kashmiri who died. And Bupi Bhaiyya, you tell me, how much the people who had no role in it had to suffer?'

'What do you mean, you tell?' I redirected the question at her.

'You know, when Article 370 was revoked, nobody talked about all those pregnant ladies who were not able to reach the hospitals on time, thanks to multiple checkposts? A lot of them had complications and a lot had miscarriages. Those patients who would have needed emergency medical aid, or those who died because they were not able to reach hospitals. And, you know, a majority of them never cared or never even knew what Article 370 was. They had to suffer because of the handful of people who have always brewed trouble in Kashmir.

'Bupi Bhaiyya, you asked me a question last time. Do I want azaadi? My answer is yes, I do. But azaadi from what? I want azaadi from suffering. Everywhere I look, people are suffering. As a Kashmiri born in the 90s, I have seen nothing but chaos and pain. A child in fifth grade shouldn't have to worry whether she'll see her family alive by the end of the day, because a crackdown and search operation (CASO) was going on in her village while she was five kilometres away at school. She should not be scared about Party No. 1 beating everyone mercilessly for no fault of theirs. She, in sixth grade, shouldn't have to worry about Party No. 2 being irked by merrymaking and celebrating a wedding and that leading to something awful like killings. There are countless examples like these. Whoever is fighting against whoever, defenceless people like the young me are suffering. I want an end to that suffering.

'Here, everyone who has a slight power over someone uses that power to subjugate others. Be it politicians, the separatists, the forces, the militants, government employees, or even common men who have power over women at home. My idea of azaadi is that no one will force something on others. When everyone, regardless of their gender, caste, or religion, will be treated fairly and will live and die with dignity. A man should be able to say without fear, "Hey, this is my house. I won't shelter you. Go away." Further, he should be able to say, "Hey, this is my house. The root of my being. You can't blow it off and render me homeless."

'And a woman should be able to say, "I've been given the right to choose my profession, whom I want to marry, and whether I want to go to masjid or pray at home. You don't have the right to dictate."

'About rights, Bupi Bhaiyya, everyone has the right to good food, quality education, healthcare, dignified employment, their faith, their bodies, and their life in general. You shouldn't be made to say a prayer if you don't believe in it in school assemblies. Why weren't your feelings taken into consideration?

'Azaadi, to me, would mean when it is accepted and followed that we are equal and different, but our differences shouldn't cause one to dominate or be inconsiderate to the other.

'In your context, do I want Kashmir to separate from India? Not at all. To me, India is an idea, a realisation of the above. Its diversity, to me, is the artistry of Allah Miyañ. So many people, climates, cuisines, arts and colours, this isn't possible unless there's a higher power, my Allah Miyañ. I bow in admiration for him when I see India. Also, to me, Indian independence in 1947 is proof that dreams do come true and that humanity wins in the end, no matter how powerful the opposition is. Why wouldn't I want to be a part of it?

'The second and most important reason why I don't want Kashmir to separate from India is because women will suffer if all power is given to people who believe in a certain ideology, which, by the way, I actually find un-Islamic. Because Allah called the prophet of Islam "mercy for the universe." He didn't say "My way or the highway." He was accepting and loving. God is accepting and loving. He isn't more mine and less yours, or the other way around. He will ask us if we were good to each other, not if we established a religious state.

'These people with certain ideologies who see religion through their narrow and unclean lenses will shut women inside with little to no rights, and that too only until women let them have their way. What do you think of these people, who celebrated the Taliban's taking over Afghanistan even after fully knowing the Taliban's anti-woman activities? Won't they do the same here? They will, if given a chance. I am not willing to give them that chance.'

Not knowing how else to react, I told her, 'That has always been the case, everywhere, throughout human history, throughout the world. In any state marred by conflict and war, the civilians are the ones who are affected the most. And any majoritarian supremacy will be bad, even for the majority. Because once a religious majority comes to power, the next step is fanaticism. Even for their own religious subjects they become suffocating.'

I thought about what Snowber said. When changes of a big magnitude came, a lot of sacrifices had to be made, voluntarily or involuntarily. And revoking the articles was the biggest, most momentous event in the history of J&K after Partition. The minorities would feel safer because of that, which to a large extent they had started to do, but then these recent episodes of killings put everything back in perspective. Whatever happened, it would be difficult to ensure a hundred per cent safe spaces for minorities in Kashmir, as of now.

'Yes, Bupi Bhaiyya. That is true. I hope things become better in Kashmir. Then everyone can live more peacefully.'

'If the Bharatiya Janata Party comes for one more term, then we will see how things develop,' I replied.

'Who else do you think can come to power? Is there any other potential choice?'

'Let's hope Kashmir stays like this, minus the killings and minority issues.'

But would that be enough for us to live in Kashmir, I thought to myself. Even if it became peaceful, we would still be micro-minorities. We would still suffer silent tortures, and we would still wonder if we have a future here.

Sunday was different, for everyone was excited about the India-Pakistan match while we were busy with our mundanities. Nobody in our house was a cricket fan. I hadn't watched a cricket match after Sachin retired, and Indu was more of a football fan. But India-Pakistan match day in Kashmir had a whole different energy level. I was hoping for India to win, not because I was a fan of the team, but because Pakistan winning meant a lot of trouble in the next few days.

The moment the result was decided, the whole of Kashmir lit up with crackers, and their sounds started echoing everywhere. Our first thought was that an encounter had broken out nearby. But then the sounds kept fluctuating, and we understood that Pakistan had won the match. Indu was stupefied at the number of crackers that blew up everywhere. For twenty minutes straight, we kept on hearing the sounds from one side or another.

'I have heard how Kashmiris celebrate Pakistan's win against India. But I never knew it was like this,' Indu told me while we watched crackers light up the evening sky from our veranda. 'They are openly supporting Pakistan,' she added.

'They have always loved Pakistan, baby. What do you think the last thirty years of the freedom movement were about?' I asked her. 'Though not everyone. There are some who want free Kashmir. Then there are some who would go with India, and then there are a handful who give zero fucks about it all.'

I added, 'This will go on and on. Let's go inside and get ready for the dinner party. They would be expecting us by now.'

Indu had been very moody all these days. There was contradicting news every day. People were being killed. It did not matter whether as militants or police or army or civilians. Nonetheless, lives were lost. There were encounters every day, sometimes nearby, sometimes at places she had never heard of. Then there were talks of peace, assurances by politicians and the army that they would punish every culprit, and that they had arrested dozens of people in connection with the civilian killings. Then there were speculations and rumours about more such killings. Even the security forces and people at the highest administrative levels said in press releases that there was a chance of more such terror incidents due to which security was being beefed up.

'Why can't it stop? Why can't India remove the forces from Kashmir, or why can't the militants give up?' she had asked me one evening.

'If anyone knew the answer to these questions, thousands and thousands of people would not be dead. It's a peculiar situation. When I was in college, I wanted to buy a bike, so I could go and take some home tuition and earn some money. But to buy the bike I need to take those tuitions and earn the money. It was a Catch-22 situation. So I did none of those things and bought a cycle. The same is true for Kashmir. One thing had to be done to achieve the other. To remove the army, militants have to stop and to stop the militants, the army has to be here. It is a non-Newtonian motion. Can't be put to rest now,' I told her.

Before going to dinner, she was still in a trance after seeing all those fireworks. I had to push her to get ready with an assurance that we could talk about it some other time.

At mamu's place, grand preparations were made for our dinner. And it was not only for Indu and me. They had invited the whole family. We were supposed to reach Bikram mamu's at 4 p.m. so that we could first have the tea and then talk and interact. And then, we were to have dinner by 9 p.m. and come back by 11 p.m. But we were already running late.

The hardest part for me, other than having meaningless conversations with people, was getting appropriately dressed for the occasion. I was used to wearing clothes closest to my arm's reach. I did not have the patience to wear matching outfits or formals or even iron my clothes. I wore what I liked and however I liked. And I was always criticised for it. Somehow everyone had the absurd idea that after marriage, my wife would hammer some sense into me and up my dressing sense. But to their surprise, Indu was equally disinterested in dressing up. The only difference was that she looked graceful and elegant while I looked unorganised and homeless. My father had put this thought in my head as a child that what mattered was not the clothes on your body, but the knowledge in your head. And I took the first half literally.

When we went to someone's house for a visit, we did not go empty-handed. We had to buy some fruits and juices for the host family. The day we started to get invites, I had to teach Indu some dos and don'ts of our culture. We already knew that everyone in the extended family loved her. The burden of good first impressions was over. To woo our relatives, she would have to greet them with Sat Sri Akal, the Sikh greeting.

We were welcomed with hugs and kisses, and after the initial pleasantries and asking Indu a dozen questions about how her study was and how her parents and everyone back in Kerala were, the conversations shifted to the issue at hand, the minority killings and what Sikhs would do now. We were served an elaborate tea, with a side of gossip about the other houses in the vicinity. While mamu and my father talked about how business was being affected, the ladies talked about someone in the neighbourhood whose daughter got married recently.

After a while, the language so easily shifted to our mother tongue that Indu got completely excluded from whatever we were talking about. I could see she was feeling left out, so I tried to bring back the conversation to something where she could be included.

'So, mami is an exceptional cook. If you could learn to make butter chicken from her, it would be fantastic,' I told Indu, raising my voice so it could gather the attention of everyone in the room.

'Not better than your mother. We all can be experts in one or two dishes. But she is the expert in everything,' mami replied. And with that sentence, the conversation died there itself. My attempt failed miserably and I joined Indu in watching some YouTube videos that she was watching on her phone.

Mamu's son, Jaiveer, was studying medicine at Jawaharlal Institute of Postgraduate Medical Education and Research (JIPMER) in Pondicherry. He was one of the only two Sikhs from Kashmir who had qualified for medicine after the NEET exam that year. All of us were proud of him. Bhavan, mamu's daughter, was still in Class XI and was under extreme pressure to perform equally well as her brother. She was busy studying, mami was busy attending to my mother while sitting next to us, and mamu and my father were engaged in the loop of pessimism that I had come to despise so much now. That left me, Indu and Ramneek to ourselves.

In between, mami would look at Indu and smile, the language barrier was so awkward. But after the important gossip was over, both my mother and mami's attention shifted to Indu.

'You could have stayed for a few more weeks. It would be very good,' said mami. 'Diwali is next week. We could have celebrated it with you,' she added.

'Oh, but Bupi was saying that it is not a Sikh festival and that you people don't celebrate it,' Indu replied. She looked a little surprised at mami's suggestion.

'No, no. We don't celebrate it, but you can celebrate it. It's your festival,' mami replied.

'No. We also don't celebrate Diwali. It is more of a north Indian festival. Hindus in Kerala don't celebrate it much. Our major festival is Onam,' Indu said.

Mami was shocked. She could not articulate a reply to it. She first looked at her, then at me, for further explanation. I was shocked, too, when I first heard that the Hindus in the south do not celebrate Diwali much. The other shock I had was when I learned that Hindus in Kerala eat beef. That was a shock I did not intend to give to any other person in my family. In north India, just talking about beef can get one lynched. It was not a thing to be joked about.

'They are Hindus. But they celebrate different gods,' I told her.

'Oh yes, yes. I remember they have Onam, Pongal and Ganpati Bappa moriya wala festivals,' mami replied. The ignorance of north Indians towards south Indians was beyond any measure. I too was ignorant before meeting Indu. I did not even know the languages and the regions they were spoken in. I just knew their names. I did not know that the movie industry of the south was so versatile, as my only exposure to south Indian movies was that of Hindi-dubbed action-packed Telugu movies. Indu introduced me to some great movies and actors from the Malayalam industry, like Mohanlal, Dulquer Salman, Tovino Thomas, Manju Warrier, Parvathy, Fahad Fasil and Mammooty, and the like. The movies like *Charlie, Trance, Bangalore Days, Ustaad Hotel* and *Lucifer* surprised me with their plot lines and story structure. There was a vast universe of knowledge in their literature. I read O.V. Vijayan, Jaishree Misra and Manu S. Pillai, who wrote in English and heard stories from Indu about the works of Benyamin, M. Mukundan, and M.T. Vasudevan Nair. I knew only about Kamla Das, Arundhati Roy and Shashi Tharoor. Before Indu could enlighten mami about the difference between Onam, Pongal and Ganesh Chaturthi, I signalled her to avoid the argument.

'Yes, mami. We celebrate Onam mostly,' she replied with a smile.

'Gurpurab is on the 19th next month. We celebrate that and a few more festivals here in Kashmir. Baisakhi, you know, in April?' mami asked.

'Yes. Baisakhi I know. We have Vishu in April, similarly,' she replied.

'Yes. In north India, Baisakhi is a harvest festival. But for us, Sikhs, it is not just a harvest festival. It's the birth anniversary of the Khalsa Panth,' said mamu, who had been quietly listening to the conversation. I noticed their conversation had paused the moment mami and Indu's conversation took the centre stage.

'Oh, you never told me this,' Indu asked me.

'I guess not. I will tell you some other time,' I replied while still watching the YouTube video on her phone.

'You should have told her about your religion. She is married to a Sikh now. She should know about Sikhism,' mamu's tone was sarcastic and judgemental at the same time. I felt a tinge of irritation and wanted to give a befitting reply that immediately formed in my head. But I just agreed with him and told him it was my mistake and that I would tell her everything about Sikhism soon.

Indu and I had discussed a lot of things. But religion was the least discussed one. It was a very personal choice, and when we married, we never considered converting our religions. She would be a Hindu, and I would be a Sikh, both of us were diluted, non-ritualistic, almost non-followers of our religions. So it was never a point of our discussion in our life. Though I felt proud of my religion and had told her a few stories that I associated with that pride, I myself had never followed any rituals. So the need never arose.

'Anyway. This Gurpurab in November is our main festival, the birth anniversary of Guru Nanak Dev ji. You know about Guru Nanak Dev? Do you?' mamu asked.

'Yes, I know. He has told me most of the basic things and philosophies of Sikhism,' she replied.

Mamu's face lit up a little. He did not expect that I would say anything about Sikhism to her.

Kashmiri Sikhs, I had come to realise, were more spirited than Sikhs anywhere else. They were very proud of their religion, and their whole life was directed and influenced by it. Being a micro-minority, it was a defensive and assertive mechanism as well. The whole community came together for such festivals, and as such, they were very important to them.

There were a few major Sikh festivals that were celebrated. The first one was Baisakhi in April. Then Guru Arjan Dev ji's martyrdom in June, Guru Hargobind ji's birth anniversary in June or July, and the last one, Guru Nanak Dev ji's birth anniversary in November. There was a commemoration festival in memory of all the Sikhs martyred during the attack on Darbar Sahib on 6 June 1984, which was held every year in Gurdwara Shaheed Bunga. Each of these occasions was celebrated in a specific gurdwara every year, so the whole of the Sikh community of Kashmir could come together from their respective towns and villages and mark it together.

All these festivals and ceremonies held a very important place in the lives of Kashmiri Sikhs. On all these occasions, an Akhand Paath was held in the gurdwaras for three days, and the big festival was held on the last day of the paath. The first day was a quiet one, and usually, very few people came to the gurdwara. But by the evening of the second day, people started to flock together to prepare for the next day's big event. Volunteers came forward to help with the preparation of langar for thousands of people who would be coming the next day. Women, men and children all take up their respective responsibilities of cutting different types of vegetables, cleaning the halls and utensils, and logistics, respectively. Tea and snacks were served throughout the evening till late at night to the volunteers and sangat.

My mamus, all three of them, were very religious. The eldest one, Manjit Singh, was a member of Sikh Missionaries and was very respected for his knowledge and philosophy about religion. The second, Harjit Singh, was the president of a major Sikh organisation. The youngest, Bikramjit Singh, where we were having dinner, was a devout volunteer in the langar hall at every festival or occasion. He would have gone to extreme lengths to explain to Indu the basics of Sikhism if she had said that she did not know much. Over time, our conversations shifted from Sikhism to Gurpurab celebrations, to where we would live in Noida and when Indu would return.

There was not much to talk about except religion, immediate politics involving the minority killings, the future of our generation and the ones to come in Kashmir, and some petty gossip about who was doing what. At mamu's place, I realised it was not only us who had grown pessimistic and kept talking about the same thing again and again. Life in Kashmiri Sikh households revolved around these issues.

When dinner was announced, it was already 9.30, and I was famished. Mami was an excellent cook, and I had an idea of what she had prepared. Her speciality, *mutton yakhni*, a mutton preparation in curd and Kashmiri masalas, was the one I loved. In addition to the yakhni, she had cooked a variety of chicken curry, mutton ristas, paneer, rajma and two different kinds of chutneys. The staple was rice. Indu, at her peak of hunger, would still eat one-tenth of what I would eat without any appetite at all. She had already told me at home to help her finish her meal if she was not able to. I used to tease her that it was a waste of food and money to take her to a buffet like Barbecue Nation or Pirates of the Grills. All of us ended up overeating.

'So now you people will come back only in March?' mamu asked after we finished the dinner.

'Hopefully not. I actually don't want to come back to Kashmir,' I replied. This was the first time I discussed this with any relative.

'What? What do you mean you don't want to come back? You have a job here. What will you do about that?' he asked.

'I might leave the job. Not immediately. I might go for unpaid leave for a year or two and see if I can manage to get some job or other earning source, or if I can settle down outside Kashmir. Only then will I leave the job,' I said. 'Anyway, Indu has to go to Australia next year, and she will come back in the summer of 2023, I still have time till then to think about it all.'

'Who leaves a government job? Don't even think about that. Whatever you do, a private job is a private job and a government job is a government job.'

'And where will you go, outside Kashmir? Jammu?' he asked.

'If in India, we are thinking of Bangalore. Otherwise, some foreign country, probably Australia or somewhere in Europe,' I replied. I could see a mixed response from Indu. When I spoke, she looked at my face and felt relaxed. When mamu spoke, she looked at him and felt anxious.

'You are wise enough to decide what is good for you. But I will still say, don't leave the job without thinking twice. You are lucky to get one. You got it easy when you were still in college. Look at the people around you. A vast majority of people are unemployed, and we in the private business don't even know if we will have work tomorrow or not. The security you have from this job. Whether you work or not, you still get money. Keep all those things in mind,' he said.

'Yes, I will. Don't worry,' I said.

For me, the plan of leaving the government job was something that was still unclear. It was a predicament of the highest level, which I would only be able to come out of when I actually came out of it. It was that absurd a problem. The moment I initiated the conversation, I knew I should not have because it would come with dozens of follow-up questions, the answers to which I myself did not know. And if this information was to reach other relatives, then the whirlpool of questions and answers would never end. I was regretting the conversation already when an unexpected question was thrown at me.

'So you are thinking of vacating your accommodation here before you go?' mamu asked.

'I don't think I would do that yet. The decision to leave Kashmir is final. But I have to come back before quitting the job for all the paperwork and all, for my documentation, etc. That I will do during my visit next year.'

I was not prepared for this question, and the answer could go both ways. A no meant I was still indecisive about leaving Kashmir which could make Indu infuriated again, while a yes meant I was making the decision in haste and there was a high possibility of regretting it in future.

When my parents, Indu and I discussed it, we decided that we would keep the property for now because we wouldn't get such a good place in case we came back to Kashmir, which was highly expected. The current move was more of an escape rather than a planned migration. And I had already told Indu that after the vacation was over in March, I would come back for a month or so and then again take leave and shift back to Noida to search for a new future outside Kashmir. And in March, I would vacate the place after selling off the furniture and moving the rest to Jammu.

'Oh, you will leave the job next year, then?' Mamu was still not able to digest it. He was the happiest when I got the job. He taught me a lot of things in the first two or three years that I lived at his home when I joined work in Kashmir. He was by far my favourite relative. I had different dynamics with all three of my mamus. With Manjit mamu, I had a more intellectually driven relationship. We talked about philosophy and religion whenever we had time. He was also the tech expert in our family. He introduced me to English movies and music when I was a teenager.

Harjit mamu was more of a rugged person, who I loved for his fearlessness and carefree life. His ideology and way of living inspired not only me but my cousins as well. He was the macho man in the family, built six feet five inches like a wild boar. And with Bikram mamu, I was more of a friend with whom I discussed my life issues and problems.

'I don't know. But I will take a long leave next year for sure,' I replied after a long pause.

My father signalled to me that we had to wind up and go home soon. During all the discussions and conversations, time flew very fast. It was around 11.30 p.m. when we told them that we should be going now. They insisted that we spend the night there. But we convinced them that we had to go home. It was always a tussle whenever we visited anyone for dinner. Mostly we stayed the night and came back home the next day after having breakfast as well. Indu had to work the next day, and if she slept late, the next day was very unproductive for her. She could not function without a full sleep. Also the next few days, she had a lot of work to do during the day and attend the dinners post-evening. She required proper sleep more than anything else now.

The last few days, because of being busy, Indu was shielded from most of the news. Her friends and relatives had gone back to their lives as no more headlines from Kashmir reached them. She did not get any more calls after she said that she had booked her flight for 2 November. And every day, I would hide the newspaper from her. I did not want any fights or arguments, for those would be the things she would remember about Kashmir forever. As humans, we tend to forget the happy moments, and are thankless about what we have, and always crib about what we did not have and remember the sad, depressing things.

During the day, I could see that my mother was a little gloomy while packing. All her life, she had been living in Kashmir. Even during the years we stayed in Jammu, we used to visit in the summers, or her siblings would visit us in winter. When I told her that I was planning to move to Bangalore or some foreign country in future, she did not say anything. No excitement, no astonishment. She was neutral. But one time, I overheard her talking to her sister over the phone, 'Bupi is saying he will go to Bangalore. We will also go with him. What will we do without him here? But then what will we do there as well, with nobody from our circle?'

In my head, I had always envisioned that I would stay together with my parents and Ramneek, wherever that was, and they had always told me that they would accompany me. Father could easily gel with people. He just needed a gurdwara nearby to engage with the community. Ramneek, who was homebound, needed his internet and electronics and me around to be comfortable and happy. Mother, on the other hand, was the most social one, despite the fact that she did not leave home much. She loved to host guests, and once in a while, she visited her brothers and sisters. Other than that, she visited the gurdwara every day. If I were to move to someplace, I had to keep in mind that at least there was a gurdwara in the vicinity so my parents could also live an active and happy life, interact outside the house, and not feel bored and alone.

With those thoughts in mind, I slept off with a slight anxiety about the next day's dinner, where the chances of a political argument were high, as Harjeet uncle was more inclined towards Sikh politics and business.

26

A Silent Migration

Srinagar, Kashmir
29 October 2021

Even before we had reached the next dinner host Harjeet uncle's house, the news of me leaving the job and Kashmir in the near future had reached them. Harjeet uncle was a firm believer that one should not leave his homeland, no matter what. He always advocated that only those who were incapable of making a living in their homelands went searching for livelihood outside. I had dozens of conversations with him about how, in my opinion, the future of Sikhs in Kashmir looked bleak. He thrashed me with his argument, saying that our generation was lethargic and lazy. They did not work hard enough to get the opportunities and avenues to get a stable lifestyle. He believed that there was no dearth of jobs for those who were capable and that one who knew how to make money could make it anywhere. That success was not dependent on the place or the time. All his assumptions made perfect sense theoretically. But with mental, emotional and psychological factors in the fray, which escaped the eyes of any overly pragmatic person, the situations turned the opposite. The question was how we could be more capable in the middle of so much stress, anxiety, tension and conflict. But at the end of all our conversations, we went home with our own opinions, sometimes after an angry exchange.

Dinner was served by nine, but the conversations started earlier.

'So you have finally decided to leave Kashmir? You've been wanting to do that for a long time,' he asked me.

In a lot of our conversations, I had told him so and, in fact, advised him to tell his children to leave Kashmir for better prospects. He had two sons. The elder one, Gurtej, was a fantastic singer and bodybuilder and had done his engineering. He earned by taking private tuitions and also was a personal trainer and dietitian to health-conscious people, and in both professions, he was very good. The younger one, Jaswinder, worked in Bangalore at a MNC and would most probably settle there if given a chance. I had told my uncle to let Gurtej leave Kashmir. With his degree and skills, he wouldn't have to struggle. Once he created a clientele base for himself, he could flourish and grow at an exceptional rate, which was hard in Kashmir.

To my uncle's question directed towards me, I replied, 'Yes, I had already decided years ago. It was just a matter of when, and I feel this is the right time. It would probably be just a year or more until Indu finishes her studies,' I replied while taking one more piece of *Khatta-meat*, a mutton dish that Gurtej had prepared. It was a Dogri (Jammu) preparation and not a Kashmiri one, and he had done complete justice to it.

'We will get more scattered. Already, we have our feet in two boats. This new generation will add a third one,' Harjeet uncle said. He had property in Jammu. Most Kashmiri Sikhs had properties in Jammu in addition to homes and properties in Srinagar town and their native villages. Some sold off their village lands to buy property in Jammu. As a result, we as a community had become seasonal migrants who stayed in Kashmir from March to the middle of December and the rest of the three months in Jammu when it was extremely cold in Kashmir. A lot of people had gradually moved out of Kashmir and gone to Jammu, with many more moving out every other year. So everyone had family and relatives in both Jammu and Kashmir.

This migration has taken a toll on us. In times of happiness and grief, we had to come together as a family to one place, which could either be Jammu or Kashmir. So for weddings, deaths, or any other ceremonies, most people had to cross borders and travel extensively to the other place. During my wedding, which happened in Kashmir, most of my relatives who lived in Jammu could not attend because of travel and time constraints.

The travel between Jammu and Kashmir by itself had taken a lot of lives. The national highway was a death route with a lot of people dying while travelling on it. During bad weather, landslides and avalanches were common, with snow storms and slippery roads adding to the risk. Every year for days, the roads were closed because of heavy snowfall and landslides, and if, God forbid, someone got stuck on the highway during those times without food and a place to stay, death was inevitable.

Whatever I did in future, wherever I would go, I would always be tied to Kashmir. All my maternal relatives would never leave Kashmir, at least in the foreseeable future, and for all those occasions, I would have to come back to participate. There were occasions and events where you did not have the option of saying no.

'One by one, everyone would be leaving Kashmir. When they won't find jobs and opportunities, when they won't have any mental peace and stability, they would have to go,' my father said. 'Now also, if you look at young people, they are leaving Kashmir. Outside Kashmir, even if they are just about surviving and struggling very hard, they still prefer to live there. The freedom and mental peace they have found in those places are more important to them than any other thing they have here.'

'But now Kashmir is changing. After Article 370 was revoked things have changed considerably,' my uncle replied. Like most Kashmiri Sikhs, the illusion of normalcy was tricking him too.

In the past three years since the abrogation of Article 370 and Article 35(a), I understood that the people who debated about those articles knew nothing about them. They had never read the text of the articles as in the Indian Constitution and, surprisingly, did not even know their breadth and scope and the provisions therein. Most people knew that abrogation meant that the special status to J&K had been withdrawn, but the majority were oblivious to the understanding of what that special status meant. For them, the only three things that the special status provided were: one, that the Constitution and penal code of Kashmir were different from the rest of India. Two, that nobody from outside Kashmir could purchase land in Kashmir, and three, that no outsider could get government jobs in Kashmir. All these were right, but there were more than a dozen provisions in the articles, which the laymen did not know.

'How do you think that things have changed for us, and why do you think that the changes are good for us?' I asked him.

'Nothing has changed for us Sikhs. If you think otherwise, then you are not grasping the situation in its entirety,' my father added.

My uncle said, 'I don't know much. But it has broken the backbone of the Kashmiri freedom movement. People now understand that they can't come out and oppose the government anymore. Ever since the abrogation, have you seen protests, hartals and strikes? Have you seen stone-pelting episodes like before? Kashmir has become calmer and more stable. Also, corruption has come down a lot, people are fearful of the Modi government, and fear consequences. Otherwise, when have you seen government offices in Kashmir working efficiently?'

To an extent, what he said was true. Now most people noticed several changes in the workings of offices. Employees were scared of the consequences. They feared that the officers above them were not their own people anymore and that they wouldn't go easy on them. The employees believed that the higher officials bore an ingrained hatred towards Kashmir and Kashmiris and that at the slightest error, the employees would be punished badly. It resulted in the efficient working of most government offices. Also, the implementation of orders and circulars became rigorous. Slowly, new orders started rolling out which aimed to Indianise the psyche of people, like the celebration of 15 August, 26 January, and other important national events that Kashmir had never even heard of. New orders enforced hosting flags in schools, reciting the National Anthem and other prayers, and likewise, things that the majority despised.

'They (Government) are going to change the demography of Kashmir. They will bring outsiders and settle them here, which will change the population ratio, voting dynamics and economic and financial scenario. We wouldn't feel like the only minority then,' my uncle said. That was the policy that everyone was talking about, changing the demography of Kashmir to effectively dilute the majority and their issues.

'Let us see. For practical purposes, we are still a minority, Muslims are still a majority, and for all reasons and purposes, we will always remain like that,' I replied. 'And the thing is that we don't have a problem with them, and they don't have a problem with us. It's in the small things, behaviours, patterns, ignorance and actions that we are being subjected to, unknowingly and unintentionally, causing trauma, stress and anxiety.'

'Yes. I have lived all my life here in Kashmir, happily and courageously. My closest friends are Muslims, and they are the first ones to come at the time of crisis, even before my family and people from my own community. I don't know why your generation has difficulty living in Kashmir. A fearless person is fearless everywhere. His surroundings, his condition and his situation did not matter. *Sher budha ho ke bhi sher hi rehta hai* (a lion, even when he gets old, is still a lion),' he replied.

I replied with some irritation, 'Some of my close friends are also Muslims. If you think I have a problem with Muslims, then you are wrong. I don't have problems with Kashmir either. My problem is with the environment, my immediate society, and the company. It's not only me, or Sikhs. Even a lot of Muslim friends have left Kashmir. They are also trying to find opportunities outside Kashmir. They too are frustrated with the Kashmir situation. Our generation wants to choose mental peace over constant fears and frustrations. And for what should we do that? For azaadi? We just want to live happily with the people we love without thinking and debating about all these issues. We want to be free to do and act without others poking their noses into our lives, which Kashmiri people are too proficient in. *Aur sher aaj kal circuson aur zoo me kutton ki tarah paley jatey hain* (And lions these days are domesticated in zoos and circuses like dogs).'

How could people not understand this simple thing?

Indu was listening to our conversation keenly. Some of it was in Hindi, but most of it was in our mother tongue, so I did not know how much she understood. The expression on her face was intense. Gurtej, on the other hand, ignored the conversation like it was not even happening in the room. He gestured at me to leave it at that. I, too, knew there was no point. Like always, it was going to be a futile one, with all of us sticking to our ideologies and opinions. But the topic was too tantalising to leave, and at the same time, the arguments were getting more intense and louder. It could have gone in any direction from there, had my father not interrupted us with a simple remark, 'We can only discuss and waste our energy. Neither you nor he is the policy maker. None of our opinions matter. So don't waste your energies.'

'*Chalo ji chhaddo parey*. You tell me where are you going to live in winter, Jammu or Delhi?' my uncle asked. With Harjeet uncle, I had a very close association. In my childhood, he influenced me a lot and would spoil me with gifts and presents. The best thing about him was that he always treated me and other kids with respect. He valued our opinions and would listen to us, and hold conversations with us. He treated us as adults. And even now, I love holding such discussions with him. Knowing that whatever the outcome of our discussion was, we would still be cool with each other, gave me more confidence to express myself freely with him.

'Delhi,' I replied. 'Bhanu and I will rent a flat together and then Indu can come whenever she has time, which she will not have much. She has a lot of pending work to finish,' I told him.

'Why is Bhanu going to Delhi?' he asked. Everybody in my extended family knew Bhanu and Sarabjeet, they were my two closest friends.

'He got a job transfer there.'

'After marriage, you should live with your wife, not with your friend,' my uncle joked, turning the conversation into a pleasant one. I gave a smile.

Indu also understood the conversation and jumped in my defence, 'I will not be able to live with him right now. I am staying in the hostel, and I have a lot of work. So it is better for him to live with Bhanu and work or enjoy and do whatever he wants.'

'Lucky you are,' my uncle mocked me again.

That night after returning home, two things happened.

First, my father asked me to go for a short walk with him. He said he felt that he had overeaten and wanted a short walk to feel light. I understood that he wanted to talk to me about something. Otherwise, he could have gone for a walk alone; he always did.

During the walk, he told me something which made me think deeply. 'I respect your decision, and I know it would be very difficult for Indu to live in Kashmir, even if it was normal or non-violent. Based on her education and hard work she has put all her life into making her career, it would be unfair if we told her to live and work in Kashmir. But still, you rethink the decisions again, and both of you talk about it. You have to move out, but is this the right time, or can you afford to quit the job now or in the next two years? Look around, there is so much despair and financial issues with the young generation. Think about all those things as well.'

'Ok,' I could not say anything more and just kept walking with him. He continued. 'When I was young, I also made the same decision. I went to Jammu when you were a child, but I could not survive there without financial stability or a permanent source of earnings. It was very difficult. Though I say that we came back because your mother was sad, I know, we came back because we could not be financially stable there, and because something in Kashmir always pulls me back. Even now, when I say I hate Kashmir, I feel leaving it behind would not be easy, not for me, not for you as well. So if you decide, stand by your decision, whatever happens.'

I was silent, I knew it was hard for him as well, but I never expected him to say it out loud. He had taken the decision to leave Kashmir twice, and still, we were in Kashmir, call it fate, circumstances, or whatever.

The second thing was that Indu asked me about Article 370 and Article 35(a) again. When the abrogation happened, we were in a newly established relationship, and at the height of it. And then one day, all of a sudden, we were inaccessible to each other for months.

In the three years after the abrogation of the two articles, I met with three perspectives about it from the Sikhs of Kashmir. First, they thought that with Article 370 and Article 35(a) gone, things would become better for the Sikhs, as government officers would come from other places and this would reduce nepotism and favouritism that worked against the Sikhs. Their problems and grievances would be heard better. People would buy lands in Kashmir and set up their businesses, and that would increase employment avenues for Sikhs as well.

The second thought was against the abrogation and felt that as a Kashmiri person, Sikh or Muslim, or from any other religion, the abrogation was unjust and unfair to them. This was a promise that was made by the state to its people but was broken regardless. The people who subscribed to this thought were in favour of a plebiscite or referendum. They wanted the reassurance of the privileges that came with the two articles which were taken from them without asking them. The third type of people were neutral and said, 'We will see how things develop. It is too soon to say anything.'

For Sikhs, who are a micro-minority, these things do not matter at all. We were the grass under the elephant's feet. If the abrogation was brought to punish the Kashmiri Muslims, we would be the collateral, and if it happened for development and progress, we would be overlooked. It could go both ways and both would not benefit us. I myself subscribed to the third perspective in a way.

I felt the impact of abrogation immediately and it was immense. I was cut off from a lot of things out of the blue, especially from Indu. We had come a very long way since her first visit to Kashmir. Though we never proposed to each other we simply knew that we belonged to each other. We started messaging and calling each other immediately after she had gone back from her visit. Ever since we never skipped a day. Even if it was for a minute or two, we would talk to each other, at least to say goodnight before sleeping.

One of my greatest fears about being in a relationship was the boundaries of freedom and individual space. But with her, I felt free and connected at the same time. The more I talked to her, the more I fell in love. Happy and content, our routines had synchronised so much that we felt we were mirroring each other.

Then in June 2019, she moved to Delhi for higher studies and became more accessible to me. But it was a new place and culture, which she was still trying to figure out. On 4 August 2019, we said goodnight to each other, but on 5 August, we were not able to say good morning. The abrogation came out of the blue and made both our futures uncertain. I had an inkling that the internet was going to shut down as that was the popular rumour going around for some days. In the days before the abrogation, we saw military forces everywhere. People were confused and then the rumours felt more and more concrete every passing hour. The buying and hoarding of groceries and supplies was the first instinct of every Kashmiri. Everyone was suspecting something was going to happen, but nobody knew what it would be and why the internet was going to be shut down. Many times I thought of telling Indu that my internet might not work for a few days, but then I held it back, thinking that it would cause panic in her, a mistake I realised later, but couldn't do anything about. I had assumed a few days of internet blackouts would do no harm. I could still call Indu or any other person I wanted to talk to if I wanted to. Or so I thought.

27

Articles 370 and 35(a)

Srinagar, Kashmir
August–October 2019

Bhanu came to Kashmir to stay with me for a month in July 2019. His return flight was booked for 5 August. During that month, we organised a lot of events, trekked and travelled, and camped at the most scenic places in Kashmir. For twenty out of the thirty days, we camped at different places. Those days we were actively working on Unfound and had roped in a lot of Kashmiri friends into our venture. Most days, we would be sitting outside the Books and Bricks Cafe, where Danny, Anam and Krushna would be our hosts. We decided to launch a book club at the Books and Bricks Cafe. Our idea was to lend books that were just ornaments on the cafe shelves. Now it could be lent to a member of our book club. The launch of the book club was decided on 3 August, and the first official meeting was to be convened during the second week of August. We had a good response, as all the cafes helped us to promote the club, and the launch was successful.

A similar initiative had been already taken by Javid Parsa, the owner of the largest chain of cafes in Kashmir, Parsa's Food for All. He had over 5000 books in Parsa's book bank, usually donations from people, and he kept them on the shelves of his cafes. He would keep a register and lend books to people. When I discussed our book club with him, he immediately helped us spread the word to his followers through his social media handles. His book bank also became a part of our book repository. He was only a year older than me, an architecture student who studied in Punjab and worked in Bangalore before returning to Kashmir and opening his cafe. From just one cafe, he became a successful entrepreneur of our generation and opened more than a dozen other outlets in Kashmir and a few in other parts of India as well, like Bangalore, Pune, Jammu, Delhi and Ladakh.

Another cafe, Winterfell Cafe, which was owned by Kamran also pitched in. Winterfell was the venue for most of our literary events as Kamran promoted art and literature, and supported artists. Whenever we used his venue, he would never charge us anything and would sometimes give out free coffee to the guests. All these prominent cafes were associated with our book club. The largest book store in Kashmir, Gulshan Book Store, promised a ten per cent discount to the members of our book club.

On 4 August, Bhanu and I were chilling outside Books and Bricks in the evening when Umair, another friend of ours and owner of Parsa's SSM (Sir Syed Memorial College) outlet joined us. We started to discuss the rumours going around, about the possible internet blackout. There was a grim premonition everywhere. During the day, everyone was downloading movies, songs and games that could be played offline because somehow everyone knew that the internet was going to be snapped the next morning, though nobody knew why and for how many days. Through different sources, we had information that there would be an imposition of curfew for the next two days, and there was a high chance that the mobile network would also be snapped.

Bhanu and I went home and told my father about the situation and suggested that we stock ration for at least a month. My father came with us, but all the shops were filled with people and everyone was stocking their essentials. We had to stand for an hour to buy our list of groceries. We bought dals, rice, oil, salt and sugar that could last for almost two months. In the evening, I went out again to the cafe, to see what else was happening around us. I was confused whether to tell Indu about any of it or not. I wanted to give her a heads-up. For the last month or so, most of the time, our conversations were focused on her work or Unfound or Bhanu and I exploring some new place. In the end, I called her, but did not say anything about what was happening, and that I was strongly suspecting a blackout. I was hopeful that whatever happened, the BSNL or the landline would work, so in an adverse situation I would be able to inform her about any further happenings.

Umair, Bhanu and I were all standing outside Books and Bricks around 7 p.m. when we saw two buses and trucks entering the indoor stadium, which was just next to the cafe. Then, two more buses came and entered Amar Singh College, opposite the stadium. All the buses had something on their roofs hidden under tarpaulin sheets. The windows of all the buses were blacked out with sheets of metal. We had a rough idea of what was happening. This was the modus operandi of the army or any other paramilitary force that used to set up bunkers and travel through cities using public transport department vehicles.

Umair got a little flustered and told us that he suspected something bad was going to happen and wanted us to accompany him to bring some of his cafe workers, who were some forty kilometres away from where we were. Bhanu and I were free and joined him.

As we sat in his car, Umair said, 'Bupi yaar, they are from Uttar Pradesh and Bihar, and they will be scared to death. More than them, their families back home will be scared if by any chance communication gets blocked.' He looked worried and added, 'And in that area, they will be under house arrest. The locals will keep them safe, but you never know what can happen in Kashmir.'

'Where would you keep them if you bring them here?' I asked him. There were three of them, all non-Kashmiris. He called Javid to ask him for advice, and they decided on the venue. For most of his cafes, Javid employed local people as workers, and that was how he was giving back to society as well, employing over hundreds of locals in his different outlets. In Srinagar, he had rented a place to accommodate his workers, and he told Umair to drop those three people at the place as well.

'For a few nights, they can stay with the other workers at the headquarters. When things are alright, we can then send them back to the cafe,' he replied. None of us knew when things would be ok. There were just wild guesses, two days, three days, a week maximum. All of us were still in the dark about that big thing that was about to happen that required such caution by the government.

When we started, it was already 9 p.m. I called my parents to let them know that I would be late again. Ever since Bhanu had come, every day we would go home late, after 11.30 p.m. after chilling and enjoying ourselves to the fullest. We spent late nights talking to friends at Books and Bricks or walking around Dal Lake. We reached the cafe where the workers were by 10.15 p.m., picked them up and started back. But on our way back, the highway looked deserted. We could see paramilitary people setting up bunkers in some places. Some of us were having trouble connecting calls, and by 11.30 p.m., our internet was down. By the time we reached our car to return home, our mobile network also blanked out. Bhanu and I hurriedly drove home. We were relieved that it was already night so Bhanu's family in Jammu wouldn't be worried, and we thought by tomorrow evening, he would be home.

I was worried about how to connect with Indu the next day. The moment I reached home, I checked my father's phone and realised that BSNL had also ceased operation at that time.

'Bro, this is fucked. No clues to what is going to happen next,' I told Bhanu.

'Good that I have a ticket booked for tomorrow. Otherwise my father would go berserk,' he replied, still scrolling through his phone. 'I have downloaded the boarding pass already. I guess we should go to the airport early in the morning. If the curfew is to be imposed, it will be imposed after 8 a.m. You should drop me off before that.'

Somehow our voices were very intense. We were talking in a distant, uneasy tone to each other. The phone had become useless all of a sudden; the only thing of any worth on my phone were some ghazals by Abida Parveen. So I played them, not knowing what else to do or how to reply to Bhanu.

'Let's sleep, and we will get up early and see,' I told him. I was still trying to figure out in my head what was going to happen the next day.

The next morning we woke up early, but my father had already returned from his visit to the gurdwara. 'So the network is gone completely, no calling also,' he told us. He was sleeping by the time the network was cut and everything was perfectly fine yesterday when he went to sleep. 'You go drop him off at the airport early. I heard there will be a curfew imposition later in the day.'

'Yes. He is already ready and packed. After breakfast, we will go,' I replied.

Around 7.30 a.m., we left the house. But the moment I left our street and reached the main road, barbed wires and paramilitary forces greeted us. Being a Sikh and accompanied by a Hindu, we received a mellower treatment. Bhanu had to show his ID cards and boarding pass to the cops to let him go to the airport, but I was sent back home. I was a Kashmiri, so I was not allowed to be out of my house. But Bhanu was a tourist, and so he was escorted by the cops, who assured me that they would take care of his transportation to the airport. And it was there we parted our ways.

I did not know how or if he reached the airport because the only mode of communication was dead. I went back and slept for another two hours. When I woke up again I told my father that I would go to Veerji's house to check on the news. My real reason was to use the landline to call Indu. Surprisingly, the landline was also dead. We, the whole of Kashmir's population, were cut off from the rest of the world with no modes of communication.

The news told me three things: I no longer belonged to the State of Jammu and Kashmir. It was now a Union Territory, and the whole governance would now be under the Central Government. Second, Article 370 and Article 35(a) were abrogated. And third, Ladakh was made a separate Union Territory. Not in my wildest dreams had I thought these articles could be repealed or abrogated. The Constitution had ensured that the articles would be difficult, if not impossible to take away. But I was wrong. So was the rest of Kashmir. On 5 August, the Parliament of India voted in favour of a resolution tabled by Home Minister Amit Shah to revoke the temporary special status or autonomy granted under Article 370 of the Indian Constitution to Jammu and Kashmir. Article 370 conferred on the state the power to have a separate constitution, a state flag and autonomy of internal administration. Though it was a 'temporary transitional and special provision', over time, it was seen as having become permanent.

During the assimilation of princely states to India, the accession of states was done on three matters: defence, foreign affairs and communication. All the princely states were told to make their own constituent assemblies, which most of the states were not able to make and hence had to follow the Indian Constituency later. States like Saurashtra, Travancore–Cochin and Mysore made their assemblies and developed model constitutions, but later their representatives, rulers and chief ministers met in the presence of the states' departments which was in charge of the princely states and agreed that separate constitutions for states were not required or necessary, and hence accepted the Constitution of India as their own constitution.

In the case of Jammu and Kashmir, the state's politicians decided to form a separate constituent assembly for the state. A separate constitution was also framed. The Indian Constitution was to legislate on the laws as in the original Instrument of Accession, and the state assembly would decide on all other matters. For this arrangement to work, an additional article, Article 370, was incorporated into the Indian Constitution. This article stipulated that the articles of the Constitution that gave power to the Central Government would be applied to Jammu and Kashmir only with the concurrence of the state's constituent assembly. This was to be a temporary provision until the state constitution was framed and adopted, however, the state constituent assembly dissolved itself without recommending either abrogation or amendment of Article 370, and ever since, it became more of the permanent article.

A safeguard that Hari Singh, the last Maharaja of Jammu and Kashmir, had put in the Document of Accession under Clause 7, declared that the state could not be compelled to accept any future Constitution of India and that the state was to decide what additional powers it would give to the Central Government to make laws for the state. Article 370's purpose was to protect those rights.

The people in Kashmir had always been assertive of their freedom, and Article 370 was an important feature of that. The idea of a plebiscite or referendum was always in the air, and in fact, every Kashmiri at one point in time would have told this statement to another, 'If India does a plebiscite in Kashmir, everyone will vote for Pakistan. That is why they will never do it.'

When the first rumours of abrogation started, people discarded it as an impossible thing to do. There would be blood on the streets, and Kashmir would burn if they abrogated the article. And what was more shocking was the revocation of Article 35(a), which defined the 'permanent residents' of the State and gave special privileges to those residents of J&K. The State of Jammu and Kashmir defined these privileges to include the ability to purchase land and immovable property, the ability to vote and contest elections, seeking government employment and availing other state benefits such as higher education and health care. Non-permanent residents of the State, even if Indian citizens, were not entitled to these 'privileges'. All these were earth-shattering developments and I had mixed feelings about them. I was concerned about how I would call Indu. If all this news reached her, she would be worried about me. Second, I did not know anything about Bhanu. Did he reach or not? Would he be safe or not? Veerji got angry about how things were done, 'What is this nonsense? Why do they have to cut the phone network?'

I replied, 'They just abrogated Article 370 and Article 35(a). What do you think will happen if they allow the network? Kashmir will go into a frenzy. Everyone will come out and assemble to protest. Do you get the enormity of what has been done?'

'This is not the way to do things. What about people, what if there is an emergency?' he asked.

'This is an emergency. Thank God they did not declare an emergency and start a military rule. If they don't cut the internet and calls for a few days, that is what would happen. Lakhs and lakhs of people would come and wreak havoc everywhere. Then it will be an easy ground for declaring an emergency,' I told him. 'Think about it. I will come back again in the evening. Let me first go and tell Papa the news.'

For the next two months, I went through unexpected and new experiences. I was angry and helpless in the first two days, thinking about why I was subjected to this lockdown. Then there was anxiety about the people I cared about and with whom I was not able to talk for the whole first week. The phone could only belt out music. Then the creativity flowed, for it stemmed from boredom, and without any distractions and engagements, reaching boredom was easy. The anxiety died along with the expectation of receiving any calls.

No more looking at the phone, no more waiting for calls and messages or emails. Life became primitive all of a sudden. Nada is a lonely place. Nothingness makes you realise how small you are. And slowly, you come to know that emptiness is a state of mind, but nothingness is just that; nothing. It amazes you when you have nothing, no thoughts, no action, are merely an existence. Some days I enjoyed being empty. It was meditative, and on other days, it was suffocating. What saved one from such swings of emotion was a hobby that was not dependent on technology. For me, it was DIYing old stuff into some piece of art, reading books, cooking and writing.

When the internet connectivity was cut off all of a sudden, I was working for a few good clients as a freelance content writer, and I could not even inform them what was happening and why I went MIA. That source of money died, but because of being homebound, the sources of expenditures were also cut off. We could not go anywhere; nobody could come to us. It became peaceful, quiet and relaxing after a point of time.

Sometimes, panic crept in when I thought about Indu and what she would be going through. I would imagine and realise that even if someone was dead, I wouldn't know, wouldn't be able to see them for the last time. And once the realisation came, the frustrations again popped their head, the restlessness accompanied them, and so did sadness and helplessness. The cycle started again, and I was angry, thinking about why I had been subjected to this lockdown.

For the next one month, I was not able to contact either Indu or Bhanu. The first contact I had with Indu was one-sided. I sent her a letter through a friend who went to Delhi. He assured me that he would deliver the letter, whatever happened. That was in the last week of August. In the first week of September, I went to a local police station, where they provided a calling facility. I stood in the queue for two hours to talk to Indu for one minute, of which forty seconds she cried. I did too. There were too many emotions flowing out, which I had to control for all the people standing behind me. We talked for a minute or so, and I told her that in a week, the landlines would be restored, and I would call her from Veerji's home.

Thankfully the landline was restored soon and calling her from Veerji's landline became a routine for the next one or two weeks. The internet was still off.

When I called Bhanu next, his mobile was still not reachable, which meant the mobile network in Jammu was also not restored. He did not have a landline and there was no other point of contact between us.

By the middle of September, Indu helped me book a ticket and sent me the PNR details so I could visit her. Everything in Kashmir was still closed, no markets, no shops, no schools or government establishments were open. There was only one shop in our locality that used to remain open from 6 a.m. to 8 a.m. when the whole area would come to shop. We had already stocked up, but some things we still needed to buy on an everyday basis, like milk. Once a week, we went early morning to buy medicines. I had no idea if I received my salary or not, for I could not confirm it from any place.

On 15 September, I landed in Delhi. The moment I reached, my phone started getting messages, thousands of unread notifications on WhatsApp, and hundreds of emails and alerts on all the apps. It went into permanent pinging mode for the next fifteen minutes.

Indu was waiting for me at Arrivals. It was a very emotional meeting. I stayed there for a week. I had a lot of friends in Delhi at that time. So I stayed a day or two at everyone's place. There I thought of helping out a bit and posted on my Facebook and Instagram pages, inviting people, students mostly, to reach out to me with letters for their families or any other essentials that they wanted to send home to Kashmir, and I would, in those hours of curfew relaxations, deliver it to them. I got a bag full of letters, air tickets, some medicines and some books to take to Kashmir. When I returned to Kashmir, I went with my father to deliver those letters whenever the administration provided a relaxation in curfew for buying essentials. I went to places I hadn't seen before, to the heart of the old city, to Kambarwari's internal colonies, to Pulwama, to Pampore, and so on. By the end of the week, I had delivered seventy-three letters and messages. Whoever I delivered them to, cried on receiving the letter. They showered blessings on me and kissed my forehead. Mothers, who hadn't heard from their sons and daughters, hugged me like I was their own son. Fathers and siblings kept thanking me over and over again while tear-filled eyes and muffled voices cracked with emotions. My father was proud of me for helping out people in this crisis as much as I could, and in a way, he never thought. When I posted my intention on social media in Delhi, it was a very spontaneous decision, and even when I received letters from people in Delhi, there was not much emotion. But when I delivered them, it was a whole different story. I felt glad that I was able to think of a way to help.

By the end of September, we could go out without many restrictions in the evenings. That was when I went to Books and Bricks Cafe and found the shutter raised a little. When I knocked, a group of my friends were already there talking about something. We spoke in detail about what was happening in Kashmir and how things were going to be for different sections of society. All of them were business people who had suffered a lot of loss due to this unexpected closure. They had edibles and running stocks worth lakhs which had gone to waste, and then a closure of over two months had made it worse. At home also, I was talking to my father about the plight of those daily wagers who had to earn to eat every day. We had no idea how they would survive. We, at the cafe, talked about this and many other things and after some time, played cards. That became a routine for me for the next one month. Every evening, I would go to the Books and Bricks Cafe.

By October, the mobile networks were restored in a phased manner, and we were called back to the schools. Eventually, by November, the shops and markets started to open up one by one, but there were still a lot of restrictions in many areas. We saw the internet for the first time in January 2020. By the time winter was over and things finally started to get back to normal. However, Covid took over, and Kashmir, along with the rest of India, was again put under a lockdown. The only good thing was that phone networks and internet had now been restored.

Most of us had a vague idea of what could have happened during the Article 370 lockdown for four months, but only a very few actually knew the extent of it. People came to know that their near and dear ones had died during that time. They came to know that hundreds of women had failed pregnancies because they could not reach the hospitals in time. Patients died without doctors. And these were just the physical outcomes. Think about a mother who carried a baby for nine months and could not deliver because there were dozens of bunkers stopping them and checking them again and again. Think about the father whose son had died somewhere and had been cremated a month ago without him knowing. Think about the students who had been preparing for the exams which they could not appear for, or those job-seekers or those preparing for PSC or other job exams and had their last chances at cracking it and could not even appear. Think of those who were not able to even send in a notice to their employers about their situation and had been replaced at their jobs already. Think of those who had invested lakhs in their new startup and then it crashed all of a sudden. The mental and emotional traumas they had gone through. Just think of those innumerable scenarios where communication and transportation were not available, where relatives and near and dear ones were not available.

All those things were swept under a big red carpet, marked danger, and labelled confidential, so no one could open them.

28

Opinions and Options

Srinagar and Baramulla, Kashmir
30–31 October 2021

On my birthday morning, I woke up early. Since childhood, I had followed this one ritual, not because I believed in it, but because my mother told me and wanted me to do that. Every year on my birthday, she would go to the gurdwara early in the morning and give Kadha Parshaad, and tell the bhaiji to pray for my well-being and prosperity. Even if I was not with her, she would go without fail on Ramneek and my birthdays.

When we came back from the gurdwara, Indu was in the kitchen. She wanted to cook her special chicken biryani for my birthday lunch. She had been ordering the ingredients from Amazon for the last two weeks. She wanted some special kind of rice which we didn't get in north India, called Malabari rice or jeerakasala rice. We decided that there would be no cake-cutting, which both of us felt was embarrassing and useless. Apart from biryani, my mother planned to make mutton rogan josh during the day.

My father was in the kitchen garden and came inside to bless me and greet me with birthday wishes, while Ramneek kissed me on the forehead and went back to sleep for some more time. Indu kept the formalities for later.

Other than the cooking for the day, we had a lot of packing to do. My mother wanted to pack the important things last so that she did not forget anything. Being seasonal migrants, it was a task we did every year, twice. Once while coming from Jammu to Srinagar in the month of March or April and the second while going back to Jammu in the month of November or December. But my mother was visibly emotional this time.

'We will come back in March if everything is alright,' she said while packing the egg boiler. There were a few kitchen appliances that we would transport every year, like the induction cooktop, egg boiler, blender and electric kettle, in addition to most of the wet stock. There were two bags full from the kitchen and another three with clothes and household stuff. That was the reason that I purchased a sedan car in the first place. The second reason was to carry more stuff in the boot during my trekking and travelling.

'Most probably we will not. If everything goes well, this time consider it a permanent migration,' I replied.

'It is not that easy,' she said.

'We have already talked about it, Maa. Easy or not, this is the only way forward,' I took the boiler from her, wrapped it in a newspaper, and placed it in the bag in front of us.

'Okay, I am happy with whatever you are happy with,' she replied with a smile.

Indu was in the kitchen overhearing our conversation. She told me later that she felt like she was going to be blamed for us moving out of Kashmir.

'Everyone will say this girl from Kerala came and took away our boy from us.'

'No one is going to say that, love. Everyone knows that one day I was going to leave Kashmir. And by the way, even if they say anything, how does it matter? Who cares about what others say? It's our life. We can live it the way we want.'

'Mother looks unhappy,' she added.

'Yes, she does. For her, it is more like home than for any of us. For me and Ramneek, it doesn't matter at all. For Papa, most of his relatives are in Jammu and he feels more active and social in Jammu than he does here. But for Mama, all her relatives are here, her brothers and sisters, and extended family, everyone. So for her, it's natural to feel like this.'

'Do you think it is fair for us to pull her away from them?' Indu asked.

'Baby, there is always a flip side to everything. If we consider each and every one of those things, we would never be able to leave from here or do anything else. And Maa too knows this. That is why whenever I told her about moving out, she told me that she would come with me. Even before I met you, that was our plan.'

'I don't know. I still feel she would not be happy away from everyone she loves.'

'That is a choice we have to make. She will adjust slowly. It might seem selfish of us. But it is better than going away by ourselves, leaving them alone when they should sit and relax and enjoy their lives. They will make a life around the place we move. She will be happy, I know,' I told her, hoping that whatever I said would turn out to be true. I already had thoughts about it, and I myself was pretty unsure about how things would develop. We would see when it came, I thought to myself.

By the end of the day, all of us were tired from cooking, overeating and packing. The biryani turned out delicious, and my mother's cooking was always par excellence. All of us enjoyed it to the fullest.

On 31 October, we had to drive sixty kilometres to my masi's home in Baramulla for dinner. We started in the evening from our home in Srinagar city to go to Baramulla. It was a Sunday and Indu was also free. She had been working hard during the day, so she could take time off during the evenings. The last three days had been pretty unproductive for her as well. As I had been busy during the days at my Covid duty centre, I, too, was not doing justice to my writing life.

Masi and my uncle lived alone with their three-year-old German Shepherd, while both their sons lived outside the state, working for some government organisations. Uncle was a landlord who owned some apple orchards and some horticulture fields, where every season, they would sow different vegetables. They were like us, seasonal migrants, from March to November they stayed in Kashmir and for the rest of the months in Jammu. Occasionally they would go and visit their children for a week or so during the summers.

Uncle was a stern and rigid person whose belief system was laid in stone, a man of words who stood by what he said and adhered to his principles strictly. When I told him that I would leave Kashmir and try to settle down in Bangalore or some other multicultural city, he was optimistic and cautious at the same time.

'Why would you uproot your mother and father from their home and take them with you?' he asked me. Most north Indian parents say that their children left them when they became old, but the fact was that they didn't want to go with their children. Just because they wanted to live their life in their homeland, they could not force their children to do the same. Nor could the children force them to come along. This created a divide and the popular belief that children discarded their parents when they were old.

'Because they choose to stay with me instead of staying away from me. A home is made by a family, and wherever we are together, it is our family,' I told him. Occasionally I had asked him why he was staying alone when he could have stayed with any of his sons, who would be happy and glad about his presence. 'And they don't have orchards and properties to take care of here. They can visit relatives here whenever they wish,' I added.

My father, mother and masi were sitting outside on the lawn while I was in the lobby talking to the uncle, who now wanted to go sit outside and take the topic along. Ramneek was watching TV in their bedroom while Indu was walking in their backyard apple garden.

My father was peeling fresh apples from the orchard and we walked to them, asking for our shares. Uncle told my father, 'He is determined to leave Kashmir. You give him some *akal*, these decisions are not to be taken in haste.'

'He is a married guy, fully responsible for his actions, and is running his household perfectly fine. He has more *akal* than me, and he can make his own decision,' My father said as he gave uncle and me a piece of apple each. 'Our time is up. We should sit back and let them take the reins now. We have to listen to them,' my father added.

'For us, they will always be children. No matter how much they grow up,' my uncle replied.

I changed the topic, 'A lot of Sikhs are moving out every year, permanently from Kashmir, settling in Jammu. They also quit their livelihood here and find new opportunities outside. I would also try to find a new job or something where I go.'

'Sikhs are spending double, quadruple on their houses in Kashmir. They are not going out. Some may go for jobs. But they will also eventually return someday. After the floods, see how much they have invested in their houses. If they wanted to go out, or leave Kashmir, they could have used the same money to build houses outside Kashmir.'

In September 2014, Kashmir saw the worst flood in its history. Most of Srinagar city was under several feet of water. Lakhs of people were displaced and had to leave their houses and waited to come back until the water receded. It took more than a month for the water to recede and then months after that to re-enter those houses, which were filled with slime and mud from the flood. Hundreds of houses fell like stacks of cards in the strong currents. Many who got insurance money or relief from the government or other agencies, rebuilt grand houses where their old houses stood. Some even used their own money to build it. They constructed new houses after razing their old ones.

'A lot of people, whose businesses and homes were destroyed, moved out of Kashmir after that,' I told my uncle, without believing the statement myself. I could not think of anyone who had done so but assumed it for the sake of argument. 'And after that, what happened? Again in 2016, they were crying about it. Why did we spend so much money? Why didn't we use the opportunity to build houses in Jammu? Remember?' I added.

Those who had invested money in their properties or rebuilt their houses were soon questioning their own decision when in 2016, Kashmir went into a four-month violence marked with protests, hartals and lockdowns after the killing of Burhan Wani, the commander of Hizbul Mujahideen. It was one of the most violent times, even stepping out of home was scary. People who were pelting stones were attacked with pellet guns. That year thousands lost their eyesight to the pellet guns. As Sikhs, we were safe, the neutral position we have always taken saved us from the wrath of the protesters as well as the Indian army.

'What can we say? There are numerous arguments from both sides. I guess it is a personal decision whether to stay or to leave. Nobody can change anyone's opinion,' Papa interrupted our argument.

'*Sukha naal gacha ji* (May he go with all our blessings). We pray that he finds more avenues and more success wherever he goes,' masi said.

At masi's house, the dinner was equally amazing, but Indu was lost in thought while having dinner. I asked her about that before we slept.

'What were you thinking? You did not even try to participate in the conversation at dinner,' I asked her.

'Why is everyone so adamant about you staying in Kashmir? How come they don't see that it is so suffocating here?' she asked.

'No idea and it doesn't matter. It's our life. We decide what we do,' I assured her.

'I guess, your community and family are so tightly and closely knit that the space and boundaries are blurred. Anyone and everyone have advice and opinions to give and try to influence the decisions, in a way interfering with one's personal life. People don't respect other's decisions and ability to run their own households,' she said. What she was saying was true. Boundaries and personal space were blurry in Kashmir. Parents and relatives were intrusive in their children's lives, creating dependent man-children instead of independent and assertive individuals. Parenting in Kashmir was a tough job, because not only your own parents but everyone in the extended family would also try to be a parent to you. I did not respond to what Indu said and just nodded along.

'And what was that about investing money in homes after the floods, uncle was talking about?' she asked.

'The floods of 2014. The areas affected had large populations of Sikhs as well. And a lot of Sikhs rebuilt their old houses into big ones, spending exorbitantly. That's what he was talking about.'

'Yes. You have told me about those times a lot. You were absorbed into relief work then,' she said. Her memory was impeccable. Whatever I had told her, even once, she remembered the exact details, names and chronology of events as if they were her memories.

About my own memories, I recollected different details of the same episode in every telling. Sometimes she asked me if I was making them up. I needed triggers to bring out a memory, Otherwise, I would not even be remembering them. About the floods, I had told her in detail, as it was one of the most engaging and active times in my life.

'You made some girlfriend also at that time. When people were hankering for food and shelter, this man was flirting and courting,' she said. 'How could you do that?' she asked me for the hundredth time. She had heard the story a dozen times and still wanted to know more about it. The times of floods were indeed engaging for me.

29

Deluge and Delusions

Kashmir
September 2014

The flood of 2014 was the most turbulent time for the people of Kashmir, for reasons other than violence. It took them years to recover from the damage. Most houses that collapsed during the floods were old mud houses, and people took this opportunity to build big concrete mansions in their place. This was what my uncle was referring to as 'spending double, quadruple money.'

During such times of adversity, the Sikhs' response to the deluge was immediate, focused and planned. When everyone was panic-stricken and clueless about what to do, a handful of young Sikhs stepped up and took the initiative to help people, which then catapulted into a large-scale rescue, relief and rehabilitation mission. It was their swift and proactive response that saved the city and thousands of its people. Even before the inundation, they helped people in the locality of Mehjoor Nagar and Aluchi Bagh to evacuate and shift their belongings to the upper and safer story of their houses. When Srinagar city lay under water and people were stuck in their houses, the residents of the Rangratte suburb rescued truckloads of people from the banks of Mehjoor Nagar, Tulsi Bagh, Jawahar Nagar, Rambagh and Chanapora, including a team of students stranded at an indoor stadium. They devised boats from foam and empty tin barrels on their own to rescue people. Those who were rescued were stationed at Gurdwara Shaheed Bunga at Baghat Barzulla, which became home to thousands of people for the next month. The grim night resonated with sobs and cries of people who were rescued.

The night of the flood, I was sleeping at Rangratte at my mamu's home safely because it was on a hilltop. For Rangratte to drown in flood, the whole of Srinagar needed to be at least 50 feet under water. We already knew that it was going to flood. The intensity, though, was what we were not prepared for, even in the wildest of our dreams. I woke up to the news of floods inundating Mehjoor Nagar, an occurrence that we had anticipated and helped to mitigate to a great degree. But during the day, the news came about more and more water entering the city, and now another area, housing the localities of Aluchi Bagh and Batmaloo was going to flood soon. Panic set in because one of my masis lived in Batmaloo and Aluchi Bagh was a Sikh-populated area. We had a lot of extended relatives and friends there.

Harjeet mamu and I decided to go to Batmaloo and bring masi to safety at Rangratte. We called her and told her to be ready. But when we reached there, water had already entered her house. She declined to come, leaving the rest of her family behind, and with the water rising so fast we did not have the patience or time to convince her. We ourselves escaped in the nick of time. By the time we drove out, the water was already reaching above the bonnet of mamu's Maruti Swift. It was frightening to see the water rise at such speed. While going back home, we stopped at the gurdwara and saw hundreds of people who had been rescued from their houses in Mehjoor Nagar and Aluchi Bagh, there. A lot of them went to their villages which were at considerable heights.

More and more homeless and water-stricken people poured into the gurdwara camp, irrespective of religion. By the evening, there were around a thousand people in the gurdwara, homeless and hungry. A langar was started to feed the people. Those who were rescued came forward to help in whatever way they could, like preparing langar, serving food, washing utensils, etc. The number increased every passing hour, so much so that even the sanctum-sanctorum, the main hall of the gurdwara, had to be thrown open for the flood victims.

I found Veerji near the library. He said, 'If this continues, we would be unable to feed all the people, and there is no arrangement of first aid, or medicine for so many people. Think about the sick people, infants and pregnant women. We have to do something for them.' Most of the phone networks were not functioning now, as towers had become dysfunctional due to the flood. Only Aircel was working, whose tower was incidentally just next to the gurdwara. I went to Sarabjeet's house and told him the situation and the idea that I would be going to Jammu the next morning to bring medicines and help set up a medical camp in the library. We roped in my father for this help. He could call his contacts in Punjab to send support, relief and emergency essentials to Jammu. The gurdwara committees mobilised their resources and called the Delhi and Punjab gurdwara committees as well, to help run the camp.

Over a span of the next two weeks, thousands of people were marooned in the gurdwara. Around 2800 kg of rice was being served per day with an equal quantity of vegetables and pulses to supplement it. The camp set up in the gurdwara premise continued to serve the people for around three months. On the first few days, an estimated three thousand people were served meals three times a day. Many, later, went to their relatives for shelter. Fourteen trucks of bottled water were brought in from Jammu and Punjab and were distributed among the people. Similarly, food, blankets, clothes and other essentials were sent from there in trucks and cargo planes over the next month. Primary kits of survival, including water, biscuits, baby food, packets of chapattis and lentils were then packed and delivered to every home. The youth, who were untrained for such missions, risked their lives distributing these kits, waddling in neck-deep water. They would take big steel drums and Sintex water tanks full of these kits and tugged them along as they floated and distributed the same to people who were still at home.

By the time I came back from Jammu with medicines, Veerji had set up a small medical camp in the library, which went on to become the largest one in the time of the deluge. More than 30,000 patients were enlisted for treatment, vaccination and other medical facilities. The gurdwara also started mobile medical camps at Bemina, Tengpura, Lasjan, Hyderpora and several other places. The camp sent out medicines to various sub-camps and even hospitals when they needed them. Medicines worth millions of rupees were distributed with proper prescriptions by in-camp doctors. Insulin and other diabetic medicines were the most distributed drugs among them.

That was where I met the girl Indu was referring to, and we both did relief work together and ended up dating for a few months. Shiromani Gurdwara Parbandhak Committee (SGPC), Delhi Gurdwara Parbandhak Committee (DGPC), and many other Sikh organisations, including Khalsa Aid, Sikh Relief and United Sikhs, distributed more than 40,000 family starting kits, including clothes, blankets, ration for a month and other important items. Hundreds of trucks of relief material were sent in from Punjab and Delhi to help the victims. After the water receded, they went from home to home, irrespective of religion, to distribute these kits. Truckloads of material were handed over to separatists as well as mainstream political leaders for distribution among the people of the state. Likewise, relief material was also provided to different mosques and NGOs, which were serving as relief camps.

After the floods, the youth did not stop their work. They went into the waters to fish out bodies of fourteen deceased from Jawahar Nagar and Rajbagh areas. The bodies were cremated by them after due legal formalities, and some were handed over to the police.

For two months, I worked with several NGOs and community organisations for relief and rehabilitation work. This micro-minority community provided much-needed relief and rehabilitation effectively to an enormously huge population. They took complete strangers to their homes for shelter and food. In the times when their near and dear ones were equally affected, they indiscriminately lent out help to the first needy soul that they came across.

Once things settled down, the majority community came forward to thank us. Every single political, religious and separatist leader thanked us and acknowledged our community's service from their respective platforms. Over the next two years or so, the efforts of the Sikh community during times of adversity were often appreciated. It boosted the Kashmir brotherhood. Like how the service of a few good men alleviated the whole community, sometimes the misdeeds of a few could jeopardise the reputation of the whole community as well.

A few years before the flood, an episode shook our community. Two people got into a fight, a Sikh from Rangratte village, to which everyone was grateful now, and a Muslim from another town. During the fight, the Sikh hit the Muslim guy on the head and injured him seriously. It was a personal fight between two people, but while taking the Muslim guy to the hospital, people started yelling, '*Sikhan ha maar seun nichu* (Sikhs have killed our child).'

Within two hours of the episode, thousands of people armed with sticks, stones and spades came to Rangratte and went on a rampage. They broke every vehicle parked on the road, threw stones at the houses, breaking their windows and outer walls, and kept yelling their slogans, '*Naar-e-takbir, Allah hu Akbar*', '*Yahan kya chalega, Nizam-e-mustafa*' and the likes. The whole suburb was gripped in fear and uncertainty about what was going to happen for the next one hour.

'Will the people break in and beat or kill us? We were gripping our swords and standing prepared to strike back if they entered our houses,' one of my cousins told me afterwards.

The police and army had to come and disperse the public before more damage was done. Then, the next day, many people from the adjoining Muslim village came and assured the residents that they would protect them if such an event was repeated. They asked for forgiveness on behalf of the mob. During the 2014 floods, when Sikhs came as saviours, their selfless service was appreciated, and the gratitude helped in fostering the brotherhood further.

Again, in 2016, during the protests against the killing of Burhan Wani, when Kashmiri students residing in different states in north India were harassed and threatened, the Sikh community became their shield, protected them, and then helped them to reach Kashmir safely. While at the same time, in Kashmir, the Sikhs were holed up in their houses for three to four months, their children without access to school education, and their youth without jobs and sources of income.

This medial position that the Sikhs had, acted as a buffer between India and Kashmir. But it also kept them safe from both. The Indian army never laid a hand on them, believing that, unlike Muslims who wanted Pakistan or azaadi, the Sikhs wanted to be with India. The Muslims or the Kashmir freedom seekers believed that Sikhs were more sympathetic to their cause, being a minority in India and who had equally suffered at the hands of the Indian majority community.

But when we looked at these incidences and temporary truces, and outbreaks of emotional mobs and the sentiments they evoked, a saying that one of my close friends used to tell me rang true.

'You have to work for heaven. But hell comes by default.'

30

Goodbyes

Srinagar, Kashmir
1 November 2021

First November was a depressing day for me, and for all of us, except for the first three hours of the morning, when we had our breakfast at masi's house and drove back to Srinagar.

Indu had some packing left, and so did my mother. With my backpacker travel experience over the years, I was the one who had to pack everything into bags and suitcases, making the best use of space. Both my mother and Indu had taken out and piled the clothes and other stuff and I was entrusted with the job of packing them space-efficiently. I knew the capacity of my car's boot. I had told my mother to keep the two suitcases and three duffel bags in which I could pack those piles. For Indu, she had a limit of fifteen kg of check-in luggage and seven kg of cabin baggage, which we used to the last gram.

In our three years of togetherness, Indu and I realised we had high separation anxiety. We were irritated and easily provoked on the last day of our stay together. More often than not, we ended up fighting just before going our way. There were short-lived fights, which were solved before we went to bed, but nevertheless, fights. We were very cautious of this throughout the day. We kept telling each other it was only for a few days, and that I would be joining her in Noida in a week or so, and then, we would be together. The anxiety and the irritability were there, but with the cheesecake date in the evening that we were looking forward to and a small drive afterwards, we were able to keep ourselves under control.

The whole week had passed by very fast. We were so engrossed in our days that we did not get any time with each other. On the days we did not have dinners, I did Covid duty during the day while Indu buried herself in her research. In the evening, I would write or edit, and Indu would spend some time with my parents and Ramneek, mostly showing them some movies on her laptop. She had this innate desire to show people the movies she loved. Sometimes I used that against her, telling her that I would watch the movie if she gave me a head massage while I watched.

I had already told Raman and Veerji that I would be going to Jammu and wanted to meet them on the evening of 2 November. Indu insisted that I meet them, for she thought I might feel a little lonely after she went to Delhi. Both of them had made a bet that this was not my final decision, that I would be in Kashmir the next year and work in my job. I told them that it wouldn't happen, and that I was determined to leave now. Veerji had asked me often, 'You have got used to this slow and laidback life, now. You work for an hour a day, and have over a hundred holidays in a year during normal times. And if there are some issues, over two hundred holidays. You get easy money and have very little expenditure here. Do you think you will get such a deal anywhere else in the whole world? This is a dream job, and you want to give this up and struggle from scratch in some other place. Would you be able to do that?'

'That is a very nice way to boost someone's confidence,' I had told him.

'I am just showing you the reality. What you want to leave behind is what most of the world is struggling for. That is why it is going to be very difficult. Not leaving Kashmir. That you will leave. But you are used to this *haramkhori*, this ease of living. Working from ground zero will be very hard for someone who has developed this lifestyle.'

'These are my crutches. They allow me to stand up, but at the same time, they stop me from running. I have been standing in the same place, for the last ten years. I deserve more, and for that, I would have to work or at least fail working towards it. But I will.'

I was confident about myself.

Raman, on the other hand, teased me, 'So from now onwards, I will be able to save some money.' He was the one who usually paid whenever we went to cafes and restaurants, which was quite frequent, almost every day before my marriage. Even after that, I met him at least twice a week.

'Good step,' he continued, 'At least you will be happy, and be the person you wanted to be, the writer you always aspired to be.' He added, 'And if you laze around there also, or keep visiting places all the time, which I am pretty sure you will do because Bhanu Bhaiyya is in the picture right now, you will come back the same person when the schools open in March.'

'Let's see. *Sab ka badla lega tera Faijal, writer ka bhi, poet ka bhi, traveller ka bhi, sab karega mein,*' I had replied in the tone mimicking and quoting from the famous meme of the *Gangs of Wasseypur* movie. I promised him that I would work on my writing, but would also keep travelling and enjoying.

Indu had said her goodbyes to both of them a few days back. I had planned for a small drive with Indu alone during the evening. Not a date, just an hour of outing. She wanted to have dinner with my parents as she wouldn't be meeting them anytime soon. Once she joined the university, she would only visit them before she had to go to Australia. That was our plan.

During the drive, I told her, 'So, finally we are leaving Kashmir.'

She looked at the Dal Lake like she was looking at it for the first time, completely absorbed in its beauty.

'Yeah. How do you feel?' she asked, still looking out the window.

'Honestly, I have mixed feelings right now. I leave Kashmir every year during the winter. So, it is not a new feeling. But when I think about it, that this is a final departure, that I probably won't come back, makes me a little restless, or sad, I don't know the exact feeling.' I replied. 'Let's park somewhere and stroll for some time.'

I slowed the car to a halt.

'We will be settling somewhere else. But Kashmir will always be your root, your home, like Kerala is for me. Wherever I go, I will always be a Keralite.'

We walked holding hands.

'Yeah.'

'Don't be sad. If everything goes well and if the situation in Kashmir becomes good over the next few decades, we will buy some land here and make a small retirement home here,' she said. For the last two or three weeks, I wanted to ask her this question. Would she still want to settle here post-retirement? But I imagined her answer in my head, 'Even after all this, you want to settle here?'

But what she said now somehow energised me. I was thinking a lot of things. Would I be able to leave Kashmir so easily? Would I come back?

Would I be able to resign from my job next year or secure a long leave? Would I be able to make a career shift? Would it be wise to do all this, would it be this and that, and so on.

'Let's not bother about that. Let's focus on what is ahead of us. You have to focus on your studies for now, I will focus on writing this winter and try to finish the book by the end of next year,' I told her, re-instilling some energy into myself.

'Yes, let's aim together. By the time I finish the studies, you should have a book under your belt. Promise me you will work towards it,' she also grew enthusiastic hearing me.

A couple's energy worked in mysterious ways. When one was happy, the other resonated with the feeling. However, if one person was sad, the other person felt down as well. The energies were transferred to each other. Mirroring, Indu called it.

'Yes. That should be our goal. We have a two-year timeline to work on our individual careers. So once we are together, we can be a little more focused on us, rather than our work,' I held her hand tighter, pulling her closer to me. 'Let's walk back.'

At the dinner table, there was not much conversation. We were not the only ones having separation anxiety. My parents were feeling low too. My mother had always been sentimental yet emotionally strong. I could never fathom her thoughts. She would be all teary-eyed while seeing me off on my spontaneous trips. But at the same time, she would take a stern stand if anyone asked me why I was going away often. She would tell them, 'Let him do what he wants. This is his time to travel and enjoy.' Before I left for these trips, she would hug me like I was going for a battle, but never stop me. Her endurance was bottomless.

She and Indu had grown very attached, and I could find similarities in their nature. Both were overly empathetic and easily provoked but strong, decisive and assertive when it came to decision-making. Father, who I thought was emotionally cold and had zero care for what others did, was the one who was teary-eyed the next morning when I went to drop Indu.

Ramneek and Indu were still developing a relationship. It was hard for her to understand his language, as he spoke in his own codified way, which only my parents and I understood. Sometimes it was hard even for us to understand him. But he liked her and understood and listened to whatever she said. That was very rare. He did not even listen to his parents sometimes. If there was anyone he had complete faith in, and would listen to without questions or ifs and buts, it was me. When Indu left, he told her to call him whenever she found time.

In the last week, I was not able to talk much to my parents, with all the dinner invitations and other work at hand keeping me busy. I was expecting a serious conversation or a depressing goodbye to Kashmir the next day. But I got neither. In my head, I imagined several conversations with them. My mother would ask, 'Are we seriously not coming back?' or my father would say, 'Take your decision wisely. Don't regret it later.' In my imagination, I would answer them that I would have to start someday afresh and that this was the best time for me, or that it was better for me to live peacefully than to live with all this mental tension. But none of that happened.

It was my first migration as a decision-making adult. I wondered if it was the same for my father and for all those people who had been through this before me. I wondered if they, too, had the conversations with themselves or if they were asked by others the same questions I was asked. I wondered if migration was a choice for them or the only option.

In my own way, I was standing up for my decision. When I slept that night, I had the most vivid dream. The souls of the mountains had come to me, sat with me at the banks of Dal Lake, and said that it would add to their grief if one more person was to vanish from their sight, whatever the reason, death or migration.

Epilogue

Kashmir
Sometime in 2022

I was teaching 'Outcomes of Democracy' to my class. It was the third period and I was explaining this to political science students of Class X: 'Social diversities can be accommodated by focusing on all the communities of the society. The majority and minority communities should be equally given attention. Democracy is not the rule of the majority.'

My phone rang and I pressed the power button to silence the vibration, which sounded louder than the ringer amidst the pin-drop silence in the class.

'It is equally important to understand that the rule of the majority is not expressed in terms of religion or languages.'

There were thirty-five students in the class, all boys. This school was one of the oldest schools in Srinagar, well-furnished and maintained, unlike my previous school.

When I checked the phone, I saw three missed calls from Veerji. I asked the students to give me a minute and called him back. Damn, not again, I said to myself.

'What, all well? Anyone killed?' I asked him the moment he answered the phone.

'What? No! One of your parcels has arrived and they are asking for the OTP,' he said. I laughed at my paranoia. 'I'll text you in a minute,' I hung up and wiped my forehead clean of sweat before smiling at the children.

In March 2022 I returned to rejoin duty for some time before I could take another leave and go back to Noida. The four months in Noida went by in the blink of an eye. Partying, travelling, writing and enjoying, that just about summed up my visit there. Mentally I was a lot freer than I had been in Kashmir. Nobody told me what to do next.

'Are we safe? Should we stay? Should we leave? Come back early. Where are you? How's the situation?' There was no use for these questions. It felt like I was completely free.

Epilogue

When I came back to Kashmir, everything seemed so good and peaceful, laid-back and slow, that I decided to stay for a minimum of one month. Indu was in Delhi, working hard, so I told her to concentrate. The final year of her studies started from July, and she had to leave for Australia to complete it around July-end. She was busy with her schedule, and my return to Noida would distract her. That was what I told her.

When I came back, I found everything as I had left it. The people, the conversations, the silence, the noise, the overthinking, everything was like it had been. The air was pure, the noise absent, and the weather pleasant, but the sun felt a little dim. I was absorbed in daily life so quickly that within a week I felt like I had never left Kashmir. The new monotony fed me day after day. It felt like home. It felt like normal.

My friends and relatives mocked me when they saw me back in Kashmir, 'See? I told you it is not easy to leave a government job, or leave Kashmir or leave your roots and go live somewhere else.'

I justified my decision one way or another, to them and to myself. I told them it was a temporary return and that I would be leaving again soon. I was never fearful of my life in Kashmir. And when I was alone in Kashmir, it felt a lot easier to live. Not just easy but a perfect way to live. For me, it was an ideal life. Live alone, work and earn, write, meet up with friends once in a while and sip coffee by the Dal Lake. But that worked if I was alone. The moment I thought about my parents, my wife and my future children, the air thinned suddenly, suffocating me.

My parents and Ramneek were in Jammu. They had decided to come in April, as the weather there was getting hotter day by day. When they returned, everything was back to normal and I convinced Indu that the episodes of minority killings were one off in a decade and that nothing like that was going to happen again. I told her that she would anyway be going to Australia, so it was better for me to be in Kashmir. I could be with family, work on my book, and wouldn't have to leave the job or take a long leave again. It was a win-win situation.

And then, on 12 May 2022, a Kashmiri Pandit named Rahul Bhat was killed. He was a PM Package employee. Within a few days, there were several other attacks on the non-locals and Kashmiri Pandits. The PM Package employees stopped going to their offices and the government decided to let them stay at home for some time. But their protests grew stronger and stronger, and most people went to Jammu for what looked like the final migration as they decided they would never come back again to Kashmir. I was equally determined last year, but here I was, back in Kashmir.

The government could not stop this new wave of killings. So they decided to provide security to the PM Package and other minority employees and, as a result, transferred us to central places from our far-off and rural postings. Most of the employees were attached to the district headquarters and posted to major landmark locations that had high security. As a result of this transfer drive, I was transferred to Jawahar Nagar, just a few kilometres from my home, in a higher secondary school which was deemed to be a secure location. After that killing, despite the transfers, many people have not joined their duties to this day. I did, along with a few other colleagues, mostly Sikhs and a handful of Pandits.

In the last week of July, I went to Delhi to see Indu off to Australia. She asked me for a promise to keep myself safe, and if I perceived any threat or danger in Kashmir, I was to leave immediately.

When I look at it now, 274 people were killed in Kashmir in the year 2021, which included 36 civilians, 45 from the security forces and 193 militants. And as of October 2022, 233 more have been killed, of which 28 were civilians and the rest a combination of security forces and militants. And yet I asked myself, 'Was there any danger? Should I leave or not?'

As I wrote this, I felt stupid for coming back again to this place, which I so wanted to leave.

Despite my privileges, I returned. Despite the chance and opportunity to leave, I came back. Despite the fact that I had all the means and ends to leave, I am still here. I think of those who don't have any of these and still left for a better future. And I think of those who don't have any of these and would never be able to leave, despite how strong that desire was.

Today when I sleep, I will write in my journal. Sikhs will continue to stay in Kashmir, no matter what. Some will leave, some will stay, some will leave and come back again, and some, like me, will leave to come back only to leave again, without knowing which one will be their last time. All of us are in this endless loop.

Like me, they would be questioning themselves: Whether to continue to live in Kashmir under such mental duress and fear of death or to leave for Jammu? They would ask themselves, as I did, and keep asking after every incident, if there would be more killings or if it was a one-off incident. They would question the reasons to stay here, justify them, placate their existence, and wonder who would be the next target.

Deep inside, all of us know the answers. We just don't want to say them out loud. Maybe we are fools who foresee what is to come and yet cannot do anything about it. But maybe that's what the roots do—they anchor, absorb and ground and sometimes they run so deep that plucking and replanting the tree becomes impossible.

Acknowledgements

I owe deep gratitude to many people for their help with this book. Without their contributions it would have been rather impossible to complete this task. It would be equally impossible to thank each one of them individually so I acknowledge the pre-eminent here.

In the making of this book, I have interviewed many people; the survivors of Mehjoor Nagar, Chithisinghpora and 1947, their friends and families and the eyewitnesses of those events. I thank all of you for helping me bring to light the stories of the Kashmiri Sikhs. I thank Kulbir and Khushdeep for letting me read their thesis and primary research which helped me understand about Kashmir and its Sikh community through a researcher's lens.

I am highly indebted to Jagjit Singh, aka Veerji, who has been a mentor, a friend and a guiding force throughout my life. The book is as much his as it is mine, for he was the one who introduced me to many of the people who have been interviewed in this book. It was in the library with him that the initial draft of this book was ideated. Without his insights and recommendations this book would have not been possible.

To my dearest friend, Raman, I owe you gratitude for helping me with the initial chapterisation and sorting out the timeline and direction of the book. Also, thanks for all the coffee and cafe outings to pull me out of the writer's blues and blocks.

Snowber has read the manuscript over and over, from its first draft to its final, and poured her wisdom and insights over long phone calls. She has been my primary go-to person for feedback. Thank you so much for being available and taking out time from your busy schedule whenever I wanted.

If not for Bhanu, Sarabjeet and C.P. Pathak, I would have taken forever to finish this book. All of you have been supporting me mentally and emotionally, helping me to ground myself and setting my priorities straight. I am thankful to each one of you.

Acknowledgements

For Indu, my wonderful wife and muse, I can write a whole book of acknowledgements and it won't still be enough. She has been my first reader and editor, meticulously reading every chapter, commenting objectively and helping me rework the manuscript every time it needed a revision. She has supported me throughout the whole process from conception to publication, offering insights, encouragements, warnings and silence at all the right times.

My parents and Ramneek, for understanding that writing is a lonely job and giving me the peaceful space and bearing with me during the course of writing this book. My mother who somehow senses my lows and mysteriously encourages and inspires me to overcome them, has been the most important pillar of support, not only for this book, but in my life as well. Though a father's contribution is always underrated, for me he has been a friend and a patron, who believes in me more than I believe in myself, and always pushes me to be better.

Finally, to the people who helped me launch my writing career and took a chance on me. My literary agent, Kanishka, who instilled confidence in me and helped me refine my work with his wonderful insights. My editor, Sarveswari Saikrishna, who chiseled the book to its current form from the manuscript that it was, and gave her corrective feedback and comments which helped me to improve my writing. Bidisha Srivastava, Managing Editor at Amaryllis, who has been constantly guiding me throughout the whole journey.

I owe immense gratitude to all of you for believing in me and helping me transition from a writer to an author.

References

Chapter: Introduction

1. 'Backgrounder, Jammu & Kashmir.' South Asia Terrorism Portal. https://www.satp.org/backgrounder/india-jammukashmir.
2. 'Document-Paper-Acts-and-Ordinances-Instrument-of-Accession-of-Jammu-and-Kashmir-State.' South Asia Terrorism Portal. https://www.satp.org/document/paper-acts-and-oridinances/instrument-of-accession-of-jammu-and-kashmir-state.
3. 'Document-Paper-Acts-and-Ordinances-Maharaja-Hari-Singh's-Letter-Requesting-Indian-Assistance-against-Tribal-Raids.' South Asia Terrorism Portal. https://www.satp.org/document/paper-acts-and-oridinances/maharaja-hari-singh%E2%80%99s-letter-requesting-indian-assistance-against-tribal-raids.
4. 'Sikhs Killed in Kashmir during Last 20 Years of Turmoil.' Komal library. https://komallibrary.wordpress.com/sikhs-killed-in-kashmir-during-last-20-years-of-turmoil.

Chapter 1: A Phone Call

1. Choudhury, Subhasish. 'Massacre in Kashmir: Decoding the Craze That Works in the Name of Jihad.' 20 January 2020. https://www.barakbulletin.com/en_US/massacre-in-kashmir-decoding-the-craze-that-works-in-the-name-of-jihad-writes-subhasish-choudhury/.
2. Datasheet-Terrorist-Attack-Fatalities.' South Asia Terrorism Portal. https://www.satp.org/datasheet-terrorist-attack/fatalities/india-jammukashmir.
3. Jammu and Kashmir: Religious Identity of Civilians Killed in Militancy.' South Asia Terrorism Portal. https://www.satp.org/satporgtp/countries/india/states/jandk/data_sheets/religious_identity.htm.

Chapter 6: Invisible

1. Holmes, J.M. 'Children of the Good Book.' *The New Yorker*. 10 May 2021. https://www.newyorker.com/magazine/2021/05/17/children-of-the-good-book.

Chapter 13: Those Who Cannot Foresee

1. Punk, Vivek. 'J&K: Attacks on Non-Locals Continue, Terrorists Kill 2 in Kulgam.' *Mint*. 17 October 2021. https://www.livemint.com/news/india/

terror-attack-claims-lives-of-2-non-local-workers-in-kulgam-area-cordoned-off-11634478051995.html.

Chapter 14: Unearthing Chithisinghpora

1. Harding, Luke. 'Killing of Sikhs Clouds Clinton Visit to India.' *The Guardian*. 22 March 2000, sec. World news. https://www.theguardian.com/world/2000/mar/22/india.kashmir.
2. Zahra, Masrat. 'Kashmir: A Reflection on 30 Years of Pain.' *Society and Culture in South Asia* 5(2). 1 July 2019. 356–63. https://doi.org/10.1177/2393861719846673.

Chapter 15: Paranoia, Alms and Pistols

1. Pandit, M. Saleem. 'After 2 More Killings in J&K, Cops Want Migrants Corralled.' India News - *Times of India*. 18 October 2021. https://timesofindia.indiatimes.com/india/terrorists-kill-2-more-non-locals-injure-1-in-jammu-kashmir/articleshow/87091250.cms.
2. '2 More Non-Native Labourers Killed by Terrorists in Kashmir; 5 Such Deaths in Less Than a Fortnight.' *News 18*. 18 October 2021. https://www.news18.com/news/india/2-killed-as-terrorists-open-fire-in-kashmirs-wanpoh-4332992.html.
3. Bhat, Sunil. 'Terrorists Kill 2 Non-Local Labourers in J&K's Kulgam, Third Attack in Two Days.' *India Today*. 18 October 2021. https://www.indiatoday.in/india/story/jammu-kashmir-terrorists-kils-non-locals-labourers-kulgam-1865831-2021-10-17.

Chapter 17: The Sikhs of Kashmir, circa 1490 to present

1. Badal, Kulbir Singh. 'State Society and Economy in Suba-I-Kashmir under Sarkar-i-Khalsa (1819-1846).' Unpublished PhD thesis, Punjabi University, Patiala, 2020.
2. Malhotra, Khushdeep Kaur. 'Precarious Citizens, expected state: Sikh Rootedness in Kashmir after the Chithisinghpora Massacre.' PhD dissertation, Temple University, Libraries, 2022.

Chapter 18: The ISI Blueprint

1. Ojha, Arvind. 'Islamic State Khorasan Warns of More Attacks in Kashmir amid Targeted Killings - *India Today*.' 18 October 2021. https://www.indiatoday.in/india/story/islamic-state-khorasan-attacks-kashmir-targeted-killings-1866275-2021-10-18.

2. 'Pakistan's ISI Conspiracy against Jammu and Kashmir Exposed, Big Conspiracy Revealed from Blueprint.' *Bharat Times English News.* 19 October 2021. https://eng.bharattimes.co.in/pakistans-isi-conspiracy-against-jammu-and-kashmir-exposed-big-conspiracy-revealed-from-blueprint/.
3. Sharma, Jitender. 'Pakistan's ISI'S Conspiracy against Jammu and Kashmir Exposed. "Blueprint" reveals a major plot'. *Zee News.* 19 October 2021. https://zeenews.india.com/india/pakistans-isis-conspiracy-against-jammu-and-kashmir-exposed-blueprint-reveals-major-plot-2403766.html.

Chapter 19: Survivor Stories

1. 'Indo-Pakistani War of 1947–1948.' Wikipedia. 13 October 2022. https://en.wikipedia.org/w/index.php?title=Indo-Pakistani_War_of_1947%E2%80%931948&oldid=1115889157.
2. The Mirpur Massacre of November 1947: 18K Hindu-Sikhs Killed, when 100 Girls in a Arya Samaj Hostel Jumped into a Well.' *Hindu Post.* 23 March 2022. https://hindupost.in/news/the-mirpur-massacre-of-november-1947-18k-hindu-sikhs-killed-when-100-girls-in-a-arya-samaj-hostel-jumped-into-a-well/.

Chapter 27: Articles 370 and 35(a)

1. 'Document-Paper-Acts-and-Ordinances-Article-370-of-the-Constitution-of-India.' South Asia Terrorism Portal. https://www.satp.org/document/paper-acts-and-oridinances/article-370-of-the-constitution-of-india.

www.ingramcontent.com/pod-product-compliance
Lightning Source LLC
Chambersburg PA
CBHW051104230426
43667CB00013B/2439